How Parliament Works

Third Edition

Paul Silk and Rhodri Walters

LONGMAN
London and New York

Addison Wesley Longman Limited,
Edinburgh Gate, Harlow,
Essex CM20 2JE, England
and Associated Companies throughout the world.

*Published in the United States of America
by Addison Wesley Longman Publishing, New York*

First published 1987
Second Edition 1989
Third Edition 1995
Second impression 1996
ISBN 0 582 21317 7 PPR

British Library Cataloguing-in-Publication Data

A catalogue record for this book is
available from the British Library

Library of Congress Cataloging-in-Publication Data

Silk, Paul.
    How Parliament Works/Paul Silk and Rhodri Walters.—3rd ed.
        p.   cm.
    Includes bibliographical references and index.
    ISBN 0-582-21317-7
    1. Great Britain.   Parliament.   I. Walters, R. H. (Rhodri Havard)
    II. Title
    JN549.S55   1995
328.41'07—dc20   94-43995
                                                                            CIP

Set by 5 in 10 on 11 pt Times
Produced through Longman Malaysia, PP

For our Parents

CONTENTS

FOREWORD

Our original aim in *How Parliament Works* was to produce an accurate, comprehensive and up-to-date guide to the day-to-day workings of the House of Commons and House of Lords. From comments we received, we believe that earlier editions of this book achieved that. Being accurate and up-to-date is always a problem when the institution described is living and changing. We are delighted, therefore, to be able to produce a very substantially revised and somewhat expanded edition of what has become, we hope, a standard work on the British Parliament. This new edition allows us to describe and analyse Parliament at the mid-point of a decade which has already seen substantial changes, in areas as diverse as the relationships between Parliament and the European Union, hours of sitting and the administration of both Houses, and which is likely to see other important developments in parliamentary life as the expectation of MPs, peers and the public about their Parliament alter.

As we emphasised in the first edition of this book, we have not written only for the students in university, college or school who need to study Parliament. We hope that our work is useful also for civil servants, researchers, journalists and lobbyists, as well as for the general reader who wants to know how Parliament operates and what its powers and defects are.

We remain greatly indebted to those who have given us advice about particular aspects of the book. So many staff and members of both Houses (as well as academic colleagues outside Parliament) have been generous with their time and their expertise that it would be invidious to name individuals. That does not diminish our gratitude. The libraries and the Journal Offices of both Houses have remained invaluable sources of information. We are also grateful to our publishers.

As in previous editions, Rhodri Walters contributed the bulk of the material on the House of Lords while Paul Silk contributed most of the rest. But the final text has been knitted together by us both, working with co-operative equanimity – testimony, perhaps, to our shared origin in South Wales.

CHAPTER 1

The parliamentary building

Most foreign tourists visiting London come to see the Houses of Parliament. The gothic extravagance on the River Thames is probably Britain's best-known landmark. They may know very little and care even less about what happens inside, but they appreciate the place as one of the greatest achievements of nineteenth-century art. Most of those who work day after day in the building remain awed by its artistic power and confidence. Parliament is first of all a magnificent building.

This book is concerned with the workings of the two Houses of Parliament, the House of Lords and the House of Commons, sometimes referred to as the 'Upper' and 'Lower' Houses respectively. There is no necessary connection between Parliament the building and Parliament the working institution. The British Parliament could meet at York or Oxford or elsewhere, and the building in London be turned into an art gallery. However, the association between parliamentarians' present meeting place and the institution of Parliament is so strong that such a suggestion appears merely ludicrous. So, before turning to the way Parliament works, we need to describe briefly the building in which it works. We also need to ask ourselves how much the building shapes the institution.

Strictly, the building is called the Palace of Westminster. Before the Norman Conquest, King Edward the Confessor established his palace on the site, and it was the monarch's chief residence until the reign of Henry VIII. The word 'parliament' derives from the French word 'parler', to speak or talk, and from the middle ages kings summoned representative advisers to their palace at Westminster to discuss the affairs of state – to be parliaments. These parliaments were different from those of today, and what they did related to the historical circumstances of their time. However, the germ of the modern institution can be traced back at least to 1265 and the summoning of a parliament at Westminster on the King's behalf by Simon de Montfort. Maintaining the long historical tradition, the parliament which met after the 1992 general election was still summoned by proclamation from the Queen, in part of which she said 'And We being desirous and resolved, as soon as may be, to meet Our people and have their advice in Parliament, do hereby make known to all Our loving Subjects Our Royal Will and Pleasure to call a new Parliament'. That parliament met in one of her royal palaces – though one which now is almost entirely under the control of the two Houses.

After Henry VIII's reign, the monarch no longer lived at the Palace of Westminster. The buildings were gradually set aside for the needs of the two Houses of Parliament, and for the law courts, though great royal occasions such as coronation feasts still took place there – George IV's coronation was celebrated in some style in Westminster Hall in 1821. The site was occupied by a hotchpotch of buildings, a few of great architectural distinction like St Stephen's Chapel and Westminster Hall, others less so.

The disaster of the great fire of 1834, which was started by over-stoking the House of Lords' furnaces, and which destroyed much of the medieval palace, with the exception of Westminster Hall, could also be seen as something of a godsend. It allowed the skilled partnership of Sir Charles Barry, the architect, and Augustus Welby Pugin, the interior designer, to construct between 1840 and 1852 the present Palace of Westminster. They recognised that the palace was primarily the meeting place for the two Houses of Parliament – theirs was a purpose-built building – and their design exhibited the enormous self-confidence of mid-Victorian Britain.

Unfortunately the growth of terrorism and the demand for tighter security have meant that the Houses of Parliament can no longer be viewed by the general public except in parties sponsored by MPs or Peers. (A plan of the building is on page 3.) Visitors begin their tour in the part of the palace still devoted to the monarch. When the Queen opens Parliament, her State coach drives under the Victoria Tower – the square tower rising to 323 feet at the south of the palace. She then ascends the Royal Staircase to the Robing Room, where she puts on the State robes and Imperial State Crown, before walking through the 110 foot-long Royal Gallery and entering the House of Lords. The rooms at the south end of the building where this ceremonial takes place are magnificent, and a great treat for those who love Victorian art. The proportions are perfect, and the decoration ornate, with constant gilded repetitions of Queen Victoria's monogram and of heraldic devices associated with earlier kings and queens. This part of the palace is not in use except for the day of State Opening, and, in the case of the Royal Gallery, on the rare occasions when a visiting Head of State addresses both Houses of Parliament – the King of Spain and the Presidents of France, Russia and the USA are among those who have done so since 1975.

From this part of the palace, the route takes visitors from the room where the House of Lords meets (known as its 'Chamber') by way of the Peers' Lobby, the Central Lobby, the Commons' Lobby, and interlinking corridors to the meeting place of the House of Commons (also its 'Chamber'). This is the centre of the building

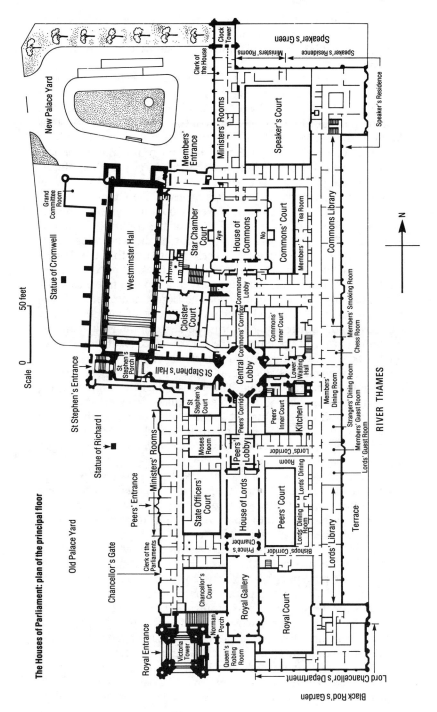

The Houses of Parliament: plan of the principal floor

Scale 0 ___ 50 feet

N

RIVER THAMES

New Palace Yard

Old Palace Yard

Chancellor's Gate

Royal Entrance

Black Rod's Garden

Lord Chancellor's Department

Statue of Cromwell

Statue of Richard I

Grand Committee Room

Westminster Hall

St Stephen's Entrance

St Stephen's Porch

St Stephen's Hall

St Stephen's Court

Cloister Court

Star Chamber Court

Clock Tower

Speaker's Green

Ministers' Rooms

Speaker's Residence

Clerk of the House

Speaker's Court

Commons Library

Speaker's Residence

Members' Entrance

Ministers' Rooms

House of Commons

Commons' Court

Tea Room

Aye

No

Members'

Members' Smoking Room

Chess Room

Commons Corridor

Commons Lobby

Central Lobby

Commons' Inner Court

Lower Waiting Hall

Peers' Corridor

Members' Dining Room

Strangers' Dining Room

Members' Guest Room

Lords' Guest Room

Peers' Inner Court

Kitchen

Peers' Lobby

Moses Room

St Stephen's Court

Ministers' Rooms

Peers' Entrance

Clerk of the Parliaments

State Officers' Court

House of Lords

Lords' Corridor

Room

Peers' Court

Lords' Dining Room

Lords' Dining Room

Lords' Library

Terrace

Chancellor's Court

Prince's Chamber

Bishops' Corridor

Royal Gallery

Royal Court

Norman Porch

Queen's Robing Room

Victoria Tower

and, when all the doors are open on the day of the State Opening, the Queen sitting on the throne in the Lords can see the Speaker in her chair presiding over the House of Commons about a quarter of a mile away.

There are similarities in layout between the two Chambers, though not in splendour. The Commons' Chamber was rebuilt after destruction in 1941 by a German bomb. It is plain and even austere. The Lords' Chamber, by contrast, is the most gorgeous room in the palace. In the Lords, the throne faces north under a gilded canopy and Cloth of Estate. In front of it is the Woolsack, on which the Lord Chancellor sits, as Speaker, or presiding officer, of the House of Lords. The Woolsack is a seat stuffed with wool which comes from the different countries of the Commonwealth. Edward III decided that a sack of wool would be a useful reminder to their lordships of the pastoral basis of the country's economy, and the tradition has persisted. In front of the Lord Chancellor are the two Judges' Woolsacks. These remind us that the Appeal and High Court Judges still receive Writs of Assistance to attend the House. Nowadays they attend only in a representative capacity on the day of the State Opening. To the Lord Chancellor's left and right are four rows of red benches for peers, divided into three sections. In the centre of the floor is the Table of the House, and on the opposite side of the table to the Lord Chancellor there are three further benches. Looking from the throne, the right of the House is known as the spiritual side, because the bishops sit there – in the front rows of the top section. The left is called the temporal side, while the benches beyond the table are called the crossbenches. As well as the bishops, government supporters sit on the spiritual side, with ministers who are peers in the front row of the central section. Other parties sit on the temporal side. Peers who do not belong to a party sit on the crossbenches.

In the House of Commons the Speaker's Chair faces south. Immediately in front of her is the Table of the House. There are five rows of green benches on either side of the Chamber, divided by a gangway into two sections. On the Speaker's right, the benches are occupied by MPs of the government party and on her left of the opposition parties. Ministers who are MPs sit on the front bench of the top section, and the main opposition party's principal spokesmen and women sit opposite them. For this reason they are known as 'frontbenchers'. All other MPs are 'backbenchers'. As in the House of Lords, the Chamber is surrounded with galleries which provide seats for the press and public. There are also special places reserved for members of the upper House and for civil servants advising ministers.

Much of the parliamentary vocabulary comes from the arrangements in the Chambers: the 'opposition' parties sit physically opposite the government; a meeting of the House is a 'sitting';

matters debated in the Chamber are debated on the 'floor' of the House; if MPs and peers hand in questions or give notice of motions they 'table' them; when the House finishes its business at night it 'rises'. Similarly, when the House votes it 'divides'; this is because those voting physically divide into two groups ('ayes' and 'noes' in the Commons, 'contents' and 'not contents' in the Lords) and walk through separate lobbies on either side of both Chambers (known as division lobbies) to be counted.

For an assembly of 651 members, the Commons' Chamber is surprisingly intimate. Its division into two sides facing one another (which is unusual compared to the semi-circular layout of most continental and American legislatures) is said to arise from the use by the Commons of St Stephen's Chapel in the old palace as its meeting place. The monks had sat in two rows of choir-stalls on either side of the altar, and when the Commons occupied the chapel in the sixteenth century, they did not change these seating arrangements. Rather fancifully, some people trace the development of the two-party system to this. Today, there are 427 seats for MPs in the Chamber and in the galleries reserved for them. MPs have no individual places and no desk or telephone or computer terminal in the Chamber. They speak from their places, not from a podium. When the House is busy, the atmosphere is made tense by the crush of MPs, and even when only a few are present for a particularly abstruse debate, the feeling of speaking to empty space, which is a problem of many foreign parliamentary chambers, is kept to a minimum.

Away from the Chambers, there are rooms used for committees on the first floor east river-front. Older MPs still refer to matters being considered in committee as being 'upstairs'. Some of these upstairs rooms are used by what are known as 'standing committees' (see index for references to further descriptions of standing committees and select committees) and are arranged very much like the Chamber, with two sides facing each other, and the occupant of the Chair sitting at one end, normally on a dais. Select committees sit around horseshoe tables, and MPs and peers do not necessarily choose their seats on party lines. Standing committees meet in public, as do select committees normally when taking evidence, and there are seats for the public at the back of the rooms.

There is a great deal more to the Palace of Westminster. It occupies an eight acre site and contains over 1100 rooms. The buildings cost £14.3 million to maintain in 1994/95. There are libraries, television rooms, dining rooms, bars and accommodation for all those who service Parliament (including a men's hairdresser, nurse and florist). Several people live in the palace, most notably the Lord Chancellor and, in rather grand apartments, the Speaker. Ministers have rooms, and most MPs now have some form of office accommodation. As recently as the 1950s, a committee of MPs reported that they were 'convinced that a substantial number of members would benefit from the provision of desks', but in the last 30 years, the parliamentary estate has expanded beyond the Palace of Westminster and now includes several nearby buildings, one of them being the old police headquarters at Scotland Yard. These outbuildings have provided considerably more office accommodation for MPs, peers and parliamentary staff, and further major development is taking place on an adjacent site above Westminster Underground station, where, after many years of controversy, a new parliamentary building containing offices for MPs and staff, committee rooms and other facilities is being constructed for occupation in 1999.

The growth of office accommodation has resulted from dissatisfaction about the facilities the palace provides. It was built as a Parliament for the mid-nineteenth century, before the days of the professional parliamentarian. Many people have compared the place to an old-fashioned gentleman's club with debating chambers attached. Certainly if being an MP means no more than sitting on comfortable leather armchairs in high book-lined rooms overlooking the Thames, eating dinners with agreeable companions, listening to political debates and voting on propositions about current affairs, then the Palace of Westminister would provide all that is needed. Today, there cannot be an MP who regards his or her job as that simple, and one of the principal constraints on MPs' ability to adapt to the needs of the late twentieth century is the physical environment in which they work. A splendid building is not necessarily a practical building, nor does it necessarily house a splendid institution. However, parliamentarians must inevitably enjoy some lifting of the spirit from their privilege of working in one of Britain's most distinguished edifices.

CHAPTER 2

Who is in Parliament?

In the introductory chapter the word 'Parliament' was used to describe a building. The word can also be used to describe an aspect of the constitution. The most narrow technical sense of the word comes when we speak of 'a parliament'. 'A parliament' is the cycle between the calling of one general election to the calling of the next. After a general election the country always has 'a new parliament'. It may well have a new government also, but even if it does not, there is still a new parliament. However, only one part of Parliament, the House of Commons, is actually affected by a general election. The other two parts – the House of Lords and the monarch – remain the same.

The size of the Commons

Before Irish independence, there were 707 members of the House of Commons or MPs (members of the House of Lords are sometimes described as Members of Parliament, though they never use the abbreviation 'MP' about themselves). After 1922, the House of Commons shrank to 615 members. Subsequent adjustments (only one of them downward) have resulted in a total since 1992 of 651 members, or one MP for roughly every 89,100 constituents. Proposals from the Boundary Commissions are likely to lead to an increase in the number of MPs after the next general election. (There are, of course, more constituents than electors – those under 18 do not have a vote, and not everyone registers as a voter. At the 1992 election, there was an average of 66,436 electors per MP.) This compares with the figures of one Congressman per 522,000 in the USA, one member of the Bundestag per 120,000 in Germany, and in France, where, like Britain, there is no federal system, one Deputy or MP per 98,000.

We could say then that the British public are comparatively well represented in the House of Commons, though in Chapter 12 we will see that some people argue that the House of Commons would do a more effective job if it had fewer MPs. In purely numerical terms, this may be correct, but the more fundamental question is whether the House of Commons is truly representative of the political and socio-economic make-up of the country.

Is the Commons representative?

Electoral method

The United Kingdom is more generous than many countries in those whom it allows to vote in parliamentary elections. There is no property qualification, since 1928 no sex discrimination, and there are voting rights for Britons who live abroad and choose to register. Commonwealth and Irish citizens resident in Britain are entitled to vote, and the only main categories excluded are those under 18, convicted prisoners still in prison, certain mentally ill people and Members of the House of Lords. It is not necessary to vote in person – the sick, those who work away from home and, since 1987, those on holiday or resident abroad can vote by post or proxy.

General elections are held after parliament has been 'dissolved' either by royal proclamation or because the maximum term between elections – five years – has expired. Since 1945, the average time between general elections has been about 3 years 6 months and no parliament has run its full term. This contrasts with the fixed terms of the US Congress or the practice of countries like Belgium or Germany where parliaments are dissolved early only in exceptional circumstances. The ending of a parliament by royal proclamation, which means, in effect, by decision of the Prime Minister, allows him or her a tactical advantage in the timing of the election, though this did not work to the advantage of the party in government in 1970 nor February 1974.

The timetable for holding parliamentary elections is set out in the Representation of the People Act 1983. The whole process from the last sitting of the old parliament to the State Opening of the new takes about six weeks, though in 1992 it took just over seven. The basic rule is that a general election must take place on the seventeenth day (excluding Sundays and Holidays) following the date of the proclamation summoning the new parliament (which nowadays usually accompanies the dissolution of the old). The 1992 timetable ran as follows:

> Monday 16 March: Parliament met for the last time, was prorogued and was dissolved by Royal Proclamation later the same day. (In 1987 dissolution followed three days after the last adjournment.)
>
> Thursday 9 April: General Election.
>
> Tuesday 28 April: Parliament met pursuant to the Proclamation of 16 March to swear members and, in the Commons, to elect a Speaker.
>
> Wednesday 6 May: State Opening of Parliament.

Electoral law on the timing of campaigns is clear, the franchise is wide and elections are frequent. However, the voting system used is also important in determining whether an election result is representative. The British method is based on the relative majority method, sometimes called the 'first past the post' principle, and makes use of single-member constituencies. This means that the country is divided up into 651 geographical areas or 'constituencies'. In each of these the elector selects just one candidate among those on the ballot paper and marks an 'X' by the candidate's name. No order of priority between the other candidates (if there are more than two) is expressed. The candidate who receives the greatest number of 'Xs' – of votes – is elected in that constituency, even if he or she does not have an absolute majority of votes.

However, not all parliamentary constituencies are the same size. Under the law, constituencies in Scotland and Wales have smaller average numbers of electors anyway, but even within England, constituency size varies. The largest electorate in England in 1993 was in the Isle of Wight (101,652), with constituencies like Kensington and Surbiton having fewer than half this number of voters. The smallest constituency in the country was the Western Isles (23,127). Each country of the United Kingdom has a Boundary Commission which has the responsibility, every 10 to 15 years, of drawing fresh constituency boundaries as fairly as possible while at the same time taking account of local ties and the inconvenience involved in altering constituencies. There are always strong pressures to resist change and the Boundary Commissions can only correct the more obvious anomalies, as in its amalgamation of inner-city seats to reflect population moves away to the suburbs. The Boundary Commissions were due to make proposals for new constituencies at the time of going to press and (if approved by Parliament) these should form the basis for any subsequent general election.

Another feature of the British electoral system is that, almost inevitably in view of the first past the post system, the party allegiances of those elected as MPs are not in the same proportions as the votes cast throughout the country for their various parties. The table below shows the results of the 1992 election (excluding parties which fought in only one part of the United Kingdom).

Party	Percentage of total vote gained	Percentage of total number of MPs elected
Conservative	41.9	51.6
Labour	34.4	41.6
Liberal Democrat	17.8	3.1

Inside the individual constituencies, some are more evenly balanced between the competing parties than others – the so-called 'marginal' and 'safe' constituencies. For example, in 1992 the percentage results in marginal Brecon and Radnor were

Conservative	36.1%	(15,977)
Liberal Democrat	35.8%	(15,847)
Labour	26.3%	(11,634)
Plaid Cymru	0.9%	(418)
Green	0.9%	(393)

while in the adjacent safe Welsh seat of Blaenau Gwent the results were

Labour	79.0%	(34,333)
Conservative	9.8%	(4,266)
Liberal Democrat	6.4%	(2,774)
Plaid Cymru	4.8%	(2,099)

Obviously, the way in which the politically non-committed voter – the so-called 'floating voter' – turned in Brecon and Radnor was of much more importance to the result there (and therefore the result nationally) than what a similar floating voter did in Blaenau Gwent.

The present British electoral system does not allow second choices and is hard on third parties. It is also hard on minority national parties: for example, in 1992 in England, 1.4 per cent of the electorate voted for small parties like the Greens. None of these is represented in parliament. Alternative voting systems, such as the different forms of proportional representation used in the Republic of Ireland (and for local elections and elections to the European Parliament in Northern Ireland) or in Germany, might result in a House of Commons with a different composition. This could have a major effect on the way in which the House of Commons operates, as Chapter 12 will outline. The rights and wrongs of proportional representation are not within the scope of this book. Whatever the merits of the system, voting is not unpopular – 77.7 per cent of the electorate voted in 1992.

Choice of candidate

MPs are chosen by their party organisations in the constituency which they represent, though usually with some involvement of the central party organisation. Both Conservative and Labour parties have central lists of approved candidates. Aspiring Conservative MPs go through a series of interviews and written applications before being placed on the list. Labour hopefuls can belong either to List A (trade union sponsored) or List B (others). In the case of the Conservative Party, the constituency selection committee may choose any candidate it wishes, whether or not he or she is on the list, although in general only candidates on the list are chosen. Labour would-be candidates must secure nomination from at least one of the constituency branches, and are selected on the principle of one party member, one vote. The eventual nominee, if not already on either List A or List B, needs to be endorsed by the party's National Executive Committee before going forward as the candidate. The Liberal Democrats have slightly different rules for selection of candidates in England, Scotland and Wales. The fundamental principles are that panels of suitable candidates are drawn up in each country, and that all party members may vote in the relevant constituency to select their candidate. Once elected, Conservative MPs can normally expect to retain their party's nomination. Labour MPs are, however, automatically subject to the selection process during the term of the parliament – so-called 're-selection'. In practice, the majority are re-selected without difficulty.

The selection of candidates is therefore subject to local democratic control within the parties, though no procedure as elaborate as the 'primary' system in the United States of America has evolved. However, unlike the USA, it is not necessary for a would-be MP to have considerable personal means. Although the deposit required from candidates has been raised from £150 to £500, this is only forfeited if a candidate receives less than 5 per cent of the votes cast. In any case, it is found by the party, as are most of the candidate's expenses. Candidates cannot buy media time themselves but there are party political broadcasts allocated by time in a manner designed to achieve a fair distribution between the parties.

Who is selected?

Despite the local democratic element in the choice of candidate, the MPs who sit in the House of Commons cannot be described as a microcosm of the electorate as a whole. In the first place, 1 in 25 of the electorate are formally disqualified from membership of the House of Commons. These are principally civil servants, members of the armed forces, police officers, judges and clergy of the Church of England, the Church of Scotland and the Roman Catholic Church. If the House of Commons were representative in an absolute sense, 26 MPs would be drawn from these professions. The principal reason why these groups are disqualified is the need for them to be politically impartial, and there is little pressure to relax the law.

But MPs are not drawn proportionately even from among the occupations which are legally qualified for membership. Of those elected in 1992, 77 per cent of Conservative MPs and 50 per cent of Labour MPs had a professional or business background, with no fewer than 60 Conservative MPs being lawyers and 76 Labour MPs teachers. Only four Conservative and 59 Labour MPs had a background as manual workers. Educational standards among MPs are also higher than the electorate as a whole – the percentages of Conservative, Labour and Liberal Democrat MPs who had been to university were 73 per cent, 61 per cent and 75 per cent respectively. Half Liberal Democrat MPs, over half Conservative MPs and around one in seven Labour MPs had been to public school.

There are many reasons why certain professions have a disproportionate number of MPs while others (e.g. nursing, engineering, manual work) are less well represented. MPs do not have secure jobs in Parliament, and often like to retain part-time work in their old professions. Some jobs are 'communicative' and more likely to appeal to aspiring politicians. Some employers are unwilling to see their employees devote large amounts of their time to politics – an essential pre-condition if one intends to stand for Parliament. Some people are too highly paid to consider the comparatively low salaries and late-night sittings which a new backbencher has to endure. However, there is no evidence that MPs vote in accordance with their old occupational loyalties when those conflict with their party or constituency loyalties, and it may be that an analysis of MPs by occupation (or previous occupation) is of no great importance.

Nor should too much importance be attached to analysis of MPs by age. In relation to the population as a whole, there are very few MPs between the ages of 21 and 30 (only one was elected in 1992) and comparatively few over 60 (around 13.5 per cent). Since the 1970s there has been a trend towards younger MPs but naturally enough constituency parties normally prefer candidates who have some experience outside politics (though there is also a trend towards choosing men and women who classify themselves as professional politicians) and those who are not too far past retirement age. The 30–60 age group is represented disproportionately, with 48 as the median age of Conservatives elected in 1992, and 49 for Labour MPs.

Two areas in which the House of Commons is most often criticised for being unrepresentative is in the comparatively few female MPs it has and the non-representation for many years of ethnic minorities. In the last 30 years, the number of female MPs has improved, as the table shows, though women remain heavily under represented.

Election	Conservative	Numbers of female MPs Labour	Liberal/SDP	Other	Total
1964	11	17	0	0	28
1966	7	19	0	0	26
1970	15	10	0	1	26
Feb. 1974	9	13	0	1	23
Oct. 1974	7	18	0	2	27
1979	8	11	0	0	19
1983	13	10	0	0	23
1987	17	21	2	1	41
1992	20	37	2	1	60

With 11 men to every woman, the House of Commons was, in late 1993, rather better than the US Senate (6 women out of 100 Senators) and much better than countries like Belize, Jordan or Papua New Guinea where there were no women MPs. However, the United Kingdom was easily outshone by a number of other European countries – Finland with 39 per cent women MPs, Norway with 36 per cent, Sweden 34 per cent, Denmark 33 per cent, Netherlands 29 per cent and Austria 21 per cent. In Seychelles, no fewer than 46 per cent of deputies were women. For the first time in some years, the proportion of women in the Commons now exceeds the proportion of women in the Lords – in late 1993, there were 79 women out of 1207 members of that House. In terms of high prestige occupations in the United Kingdom, the ratio of women to men in the Commons is better than that in the Institute of Directors or among university professors, though worse than among medical consultants. Each political party has a policy of encouraging female candidates (the Labour Party has a policy of having all-women shortlists for candidacies in half the seats it regards as winnable), and a pressure group (the 300 Group) exists specifically to promote a higher female membership of the House. The reasons for the present low figures have been analysed by writers who suggest that those inside the constituency parties who select candidates may have a traditionalist approach to women's role in society, while at the same time many women are not attracted to the House of Commons precisely because the institution has been shaped by men in the past – as Shirley Williams, the former Cabinet Minister, was quoted as saying in *The Times* on 30th July 1985 'it's not so much a gentleman's club as a boys' boarding club'.

There have been black members of the House of Commons in the past (a Liberal, a Conservative and a Communist who each sat for brief periods between 1892 and 1929) but since the substantial immigration into the United Kingdom from its former colonies in the West Indies and the Indian sub-continent in the 1950s no representative of these communities had been elected to Parliament

until 1987 (though three had been created life peers). There is still
no representative of the substantial ethnic Chinese community.
Efforts have been made in all parties to nominate ethnic minority
candidates, but the six black or ethnic minority MPs elected in 1992
represent less than one per cent of the membership of the House,
and this compares adversely with the 4.5 per cent of the population
of the United Kingdom who are estimated to come from ethnic
minority communities. However, it is interesting to note that there
was only one black member of the US Senate in 1994.

Who are the Lords?

This book concentrates on the House of Commons. The Commons
became the dominant element of Parliament because they were
representative in the sense of being elected – even if, as we have
seen, they do not mirror the community at large. The Lords,
however, are representative in this sense of no one but themselves.
Their membership consists of several different elements.

Archbishops and bishops

The Anglican Archbishops of Canterbury and York, the Bishops
of Durham, London and Winchester and the 21 senior diocesan
bishops from other dioceses of the Church of England are the
'Lords Spiritual'. All the other Lords are known as 'Lords Temporal'. In the medieval Parliament, the Lords Spiritual (bishops and
mitred abbots) made up about half the membership. Currently they
represent about 1 in 50. Only the Church of England is represented.
The other 'established' church, the Church of Scotland, has no
nominees, nor do other religious denominations, non-Christian
religions or the Anglican churches outside England. When the
then Chief Rabbi, Lord Jakobovits, was made a Peer in January
1988, it was personal to him.

Hereditary peers

On 3 November 1994, 773 members of the House of Lords sat as
hereditary peers. Fifteen of these were 'hereditary peers of first
creation' – in other words they were the first to receive their
title, but may pass it on to their descendants – the others being
'hereditary peers by succession' or peers who have inherited their
title and who may pass it on in turn to their descendants. The
principle of a hereditary peerage is that, at some historical point,
an individual is created a peer or lord (in one of the different ranks
of dukes, marquesses, earls, viscounts or barons) and the legal
document conferring that peerage (the 'letters patent') stipulates

that his heirs (normally only the males) may inherit his title and with it the right to sit in the House of Lords. Some peerages descend through the female as well as the male line, and since 1963 women holders of hereditary peerages have been able to take their seats in the Lords.

The oldest English title is that of Lord de Ros. He is the twenty-eighth Baron, and his title dates back to 1264. The most recent hereditary peerage (excluding the royal Duke of York) – the Earldom of Stockton – was created in February 1984 when the former Prime Minister, the late Harold Macmillan, received this title. Two other hereditary peerages were created in 1983, but before that no new hereditary peerages had been created for almost 20 years. Under the Peerage Act 1963, it is possible to disclaim a hereditary peerage for one's lifetime. It was this which enabled Tony Benn eventually to remain as an MP in the House of Commons on the death of his father, Viscount Stansgate. Proposals for the reform of the House of Lords which have been canvassed in the last 70 years have usually suggested the removal of any hereditary right to sit or to vote in Parliament.

Life peers

The most significant reform of the twentieth century came with the passing of the Life Peerage Act 1958. Under this legislation, men and women could be created peers for life. The title would cease on their death. In November 1994 there were 383 life peers. Many of them are politicians, often those who have worked for their party outside Parliament or who have retired from the Commons or been defeated in elections. Other life peers have been drawn from different aspects of national life and have brought considerable and very valuable expertise to the House of Lords – former senior servicemen and civil servants, heads of nationalised and large private sector industries, trade union leaders, doctors and academics and even the occasional actor or teacher. The power to create peerages belongs formally to the Crown but in effect new peerages, including hereditary peerages of first creation and, since 1958, life peerages, are a gift of the Prime Minister of the day. This is obviously a considerable source of patronage for the Prime Minister. By convention, other party leaders are also asked to make nominations for new peerages. This is often the only way open to opposition parties to strengthen their teams of frontbench spokesmen.

Judicial life peers

Separate from its other functions, the House of Lords acts as the supreme court of appeal for the whole United Kingdom in civil cases and for England, Wales and Northern Ireland in criminal cases. About 70 cases a year are heard, and the business is done in the Appellate Committee, though judgments are delivered in the Chamber at specially convened sittings. When Parliament is not in session, the appeals themselves are also heard in the Chamber. The Lord Chancellor and Lords who hold or have held high judicial office may sit in the Appellate Committee provided that they are under 75 years of age, but the backbone is provided by up to twelve Lords of Appeal in Ordinary, salaried life peers appointed under the Appellate Jurisdiction Act 1876 specifically to hear appeals.

Who is active?

From the total membership of 1204, 161 are not active. A few are under 21, while some do not wish to participate and have not bothered to go through the necessary formalities on inheriting their title. They therefore do not receive Writs of Summons to Parliament. Others, while receiving a Writ, have obtained leave of absence. A further 11 have taken the most radical step of all and disclaimed their peerage for life. Thus of the potential membership of 1204 only 1032 are likely to sit. Actual attendance is far less. For example at the end of the 1993–94 session, of the 1032 potentially active peers, 876 attended at least once. 450 members attended on at least one-third of the sitting days; 370 members attended on at least half the sitting days; and 292 members attended on two-thirds or more of the sitting days. Taking these latter as the 'regular' attenders, 151 were life peers, three were hereditary peers of first creation, and 138 were hereditary peers by succession. Average daily attendance over this period was 378.

Because members of the House of Lords (except the bishops) are members until they die, some are too elderly to take an active part in the House – though this did not inhibit Lord Shinwell, born in 1884 and still active until his death over 101 years later in 1986.

Peers are unpaid, although they receive expenses and allowances of various kinds. The most important of these allowances are free travel to and from Westminster, an overnight and day subsistence allowance, and a modest secretarial and office expenses allowance. If all expenses are claimed, a peer can receive up to £134-50 for every day of attendance, excluding travel expenses. But this does not amount to a full-time salary, nor is it meant to. Consequently many peers have important and full-time jobs elsewhere – from Lord Camoys, a leading banker, to the Earl of Rosslyn, a policeman in his thirties.

In November 1994, figures for party allegiance among active peers were as follows:

Conservative	456
Labour	109
Liberal Democrat	54

A further 293 Lords (including the bishops and Lords of Appeal in Ordinary) declare themselves as independents or 'crossbenchers'. Although Conservatives outnumber adherents of other political parties by over two to one, as we shall see later, it has been common for the House of Lords to vote against some of the policies of the Conservative government since 1979. Free from the need to seek re-election or to court popularity with a constituency party, all members of the House of Lords have a latitude to act which is sometimes envied by their colleagues down the corridor. The crossbenchers ensure that the Conservative Party, though the largest party in the House, does not always have an absolute majority.

The Queen

Earlier in this book, the gorgeous Royal Robing Room and the Royal Gallery of the Palace of Westminster were described. And, of course, the whole Parliament building is a palace. These remind us that the sovereign is a part of Parliament – one of three branches of the legislature. The sovereign must give the Royal Assent to all legislation passed by both Houses of Parliament. She opens Parliament and dissolves it. She formally makes treaties with foreign states, creates peerages and makes many of the top appointments in the civil service, armed forces and judiciary. The form of delegated legislation known as Orders in Council are made in her name. But these powers are not exercised in anything other than name. The Queen is constitutionally bound to take the advice – in other words, to act in accordance with the wishes – of the Prime Minister. As the nineteenth-century writer Walter Bagehot put it, the Queen 'must sign her own death-warrant if the two Houses unanimously send it up to her'.

The last sovereign to refuse to give the Royal Assent to legislation was Queen Anne in 1707. But since the eighteenth century sovereigns have progressively distanced themselves from the business of politics. The conventional phrase is that the Queen 'is above politics', or as Bagehot wrote of royalty 'Its mystery is its life. We must not let in daylight upon magic. We must not bring the Queen into the combat of politics, or she will cease to be reverenced by all combatants; she will become one combatant among many'.

So is the Queen's role in Parliament merely ceremonial – just a question of riding in the State coach, escorted by the Horse Guards, from Buckingham Palace down to Westminster once a year to put on the Crown and the State Robes and deliver the Queen's Speech (a speech written for her by the government and announcing their legislative programme for the coming session)? In normal circumstances, when a government is in office and is supported by a majority of the House of Commons, this is so, but the Queen's role would be heightened if a general election produced a result which did not give a clear majority to any one party.

One of the Queen's formal responsibilities is to appoint a Prime Minister. The constitutional convention is that she should choose the leader of the party which has a majority of seats in the House of Commons after a general election, or the successor as leader of the party if the leader resigns in mid-term, as Harold Wilson did in 1976. Since 1945, the sovereign has had a clear indication after the election result as to which party leader should be asked to be Prime Minister. But if a general election resulted in substantial numbers of seats for three different parties, there is no clear constitutional convention which lays down what the Queen should do if the leader of the largest party is known not to have the support of either of the other two parties, or, if appointed Prime Minister, is defeated on a motion of no confidence in the House of Commons. Should the Queen appoint the leader of a rival party as Prime Minister at the outset if he or she is more likely to achieve a compromise? Should the Queen dissolve Parliament to allow a second election to take place if the leader of the largest party is appointed Prime Minister and advises her to do so? And if she does so, and the second election comes up with a similar result to the first, what should she do then?

The problem for the Queen in such a situation is that she may appear to become embroiled in the power-broking which goes with coalitions or minority governments. That might tarnish the magic about which Bagehot wrote and even discredit constitutional monarchy. In Australia in 1975 the Queen's representative, the Governor General, dismissed the Prime Minister in a constitutional crisis, and this has helped to fuel pressure for a republican form of government there. By contrast, in Belgium, where coalition governments are the norm, there was no real adverse comment directed towards the King in 1985 when he refused to dissolve Parliament as soon as the Prime Minister had requested, after the coalition had broken down.

It has been suggested that the Queen's powers to dissolve Parliament and to ask one of the party leaders to form a government should be delegated to the Speaker of the House of Commons as is the case in Sweden. But this would hardly resolve the problem, and it could exacerbate it by compromising the political neutrality of the Speaker. From years of experience and by taking advice from a variety of sources, the British sovereign can be relied upon to remain as objective and as much of a non-combatant as possible; and the resulting decisions to be pragmatic and right in the particular circumstances.

CHAPTER 3

Officers, officials and helpers: Parliament's administration

Any continuing organisation – whether a company or a public service – needs a permanent staff. And, beginning at the top, every sort of meeting, especially very large assemblies like the Houses of Parliament, needs someone in the Chair. The role of presiding officer in the two Houses has evolved rather differently, and the similarity between the maces and black satin robes which are accoutrements of both the Speaker of the House of Commons and the Lord Chancellor are misleading. Their functions are very different.

The Speaker of the House of Commons

The title of the Speaker (Madam Speaker or Mr Speaker, as she or he is always referred to in the House) comes from his or her position as the official spokesman of the Commons to the Monarch – a rather more arduous task in times when sovereigns and Commons were frequently squabbling than it is today. The Speaker still delivers formal speeches at State occasions such as the Queen's Silver Jubilee, and is responsible for other formal communications on behalf of the House, whether to the Indian Parliament on the assassination of Mrs Gandhi or – if the circumstances ever arose – to the governor of Brixton Prison authorising him to hold in custody someone who had committed a contempt of the House. The Speaker's more onerous modern duties are more inward-looking, but have considerable repercussions on the way in which the House operates.

In most foreign parliamentary assemblies, the presiding officer is a party politician. In the US House of Representatives, for example, the Speaker is a leading party politician and frequently takes part in controversial political debate. The pattern in Germany is for the Bundestag to elect as its President a senior member of the party in office who will continue to play an active part in his party's affairs. The same is true in France.

In Britain the person elected as Speaker is invariably an experienced MP. Moreover until Betty Boothroyd, a former Labour

MP, was elected Speaker in 1992, Speakers since 1940 had always been members of the government party when first elected to the Chair. However, although the Speaker will have been active in party politics for many years, the tradition of impartiality in the Speakership, which began with Arthur Onslow (Speaker for 33 years from 1728), is so strong that everyone accepts that a new Speaker will renounce party allegiance and become genuinely independent. A Speaker is an MP and has a constituency like all other MPs. If a general election is called he or she is obliged to stand if wishing to remain as Speaker. Because of the tradition of impartiality he or she does not campaign, but stands as 'The Speaker seeking re-election' and has in the past sometimes not even been opposed by the main opposition parties. If a change of government results from the election, the former Speaker can expect to be re-elected to the Chair – as Speakers who were former members of the Labour Party were in 1970 and 1979 and former Conservatives were in 1964 and 1974.

The choice of a Speaker is by election with MPs each having one vote. It is a choice which backbenchers take very seriously, and though the Cabinet and Prime Minister will often be known to favour a particular candidate when a vacancy occurs, backbench support is vital. In 1992, the former Cabinet Minister, Peter Brooke was defeated by 372 votes to 238, and Betty Boothroyd elected instead. Generally, however, a vote is avoided, and a Speaker is elected by his or her fellow MPs without opposition. Traditionally Speakers were backbenchers who had not been ministers, but the last seven Speakers have had some experience of government, three of them in the Cabinet. Speaker Boothroyd has not had departmental experience, but was a government whip between 1974 and 1976. Since he or she continues as an MP, a Speaker retains responsibility for constituents. However, work on their behalf cannot be pursued in a public way – for example, a Speaker cannot table parliamentary questions, though he or she can (and does) write to ministers about constituency issues.

The central function of the Speaker and the most obvious since broadcasting (and now televising) of the Commons began is to maintain order in debate. All speeches made in the Chamber are addressed to the Chair and the Speaker is responsible for 'calling to order' any MP who strays from the rules of the House, some of which are laid down in Standing Orders or in past resolutions of the House, but many of which are contained in the book commonly known as *Erskine May* – an exhaustive description of parliamentary practice, which has been published in successive editions since the nineteenth century, under the editorship of Clerks of the House. Rules range from the relatively trivial, like those obliging MPs to refer to each other by constituency rather than name, to the serious, like the *sub judice* rule (see page 90). In a democratic assembly, passions can run high and tempers flare. In these situations the Speaker has powers to discipline individual MPs, either by ordering them to leave the Chamber for the day or, for more serious offences, 'naming' them. After a member has been named, a motion is moved by the senior minister present, which the House invariably agrees to, and which has the effect of suspending the MP, so barring him or her from the building for five sitting days on the first occasion, twenty sitting days on the second and indefinitely on the third. If disorder in the Chamber is general, the Speaker can suspend the sitting.

Speaker Boothroyd's predecessor, Speaker Weatherill spoke in 1985 of the 'difficult task imposed on the Speaker . . . to balance the diverse and urgent claims of honourable Members, both backbench and frontbench and of nearly a dozen parties.' In MPs' eyes, the most important job the Speaker has is to balance the rights of the minorities in the House, or of those who hold unpopular views, against the majority, · and to hold the balance between the government and backbenchers in general. Politicians are in the business of getting their own views across, and the juggling act between these competing views is not easy for any Speaker. The way in which it is done affects the style of the House and every Speaker comes in for a certain amount of criticism, either for favouring backbenchers, or the government or the main opposition party too much. Generally Speakers are criticised on all fronts simultaneously.

The Speaker has a considerable number of discretionary powers and the way these are used is carefully scrutinised by those who feel hard done by. A former Speaker, George Thomas, wrote that his most potent weapon was the 'right to decide who to call to take part in debate or to ask questions'. The Speaker normally calls MPs to speak or ask questions from the two sides of the House alternately, but time is limited and some MPs are almost inevitably not called to speak in the popular debates. To be called during the half-hour a week devoted to Prime Minister's question time is especially prized, and successive Speakers have said that they keep records of those whom they have called in the past so that they can even out the score as much as possible. In one-off debates, it is harder to please everyone. Let us imagine a half-day debate on a proposal to end all ferry services between Scotland and Belfast. At least an hour of the debate would be taken up by the main speakers of the government and the main opposition party. Competing for the remaining two hours would be the main speakers of the smaller parties, Scottish and Belfast MPs with constituency interests, perhaps Labour MPs who were sponsored by the union representing seamen and those MPs who specialise in merchant shipping. When there is so much demand to speak on a relatively narrow issue like this, it is easy to imagine the competition to speak in major debates on defence, health or economic policy.

The Speaker also has discretionary powers to limit debate. He or she can select amendments or choose not to select them. This has an effect principally on debates on legislation, and will be described in Chapter 6. In Chapter 5, the closure will be described. This procedural device can be used to limit any debate, but the initial decision about whether an MP may attempt to use it rests with the Speaker. The Speaker can also intervene to prevent deliberate time-wasting by MPs either speaking repetitiously or calling for unnecessary divisions.

Three important procedures are allowed at the Speaker's discretion. Two of these permit the House to consider a matter urgently – the private notice question and the emergency debate. They are described in Chapters 8 and 9. Neither is generally welcome to the government, and both usually arise on matters of controversy where there are weighty political pressures pulling in two different directions. The third procedure is also contentious. Before 1978, complaints of breach of privilege were frequently raised on the floor of the House. In essence, a complaint can be made if someone is alleged to commit a contempt of the House, as defined by case law going back many centuries. In the 1976–77 session there were nine complaints of breach of privilege made on the floor of the House. In 1978 it was decided that complaints should be made initially in private to the Speaker who would decide whether the complaint could be raised in the House. A dramatic reduction in the number of complaints made openly resulted – there were only six in the ten years to November 1994. The use of the Speaker as a first hurdle has prevented the frivolous and ill-founded complaints which occurred before.

Although these powers are described as discretionary, as George Thomas wrote, 'a Speaker's greatest ally is precedent'. In deciding whether to allow a closure on a private member's bill, select an amendment defeated in standing committee by the casting vote of the Chair or call the leader of the opposition to ask a third supplementary at Prime Minister's question time, the Speaker will be aware of the way previous Speakers have acted. He or she has discretion, but that is tempered by these precedents.

In two areas in particular the Speaker always acts in a way which is governed by precedent. When the House is adjourned for a recess (or even over a weekend, as happened in the Falklands War) the government may ask the Speaker for a recall if the 'public interest' requires. The Speaker invariably allows this request. Secondly, the Speaker, while never normally voting, retains a casting vote when there is a tie. This was always possible during the 1974–79 parliament after the government lost its majority. During this period the Speaker's casting vote was used on seven occasions. The principles on which a casting vote is given were laid down by Speakers in the 1790s and 1860s and broadly are intended to give the House another chance before any irrevocable decision is taken. Speakers stick rigorously to these principles to avoid any appearance of partiality – there are few moments as tense as a tied vote on a crucial issue. A dramatic recent use of the casting vote was on 22 July 1993 when there was a tied vote – 317 to 317 – on the Leader of the Opposition's Amendment to a Motion on the Social Protocol of the Maastricht Treaty which had been moved by the Prime Minister. The Speaker voted against the Amendment on the principle that a decision to amend should only be taken by a majority vote. The occasion was very tense, but the neutrality of the Speakership was protected by the certainty that Speaker Boothroyd would vote in accordance with precedent.

In certain areas the Speaker has statutory responsibilities. The one which causes the most day-to-day work is his or her membership – and chairmanship – of the House of Commons Commission. This is the body which, as we shall see, employs virtually all the permanent staff of the House. *Ex officio* the Speaker is also Chairman of each of the Boundary Commissions mentioned in Chapter 2, though the effective work is done by the other members, led by a High Court Judge (or Scottish equivalent). In the past, Speakers have also been asked to chair a Speaker's Conference on Electoral Law where major proposals for change in the law governing elections are to be made and the government of the day thinks it wise to consult parliamentary opinion in advance.

Although the fact that the Speaker is governed by precedent has been emphasised, the problems with which the Commons have to deal are always changing. Thus, each Speaker has a responsibility for setting new precedents by his or her rulings. These new precedents can be as far-reaching as the procedures adopted by Speaker Brand in the 1870s and 1880s to deal with the Irish Home Rule MPs who were obstructing the Commons' business – before his unilateral action to limit MPs' rights to speak, MPs could speak for as long as they liked on any question they were asked to debate. More often, small changes occur as a result of Speakers' decisions which gradually and imperceptibly alter the procedures of the House.

The Speaker's job is a lonely one. By tradition he or she does not mingle with the other MPs in the dining rooms or bars. Formal dress is worn (though Speaker Boothroyd dispensed with the traditional full-bottomed wig when she became Speaker). A trainbearer walks in front of the Speaker when he or she is outside the Speaker's residence, and anyone who passes the Speaker in the corridors – from the Prime Minister down – is obliged to stop and bow. In private the Speaker comes under pressure from backbenchers and frontbenchers from all sides of the House. If any trace of partiality were displayed, it would be pounced on and a motion critical of the Chair would be tabled. Casual criticism of the Speaker is not allowed, but he or she is not protected, as the German Speaker is, from criticism, as long as it takes the form of a substantive motion. To avoid this, the Speaker's aloofness is almost essential. There are material compensations – the salary of a Cabinet Minister, the use of the Speaker's House, which contains some of the most splendid rooms of the whole palace, and a peerage on retirement. But a Speaker's chief reward must be the satisfaction of doing the job for which he or she was elected – making sure that the institution runs well, effectively and fairly.

The Speaker is assisted by three deputies – the Chairman of Ways and Means and two Deputy Chairmen. The Chairman of Ways and Means has special responsibilities for private bills (see Chapter 6), and he presides when a Committee of the Whole House is sitting. Committees of the Whole House are the one part of the proceedings in the Chamber for which the Speaker is not responsible. Both Speaker Thomas and Speaker Weatherill served apprenticeships as Chairman of Ways and Means before becoming Speaker, while Speaker Boothroyd was one of the Deputy Chairmen of Ways and Means.

The Lord Chancellor

The Lord Chancellor's residence is at the other end of the Palace of Westminster from the Speaker's. His job is also remote from that of the Commons' presiding officer. In him are combined the three functions kept constitutionally separate in the United States of America – the judiciary, the legislature and the executive. The Lord Chancellor is first and foremost an appointee of the Prime Minister, and a member of the Cabinet, heading a department responsible among other matters for the administration of the courts. Only distinguished lawyers are appointed to the Lord Chancellorship because of the Lord Chancellor's second role as head of the judiciary and his function of presiding over the House of Lords when it sits in its special judicial capacity (a function he is able to perform only occasionally). His tasks as Speaker of the House of Lords are, on the whole, subsidiary to his work as a member of the government.

The Lord Chancellor's powers as Speaker of the Upper House (which are shared equally by Deputy Speakers) are very limited indeed. The Lord Chancellor does not arbitrate on rules of order. The preservation of order in the House is the responsibility of all the Lords who are present and any Lord may call the attention of the House to any breaches of order or laxity in observing its customs. If the House finds itself in need of advice on matters of procedure and order it is to the Leader of the House (also a government minister), rather than the Lord Chancellor, that they look. And the Leader – or in his absence, the Government Chief Whip – will often intervene to interpret and give voice to what he considers to be the wish of the House when procedural difficulties occur.

The Lord Chancellor and Deputy Speakers do not call Lords to speak. As we shall see on page 91, order of speaking in debates is pre-arranged. The Lord Chancellor or his deputies will call members to speak to their amendments when the House is considering legislation, but no one calls the subsequent speakers in a debate on an amendment.

The Lord Chancellor cannot curtail debate, and when debate is concluded, his function is limited to 'putting the question' – announcing what it is on which the Lords are about to vote – and then declaring the result of the vote. He votes just like any other Lord, and, if the vote is tied, he has no function – the Standing Orders of the House then govern the result. Like the Speaker of the House of Commons, he is empowered to recall the House of Lords whenever it stands adjourned if public interest requires it – for example, for the debate on the outbreak of the Falklands War. But because of his position as a Cabinet Minister, there is no suggestion that the Lord Chancellor should be impartial. He speaks in debate in defence of government policy, and votes accordingly. With the agreement of the House, he does from time to time represent it on ceremonial occasions. Unlike the Speaker in the Commons, the Lord Chancellor plays no part in the day-to-day administration of the House. This role is undertaken by the Chairman of Committees.

Other parliamentary officials

House of Lords

The Houses of Parliament have a relatively small permanent staff. In the House of Lords, all of the staff come under the direct control of its clerk, the Clerk of the Parliaments, under the Clerk of the Parliaments Act 1824. As Accounting Officer and Corporate Officer, his own functions are very similar to those of the Clerk of the House of Commons, who will be described later, though the Clerk of the Parliaments is also Registrar of the Court when the House of Lords sits in its judicial capacity. Different offices under the Clerk's control deal with accounts, committees, establishments, overseas business, the journals of the House and public information, judicial business, the Official Report or *Hansard*, printed papers, private legislation, public legislation, historical records and refreshments. These offices are staffed by other clerks and officials appointed by him. There is also a librarian with a small staff who is responsible for the library and for a research service for peers. One officer not directly controlled by the Clerk of the Parliaments, although he is financially accountable to him, is the Gentleman Usher of the Black Rod, commonly called Black Rod. Black Rod achieves high public visibility each year when he marches down to the House of Commons to summon them to attend in the House of Lords where the Queen is waiting to read the speech with which Parliament is formally opened. As he arrives at the Commons, the door is slammed in his face to symbolise the historic independence of the Commons from the Crown, and he knocks three times with the black rod, which he carries and which gives him his name, before being admitted. In addition to this – and other – ceremonial duties, Black Rod is appointed as Agent to the Administration and Works Sub-Committee and as such is responsible for accommodation, security and services in the House of Lords. He is usually a retired senior member of the armed forces.

Another key figure is the Chairman of Committees, a member of the House who is sessionally appointed by the House to take the Chair in all Committees of the Whole House. He is also principal Deputy Speaker and organises the panel of deputy chairmen and deputy speakers to assist him and the Lord Chancellor to preside in the Chamber of the House. As Chairman of the Select Committee on House of Lords Offices and of its two key sub-committees on Administration and Works, and Finance and Staff, he is a very influential figure. He is paid the salary of a Minister of State.

The total number of House of Lords staff – the clerks, secretaries, clerical grades, doorkeepers, attendants, housemaids, refreshment staff and staff of the Official Report (*Hansard*) – is just over 300.

House of Commons

Leader of the House

The Leader of the House of Commons is an MP and a minister of Cabinet rank, and, of course, therefore appointed to his job by the Prime Minister. But although he has collective Cabinet responsibility for defending the government's policies in the House, he has a wider task of upholding the rights and privileges of the House. Along with the government whips, the Leader is one of the House's business managers. He has important functions in the cabinet committees concerned with the legislative programme; he reports weekly to Cabinet on forthcoming parliamentary business, and he announces that business to the House, and answers questions on it, every Thursday. When guillotine or Business of the House motions – or motions disciplining individual MPs – need to be moved, he is usually responsible for doing so. In any procedural debate, he sets out the government's view. He is a member of the House of Commons Commission, and of the Finance and Services Committee and chairs the Committee of Privileges. He often stands in for the Prime Minister when the latter is absent from the House, and sums up at the end of major debates – on the Address at the beginning of the session, or on any motion of confidence. A shadow leader of the House is appointed by the opposition. There is also a Cabinet minister Leader of the House of Lords, who performs similar functions to those of the Commons Leader. Individual areas where the Leaders of each House operate are described in more detail elsewhere in the book.

Clerks in the Commons

The senior permanent official of the House of Commons is its clerk. Unlike the Clerk of the Parliaments, the Clerk of the House of Commons does not have the other departments of the House under his control, though he is responsible for accounting for all the money spent by the House. The clerk's formal functions have come down from the middle ages – there has been an unbroken line of clerks since 1363 – and derive from a time when literacy was not universal. He is still responsible for keeping a faithful record of the House's decisions and for reading out the items of business which the House is due to consider. He sits at the table of the House, immediately in front of the Speaker, and is usually joined there by one or two colleagues who will also deputise for him at less busy times. Although these 'Clerks at the Table' dress in wig and gown, they are not usually barristers. Their expertise is in the procedure and practices of the House of Commons which make up part of the law of Parliament, and their principal modern function is to advise the Speaker, government, opposition and backbenchers of the way in which the House's procedures can be operated.

The Clerk heads a department which provides clerks for every standing committee and select committee and others who give advice to MPs on parliamentary questions, public and private legislation and other aspects of the procedure of the House. A large proportion of the staff of the department work for select committees. They are the only permanent staff of these bodies. All clerks are recruited in the same way as the administrative grades of the civil service and diplomatic service. However, they are not civil servants. They remain independent of the government, and they have a duty to give advice equally freely to any MP who asks for it, from the government chief whip to the newest or most eccentric backbencher. Also within the Clerk's Department are the Vote Office, which provides MPs with the documents they need, and the Parliamentary Office of Science and Technology (POST). POST was set up initially in 1988 with business sponsorship in order to help MPs have better access to scientific thinking. It became part of the House's service in 1993.

Clerks, like the majority of the staff of the House, are formally employees of the House of Commons Commission (see below). However the Clerk of the House himself and his principal deputy, the Clerk Assistant, are appointed by the Crown, which emphasises their independence.

Serjeant at Arms

The Serjeant at Arms's first recorded predecessor was given office by King Henry V in 1415, the year of the battle of Agincourt. Traditionally the Serjeant has been an ex-serviceman. In previous centuries he was responsible for executing the orders of the House, including making arrests, and the mace, which he still carries in ceremonial, was a necessary symbol of authority. His modern function of security is no less tricky in an age of terrorism, and he and his staff are responsible for maintaining order inside the precincts of the House and preventing any demonstrations or other misconduct taking place. The separate function of housekeeping involves the provision of office accommodation and linked services for MPs. The Serjeant's Department also shares with the House of Lords the responsibility for the parliamentary works directorate.

The Commons Library

The library department provides much more than simply library facilities. Its information and research services have steadily expanded, and are often the only – and therefore very welcome – research facilities available to backbench MPs. Different sections within the library undertake research on international affairs and defence, economic affairs, education and social services, home affairs, science and environment and statistics. The senior researchers are highly qualified, and their work is greatly respected inside and outside the House. The library also contains a public information office which deals with a large number of queries of all sorts from the public outside. The office can be telephoned direct.

Other permanent staff of the Commons

Other departments within the House of Commons service deal with the complex of refreshment and banqueting facilities in the House (the turnover in 1992–93 was £3.3m), with the Official Report (*Hansard*) which is the verbatim record of the debates in the Chamber and in standing committees, and with the finance and administration of the House including salaries and allowances of MPs and staff.

A computer officer works within the administration department. Both Houses are gradually, but for an increasing number of computer-literate MPs, too slowly, expanding their use of computer applications. MPs are responsible individually for purchasing IT equipment for themselves and their staff (though in June 1994, the House agreed that general recommendations would be offered centrally). The Parliamentary On-Line Information System (POLIS) has been available for some time and is being upgraded to enable easier access by MPs, their staff, Library staff and others. The system provides indexes to, among other things, *Hansard*, parliamentary publications, early day motions and the Library's book holdings. The Information Committee (see pages 31 and 210) has reported on a pilot experiment in a parliamentary outbuilding of a Parliamentary Data and Video Network which provides access to POLIS and external databases, fax facilities, electronic mail, a bulletin board and diary facilities. Its conclusions were broadly favourable and were endorsed by the House in June 1994. The introduction of a full Parliamentary Data and Video Network throughout the House and its outbuildings is now expected to take some six or seven years – a period which will no doubt see rapid development of new computer applications.

The total number of staff employed by the House of Commons Commission was 1285 on 1 November 1993.

Parliamentary administration

How, then, do these officers and other staff fit together in the administration of the affairs of the two Houses? The internal administration of Parliament is frequently passed over in commentaries on the UK parliamentary system – possibly because it is by no means straightforward to understand or because it is thought not directly to affect those activities of Parliament in which commentators are most interested. But the internal organisation of Parliament has done much to condition the environment and resources available to the two Houses for the conduct of their business. And it is frequently the case that backbench members can worry about the activities of the respective catering departments or the facilities in the Libraries as much as the provisions in a bill or the subject of a debate.

Each House regulates its own affairs using a broadly comparable system of domestic committees of members to decide issues of policy. The full-time officers, most of whom we described above, work with these committees and implement their decisions. On 1 April 1992, following the report of a committee chaired by Sir Robin Ibbs on the administration of the House of Commons, both Houses took on a more complete responsibility for their own financial arrangements than hitherto; previously the Department of the Environment had funded works and Her Majesty's Stationery Office, printing and publication costs. This ended. Both Houses underwent a reorganisation of their domestic committees to reflect their new responsibilities. The current position is as follows.

House of Commons

The chief decision-making body in the administration of the House of Commons is the House of Commons Commission, first set up in 1979 following the passage of the House of Commons (Administration) Act 1978. It is chaired by the Speaker and consists of the Leader of the House, a member nominated by the Leader of the Opposition and three backbench members, one from each of the main political parties. The Commission is the employer and paymaster of virtually all the permanent staff of the six House Departments (Clerk's, Library, Serjeant at Arms, Administration, Catering, Official Report) and responsible for expenditure on all the services provided by the House, including buildings. (The Treasury retains responsibility for payment of MPs' salaries and allowances only.)

This expenditure falls under two 'Votes' in the annual budgetary cycle – for the Administration of the House of Commons (£69m in 1994–95) and for Works Services (£38m in 1994–95). (MPs' salaries come under a third Vote.) Most government expenditure is closely controlled by the Treasury, but the two Commons' Votes are presented directly to the House by the Speaker on behalf of the Commission and are subject to no formal control by Government (for example, they are not 'cash limited'), although the Treasury is associated closely in the process of arriving at each year's Estimates. But the Commission exercises a self-denying rule whereby it will not make financial provision for any new major service which has not been approved in principle by the House of Commons itself or, in minor cases, by the relevant domestic committee.

The heads of the six Departments (the Clerk of the House, the Librarian, the Serjeant at Arms, the Director of Finance and

Administration, the Editor of the Official Report, and the Director of Catering Services) are individually responsible to the Speaker and the Commission for the activities of their staff. Together, they make up a Board of Management which provides collective management advice to the Commission, and they invariably hold preparatory meetings before the Commission meets. The Board also implements the tighter budgetary discipline and financial management which have been introduced since the Ibbs Report.

In deciding the kind of services to be provided to MPs and the levels of expenditure to be authorised, the Commission is assisted by five free-standing 'domestic' select committees. Of these, four are designed to give expression to MPs' views on the provision of services in the areas of *Accommodation and Works, Administration* (i.e. general services), *Catering*, and *Information* (including the Library). The fifth, the *Finance and Services Committee*, considers all proposals for new services which are expected to involve additional expenditure before they go to the Commission. The Chairmen of the four other Committees are members of the Finance and Services Committee and its Chairman is a member of the Commission.

The Clerk of the House is Accounting Officer for the expenditure of all six Departments and he is also Corporate Officer of the House of Commons – that is to say its legal representative. This, together with the antiquity of his office, makes him *primus inter pares* in relation to the other departmental heads.

House of Lords

The chief decision-making body in the administration of the Lords is the Select Committee on House of Lords Offices, under the Chairmanship of the Chairman of Committees. The Leader of the House and other party leaders and chief whips sit on it, and its total membership is 29. The Offices Committee, unlike the House of Commons Commission, does not, however, employ the staff in the Lords. In the Lords, there are two administrative Departments – Black Rod's Department and the Department of the Clerk of the Parliaments (also known as the Parliament Office), which includes all other administrative units like the Library, the Official Report and the Refreshment Department. All staff in the Lords are employed by the Clerk of the Parliaments under the Clerk of the Parliaments Act 1824. (In discharging his duties, however, he is answerable to the Finance and Staff Sub-Committee of the Offices Committee.) There is no equivalent of the Board of Management in the Lords. The Clerk of the Parliaments – like his Commons counterpart – is Accounting Officer and Corporate Officer.

Rather as the House of Commons Commission use the five

'domestic' Select Committees, the decisions of the Offices Committee are informed by the prior deliberations of four domestic sub-committees of the Offices Committee – on *Finance and Staff, Library and Computers, Administration and Works,* and *Refreshment*. In their respective fields, these sub-committees act as a sounding board for the opinions of members and may take decisions which need not be referred to the Offices Committee. All matters involving expenditure will, however, be referred to the Finance and Staff Sub-Committee for decision and reported to the Offices Committee. The importance of the Finance and Staff Sub-Committee is reflected in its membership, which includes the leaders of the political parties. To the extent that the House of Lords has an equivalent to the House of Commons Commission, it is the Finance and Staff Sub-Committee.

Like the Commons, Lords expenditure falls under two Votes – for Administration (£26m in 1993–94) and for Works (£15.5m in 1993–94). Peers' expenses are included in the Administration Vote. The Lords Votes are not presented directly to the Commons for approval but by the Treasury, rather as is the expenditure of a Government Department. The Lords, unlike the Commons, are not their own paymasters! But expenditure is not cash limited.

Parliamentary Works Directorate

As we have seen, both Houses have Works Votes. Through these Votes, each House funds building work and maintenance. But the two Houses share a common building of great historical significance. Thus, under a Memorandum of Understanding, all maintenance and any new works in support of common services are funded jointly by the Commons and Lords in the ratio 60:40 – in line with the space occupied by each House in the Palace. New works of benefit to a single House or expenditure on other buildings in single occupation are funded by one House alone.

These funds are spent through the Parliamentary Works Directorate (PWD) headed by the Director of Works. The Directorate is part of the Serjeant at Arms' Department in the Commons, but it serves both Houses equally and is answerable to both. It employs 190 staff. Of these, there are 100 directly employed labour craftsmen; 65 engineering/professional staff; and the balance are administration personnel. In addition, PWD engages outside contractors for major projects, numbering many hundreds in the usually very busy summer recess.

Financial Management

The Ibbs scrutiny has not only helped to shape the current administrative framework of the two Houses. It has imbued the administration with what, for Parliament, is a largely new concept of financial management. Bringing works expenditure and printing costs into the respective Votes, and re-organising the domestic committees were the most conspicuous features of improved financial management. But more significant for those who work in Parliament has been the introduction of departmental budgeting, of devolved budgetary responsibility to departmental managers and an increased awareness amongst all staff of the need to have regard to costs and value – whether in planning expenditure, taking on commitments or authorising payments. This is not always easy in a 'demand-led' organisation like Parliament and it has, for some, undoubtedly been something of a culture shock.

The Comptroller and Auditor General

There are two other important officers of the House of Commons. Neither works within the palace, nor plays any part in parliamentary administration, but both control large staffs and do work of national importance which is of particular relevance to the House of Commons in its two principal historic roles – the control of public expenditure and the redress of grievances. They could be described as 'semi-parliamentary' officials. The first of these is the Comptroller and Auditor General. His full title is 'Comptroller General of the Receipt and Issue of Her Majesty's Exchequer and Auditor General of Public Accounts' but he is normally just known as the C & AG. He heads a staff of just under 1000 in the National Audit Office, whose main buildings are a mile or so away from the Houses of Parliament. The C & AG has direct responsibility to Parliament and works closely with the House of Commons Committee of Public Accounts (see page 208). This relationship is recognised by his personal status as an Officer of the House of Commons.

All government departments and a whole range of other public sector bodies have their accounts certified by the C & AG, and the reports on these accounts are regularly presented to Parliament as parliamentary papers. However, some of the most interesting work of the C & AG comes in his value-for-money examinations of economy, efficiency and effectiveness in the use of resources by the bodies which he audits. Here he can select any topic he wishes, conduct an in-depth investigation and report to the Committee of Public Accounts. The committee will in turn usually take evidence from the body audited, and expect to see a Treasury response to their report. Though value-for-money examinations have usually concentrated on particular areas of waste, the C & AG is increasingly concerned with larger-scale, broad-based studies which should help public bodies to achieve value-for-money rather than merely criticising them for what has gone wrong in the past.

The C & AG is not subject to operational direction from the Committee of Public Accounts, nor from the House of Commons itself. He alone decides what to investigate and what he will say in his reports. However, the certainty that any criticisms he levels will be taken up by the Public Accounts Committee enhances his status, while the committee's work is made more credible by the back-up of the C & AG and his staff. In this sense the C & AG is like the ombudsman – both their independence and co-operation with Parliament are vital for them to help Parliament do its job of attempting to check abuses in government.

The Parliamentary Commissioner for Administration

The Parliamentary Commissioner for Administration is more commonly known as the Ombudsman, a Swedish word reflecting the fact that the first such officials were established in Scandinavia in the nineteenth century. Assisted by a staff of about 140, he investigates complaints of maladministration made by aggrieved members of the public against government departments and various other public sector bodies. Britain has had an Ombudsman since 1967 when the Parliamentary Commissioner Act was passed. The Ombudsman is usually an ex-civil servant or lawyer and, since 1973, has had the additional duty of Health Service Commissioner, investigating complaints of maladministration in the National Health Service.

The Ombudsman cannot examine questions of policy or clinical judgment, for instance the merits of a certain taxation system or whether a doctor's diagnosis was correct. Instead he looks at the quality of administrative actions. Examples of maladministration include rudeness by staff, delays in correspondence, failure to grant compensation or benefits, and ineffective complaints systems within departments or hospitals.

In NHS matters members of the public can approach the Ombudsman directly but other complaints (that is, those to the Ombudsman as Parliamentary Commissioner) must be referred to him by an MP. In 1992 as Parliamentary Commissioner he received 945 cases from MPs. 269 new cases were accepted for investigation. As Health Service Commissioner he received 1227 complaints in 1992–93. 164 complaints were accepted for investigation. Both the number of complaints received and the number of investigations undertaken have been increasing significantly in recent years.

The Ombudsman enjoys wide powers in his investigations. He has access to all documents apart from Cabinet papers and can require the attendance of witnesses. At the end of the investigation he produces a report which contains his findings on the complaint and any recommendations he might have. These recommendations may include both redress for the individual complainant, for instance the granting of financial compensation, and general improvements to administrative practice. The Ombudsman has no power to force a Government department or hospital to comply. Invariably, however, they do as he recommends. The Ombudsman's 1989 Report into the Barlow Clowes affair was a rare instance in which the Government disagreed with the Ombudsman's conclusions. They nevertheless agreed, out of respect for his Office, to make a substantial payment in compensation as he recommended.

The Ombudsman makes reports to Parliament in which the most significant cases are published in anonymised form and general lessons are drawn from his investigations. These reports are considered by the Select Committee on the Parliamentary Commissioner for Administration (see page 209). The Committee is concerned to learn why maladministration took place and what action has been taken to prevent such events happening again. The possibility of appearing before the Committee no doubt plays a part in encouraging departments and hospitals to agree with the Ombudsman's reports. The Committee also makes general recommendations relating to the Ombudsman's work and has frequently argued for extensions to his jurisdiction.

The effect of the Ombudsman's work extends beyond the individual complainant. On occasion the single case will alert the Ombudsman and a department to many others, sometimes thousands, similarly affected who will thus receive the same redress. The success of the Ombudsman can be judged by the creation since 1967 of other ombudsmen in the United Kingdom. There are Northern Ireland and Local Government Ombudsmen established by statute and others in both public and private sectors. The Ombudsman has demonstrated the value of his Office to the individual in the resolution of complaints and to Government in the improvements made to administration as a consequence of his reports.

Since April 1994, the Ombudsman has also had the responsibility of receiving complaints from individuals who believe that government departments have denied them information to which they have a right under the 'Code of Practice on Access to Government Information'.

MPs' assistants and pay and allowances

MPs have their own personal staff. The numbers of these have increased greatly in recent years, mainly through upgrading of the allowance (now known as the office costs allowance) payable in part for the employment of staff. An allowance of £500 was first introduced in 1969. This was increased from time to time in the twenty or so years which followed, but never to the level which many MPs felt they needed to perform their work adequately. Opposition to increasing the allowance came from successive governments. This arose from a number of factors: ministers wish to save public expenditure and, while they are backed up by civil servants themselves, they are reluctant to give backbenchers better resources to scrutinise the executive. Nevertheless, government proposals in 1986 and 1992 to increase the allowance by amounts which were regarded by backbenchers as over-modest were defeated by backbench revolts. In 1992 the effect of the House's decision was, in broad terms, to accept the level of allowance which had been assessed as appropriate by the Top Salaries Review Body in a 1992 report. This would then be upgraded in line with movement in appropriate civil service pay scales in subsequent years. In July 1994, it was decided that upgrading would reflect changes in the retail price index. For the year ending 31 March 1995, the office costs allowance stood at £41,308 – which remains a relatively modest sum for the employment of staff and the provision of office equipment such as computers and fax machines. Members of the German Bundestag and the European Parliament received almost twice this amount three years earlier in 1992, while members of the United States House of Representatives were provided with around £350,000.

Patterns of staff use by British MPs vary. Save in exceptional circumstances, an MP is only allowed to employ three staff eligible for passes to enter the parliamentary building. On average, MPs employ two staff, often a secretary and a political hopeful as a research assistant. But some MPs see their base as their constituencies and prefer to concentrate their staff there rather than at Westminster, and perhaps to share secretaries or researchers at Westminster. Some also employ temporary research assistants or 'interns' on the USA model – individuals who work more for the experience than the pay. An alternative route is for external organisations to fund research assistants who will work largely for them, though nominally working for an individual MP.

The Top Salaries Review Body's 1992 Report concluded that extra staff were necessary because of the increased demands on MPs from constituents and others. While this is undoubtedly true, the growth in staff has itself generated more activity in parliament in terms of, for example, numbers of questions or amendments tabled. An indication of the increase in the workload comes from the number of requests from researchers logged by the Library. In 1978 there were 144; by 1984, there were around 17,000, and by 1993, over 30,000.

In addition to the office costs allowance, MPs' allowances cover travel on parliamentary business for themselves, fifteen free return journeys a year between constituency or home and London for their spouses and children under 18, free stationery, telephone calls and postage within the United Kingdom, and, for those with constituencies outside London, over £11,000 a year to cover overnight accommodation away from home. Financial allowances are uprated annually in accordance with the retail price index.

In addition MPs are paid a salary. The setting of this salary has always been controversial. The press are particularly interested in MPs' pay, and MPs are one of the few groups in the country who can vote to set their own pay scale. There have been several attempts to remove pay-setting from an annual atmosphere of controversy. After a lengthy debate in July 1983, MPs decided to set the levels of their pay for the next five years, and then to link it to the civil service grade which earned £18,500 per annum in 1983. This policy was confirmed after the 1987 General Election.

In 1992 new pay arrangements were introduced for the civil service, while the House agreed to freeze MPs' pay for 1993 at 1992 levels. There was a great deal of dissatisfaction at this decision, and the Prime Minister announced in July 1993 that the Top Salaries Review Body (which would be renamed the Senior Salaries Review Body) would in future be asked to report from time to time on the pay, pensions and allowances of MPs (as well as Peers' allowances). In November 1993, MPs took decisions which had the effect of paying themselves £31,687 in 1994, £33,189 in 1995 and thereafter increasing pay by the equivalent of the average increase paid in the previous year to civil servants of grades 5 to 7. In real terms, MPs' salaries in January 1994 were almost as high as they had ever been. Nevertheless, they remain modest in comparison with other professional salaries and with the pay of members of a number of other parliaments, including Italy, Germany and France, let alone the USA. Some critics of MPs have alleged that there are MPs who use their allowances to boost their salaries – in other words, they claim allowances to which they are not strictly entitled. Others criticise the paid directorships, consultancies and so on which some MPs hold, and argue that MPs should receive no sources of finance other than their salaries and allowances. Issues such as these are likely to be considered by the Nolan Committee on standards in public life (see page 54). One thing is certain: there are few groups whose remuneration is as open to scrutiny as MPs.

Salaries and allowances are not the only factors which matter. The first chapter described how the present building was constructed with the needs of the nineteenth century in mind. Recognition of the need for decent accommodation has led to the conversion of a number of outbuildings in recent years – the old Scotland Yard buildings (now known as Norman Shaw buildings) now contain around 130 offices for MPs (about 40 of them shared), while the more recently converted 1 Parliament Street and 7 Millbank buildings provide rooms for almost 200 MPs and their staffs, as well as accommodation for many of the permanent staff of the House. Virtually all MPs now have their own offices, though there remains an underprovision of interview rooms and accommodation in the main building: MPs can still be seen interviewing constituents in the Central Lobby or dictating letters to their secretaries in the corridors. After the opening of the new parliamentary building in Bridge Street in 1999, there should at last be reasonable physical circumstances in which MPs and parliamentary staff can work.

CHAPTER 4

Parliament's powers: theory and practice

The constitutional theory of parliamentary sovereignty

The 'sovereignty of Parliament' is a principle of the British constitution. As we will see, this does not imply any theory about where political power actually rests in Britain. Parliament is described as sovereign because it is a settled part of the way the British State operates that any Act of Parliament can make or unmake any law whatever. No one can question the legality of an Act of Parliament. An Act could be passed to make all Welshmen wear kilts or for only orange jellies to be sold in supermarkets. More fundamental and serious laws could be passed – to ban all political parties except one, for example – and no court or other authority could say 'this law is unjust or foolish or unconstitutional' and order its overturn.

The principle was set out elegantly in 1844 when Thomas Erskine May published the first edition of the work (Erskine May's *Treatise on the Law, Privileges, Proceedings and Usage of Parliament*) which was to become the authoritative source book for the procedure of Parliament. He began his second chapter with a paragraph which read:

The legislative authority of Parliament extends over the United Kingdom, and all its colonies and foreign possessions; and there are no other limits to its power of making laws for the whole empire than those which are incident to all sovereign authority – the willingness of the people to obey, or their power to resist. Unlike the legislatures of many other countries, it is bound by no fundamental charter or constitution; but has itself the sole constitutional right of establishing and altering the laws and government of the empire.

This theoretical sovereignty is, of course, subject to practical limitations. R. A. Butler, in a famous phrase echoing Bismarck, called politics 'the art of the possible'. Laws cannot be enforced which do not recognise realities, and the most important of those realities was what Erskine May called 'the willingness of the people to obey or their power to resist'.

In the process of dismantling its colonial past the British Parliament passed the Statute of Westminster in 1931. Its preamble reads 'no law hereafter made by the Parliament of the United Kingdom shall extend to ... the dominions'. Britain no longer had power in some of its former colonies to make laws because it no longer wished to resist the power of the people of these countries to run their own affairs. Similarly, in Britain today the base line when we talk of the 'sovereignty of Parliament' remains the willingness of the people to obey the law.

There are other limitations to sovereignty which result from the radical changes in society which have occurred since the 1840s. Multinational business or the information technology revolution have in their own way limited the practical power of the law as enacted by Parliament. For example, as a result of the development of information technology, no one can actually physically control the flow of money abroad from the City of London when millions of pounds can be invested elsewhere at the press of a button. If we say that Parliament is sovereign over the financial institutions of the City of London, that may be true in constitutional theory, but it is not clear what is meant in practical terms.

As well as these practical constraints on parliamentary sovereignty, the fact that the United Kingdom is a member of the European Union (EU), with all the obligations that implies, has raised fundamental questions about the principle of sovereignty, at least in those areas where the EU has power to make law directly. The British courts have in effect overturned domestic legislation where it is incompatible with European law, but the question of how they would react to any law passed by the British Parliament which purported to abrogate an EU Treaty obligation is not clear. EU law supremacy and parliamentary sovereignty are two concepts which it is difficult simultaneously to uphold. Interested readers are recommended to follow the arguments in one of the standard text books on constitutional law, and they will find more on Europe in Chapter 11.

The dispute about the effect of European Union membership, which was brought about through Acts of Parliament (the various European Communities Acts), reminds us that parliamentary sovereignty is a legal concept. It should be distinguished from the more political concept of the power of Parliament as a working institution. Acts of Parliament may be able to do anything, but just because an Act has been passed, we must not necessarily assume that Members of Parliament originally saw the need for the Act or devised its wording or thought about its relationship with other Acts of Parliament, nor even that they discussed it thoroughly and dispassionately.

Let us assume for the moment that 'real power' has not passed outside Britain altogether. If we were then asked the question 'where does power rest in Britain?', we would probably say that it rested with the executive, what we in fact normally call the 'government' – the departments of State with their permanent staffs of civil servants which are headed by ministers, with the Prime Minister at the head of them all. We would have to accept that Parliament with its limited resources cannot govern a complex modern society such as the United Kingdom.

For a period in the nineteenth century Parliament could have been described as governing the country, but a number of factors have meant that in the twentieth century the power of governing has passed to the executive. These factors include the growth of democracy through the principle of one person one vote, the development of political parties, the increasing prominence of party leaders, the mass media and above all the growing and complex business of running a modern state.

Here we seem to have a dilemma. We do not talk about the 'sovereignty of government'. The constitutional concept is still 'the sovereignty of Parliament'. The courts would not accept that a government could simply make laws by announcing that it had done so. New statutes can only be made through endorsement by Parliament. Because of this, governments are still obliged to secure the approval of Parliament for what they do.

The initiative may be the government's, while for the most part Parliament allows itself to be controlled by the government which it in turn supports in office. However, Parliament retains important powers to validate or reject the actions of the government. What these powers are, and how Parliament exercises them, will be the subjects of Chapters 6 to 10, but first we will ask why Parliament acquiesces in the control which the government exercises over it, and how parliamentary sovereignty can be reconciled with government power.

Controls and influences on the House of Commons

The government's control

In the twentieth century, the dominant House of Parliament has been the House of Commons, and it is here that government's control is both most obvious and most effective. Why is this acceptable to MPs?

The main reason is because the governing political party is determined as a result of a parliamentary election. No-one should be surprised that MPs of that governing party should normally wish to support the government. After all, it only is the government because of their support – and they have only been elected because they were candidates for that party. Even if backbenchers on the government side may from time to time rebel on individual issues, they will normally want the government to get its way, and will favour practices and standing orders in the Commons which allow this to happen.

In addition, the party of government chooses the bulk of its ministers from among MPs, with a minority drawn from the House of Lords. The chief figures in the government, the ministers, are thus drawn from Parliament. In both Houses, even the 'Leader of the House' is a senior government minister, appointed by the Prime Minister, and ultimately responsible to him or her. In February 1994, there were 20 MPs and 2 Lords who were Cabinet Ministers and 50 MPs and 14 Lords who were ministers outside the Cabinet (excluding whips). Only very occasionally are non-members of either House appointed as ministers, and then they are normally created peers (Lord Young of Graffham was brought into the 1984 Cabinet by this route and he was a minister for a while before he became a peer). The only minister never to have been a peer or an MP was the South African leader, Smuts, who sat in Lloyd George's War Cabinet. MPs who are ministers – and their parliamentary private secretaries* – can be guaranteed to support the government because of the constitutional doctrine of 'collective responsibility'. Under this, a minister may disagree privately, but he or she is obliged to support any public statement of government policy, or to resign. Because they can be relied upon to support the government in any vote, ministers and their parliamentary private secretaries are sometimes called the 'payroll vote'.

While the majority of the House are thus either ministers or backbenchers who support ministers, whether because of their position as PPSs or their hope of becoming ministers themselves or simply through party loyalty, the government can be expected to dominate the House. As a result of this, the modern House of Commons has allowed Standing Orders to develop which give the business of the government precedence over any other business on all days the House meets, except for twenty days a year controlled by the two main opposition parties, three days controlled by select committees and certain periods reserved for backbenchers' bills and other backbench-initiated business. This means in an average session that more than three-quarters of the days are reserved for government business.

---

*Parliamentary private secretaries (or PPSs) are backbench MPs from the government party who are chosen by individual cabinet ministers or ministers of state to assist them in their parliamentary duties. They act as a channel of information between backbenchers and ministers, for example. They are not paid a salary and are not ministers of the Crown. However, they are not expected to vote against government policy, serve on select committees or take part in debates on their ministers' subjects of responsibility. To be a PPS is often regarded as the first step on the road to high office, though it is not necessarily so.

It is not just time which is controlled by the government: only it has the power to use some procedures or to introduce most financial measures. And if the Standing Orders do not allow the government enough flexibility, the government can propose their temporary suspension with the expectation that its supporters will approve. The arrangement and timetabling of government business in the House is in fact the responsibility of the government chief whip (the role of the whips will be discussed more fully on page 47). Because of the dominance of government business, to all intents and purposes, the government manages all the business of the House of Commons, in consultation with the other parties.

A government does not have absolute powers. It depends on the support of a majority of the House of Commons. When it no longer has this, as happened to the Labour government in 1979, it must resign and call an election. By 1979, Labour no longer had an overall majority in the House, and relied on other parties for support. Since 1979, each government has had a majority (though the small majority of 1992 – exacerbated in late 1994 by the withdrawal of the whip from 8 rebel Conservative MPs – brought back the spectre of lost votes on the floor of the House). What stops a party with a large majority from suppression of the other political parties? Such a government could use its majority to suspend Standing Orders in their entirety; it could introduce an 'enabling bill' at the beginning of the session which would provide that all future legislation should be by ministerial order rather than Act of Parliament; it could even expel all members of the opposition parties from the House of Commons. In other words, it could act, in the former Conservative Lord Chancellor, Lord Hailsham's famous phrase, as an 'elective dictatorship'.

Some people think constitutional reform is necessary to prevent an 'elective dictatorship' acting in this way. Government powers, they say, need to be checked, and Parliament needs to be strengthened. Fundamental questions about constitutional reform are outside the scope of this book, but some methods with a special bearing on Parliament will be mentioned briefly in Chapter 12.

However, the freedom of opposition MPs to criticise the government is protected in a variety of ways. Most important of these is the political culture of Britain, backed up by the media, the educational system and popular opinion: we expect to be able to discuss issues freely and to allow the whole range of political opinions to be expressed. This is in a sense an unwritten constitutional rule, and a government which tried to break the rule by using its parliamentary majority to suppress the views of its opponents would lose popular support. Individual MPs realise this, and they know that they need popular support to be re-elected. Although government control of the Commons rests, as we see in the next section, upon party cohesion, control which amounted to abuse would not be tolerated by MPs. They are individuals, chosen by individuals inside their constituency parties and elected by individuals in the constituency. It is the individuality of the MP – as well as their liability to re-election at least every five years – which is one of the ultimate strengths of the present system.

There is a more pragmatic reason why the present system of government domination of the Commons has developed. The principal opposition parties hope that, after a future general election, they too will occupy the government benches. Then they will want the system to operate to their advantage, allowing them to secure the passage of their legislation. Meanwhile they accept that the government of the day (which they oppose) has a similar right. For their part, government MPs recognise that they might at some time in the future form the opposition. For this reason it would be counterproductive for them to whittle away at the opposition's rights. There is a sense of fair play about this mutual acceptance on both sides of the House that the government has the right to govern. This view is, however, largely dependent upon an expectation that the party of government will from time to time change, and it is noticeable that long periods when one party remains in government have brought strains and accusations of government indifference or even arrogance towards legitimate opposition aspirations. This was apparent in early 1994 when the Labour Party broke off normal working arrangements with the Conservative government for some months.

The party – the basis of parliamentary politics

If 651 people were chosen at random as a sort of jury and asked to decide whether laws should be approved or not, they would decide for a whole number of personal reasons. Only a small proportion of them would be members of political parties and, of these, not all would vote in accordance with their party's policy – they might not even know what it was. The 651 MPs by contrast are all members of political parties – with the exception of the Speaker – and seldom vote without thinking what their party's policy is on the issue before them. In a sense, political parties are a limitation on MPs' freedom of action, but they are essential in a democracy as the way in which people active in politics and the electorate in general can control the MPs whom they send on their behalf to Westminster.

Individuals become members of political parties because they believe that their party's policies are broadly correct, though they may disagree in a few specific areas. When the party members in a constituency select their parliamentary candidate, not all of them will share his or her views on every issue. Some would have preferred a more left-wing candidate and some more of a right-winger. Most party supporters in the constituency and a large number of floating voters who are attracted by the party's policies will vote for the candidate at the general election simply because he or she is the candidate of the Labour or Conservative or Nationalist or whatever party, and they agree broadly with the policies put forward by their favoured party in fighting the election campaign. Only a small number of the people who vote for the candidate will know anything about his or her personal views. Candidates are elected, and arrive in Parliament because of their parties' endorsement. Their party allegiance and those of their opponents in the election were the way in which the electors were able to choose the broad political philosophy which they wanted to underlie the way in which the country was governed over the following five years. Each MP has a small amount of latitude to rebel against his or her party on issues on which they feel strongly, but they must always remember that they are only MPs because each of them has a party label.

The classic doctrine of Edmund Burke, set out in his address to the electors of Bristol of 1774, was that, once elected, an MP was responsible for making independently his own judgements on the issues before him in Parliament. Sometimes today, especially when moral questions like abortion or the death penalty are before the House, there is no party recommendation on voting, and MPs follow their own conscience. But for the majority of political business in the modern House of Commons, MPs are first of all responsible to their political parties – and in at least nine out of ten of the divisions in the House of Commons, an MP's party will tell him or her which way it wants them to vote. Individuals who say that their judgement is always different from that of their party leaders are going to find it pretty well impossible to convince their local parties to re-select them as candidates. They might enjoy a few years of glorious irresponsibility in the House (an MP cannot be sacked between elections), but their political career will probably be at an end when the next election comes round. Perhaps the best known case of an MP who kicked over the party traces completely was that of John Stonehouse, a Labour MP who 'disappeared' in Florida and then reappeared in Westminster as the sole member of the English Nationalist Party. Elected MPs can change their party allegiance in less bizarre ways, and a number did so to form the Social Democratic Party during the 1979–83 parliament, after originally being elected as Labour MPs (one as a Conservative). Over twenty of them lost their seats at the 1983 election, so appearing to demonstrate that party rather than personality was the principal reason for their original election.

This large change in allegiance was the product of special

circumstances. Generally, although the press like to exaggerate any tension between individual MPs and their party's leadership, MPs are elected as Conservative or Labour or Nationalist MPs because they support the policies of the leadership of the Conservative or Labour or Nationalist parties. Because they support these policies, they will vote along party lines on most occasions. It is a two-way street, and it is perhaps more accurate to see MPs as only having any power at all because they are members of political parties than saying that their parties limit their power. That said, there will always be occasions, as we will explain later, when individual MPs feel that they cannot endorse their party's line – as happened most obviously during the passage in the 1992–3 session of the bill designed to implement the Maastricht Treaty, the European Communities (Amendment) Bill.

MPs, then, all have party loyalties. The 1992 election result meant that the House of Commons did not consist of 651 individuals but of 336 Conservatives, 271 Labour MPs, 20 Liberal Democrats, 4 Welsh and 3 Scottish Nationalists and 17 MPs representing the different political parties of Northern Ireland. The most important function of this party composition of the House of Commons is to determine which party will govern, and which party will have the privileges of being the 'official opposition'. In the two-party system there is usually no doubt about this. Because Conservatives were the largest number, their leader remained Prime Minister. The leader of the Labour Party remained leader of the opposition because his party was the second largest. Since 1937, the leader of the opposition has been paid a salary and has various important rights conceded by successive governments.

We have described earlier how the Queen's job of selecting a Prime Minister could be more difficult when a result is close, but when it is as clear-cut as it has been in every election since 1945, it is obvious from the make-up by party of the House of Commons which party should be in government. In 1992, the Conservatives, with an overall majority of 21, could expect that their policies would be voted for by a majority of MPs.

Once an election has decided which party will be in government, the House of Commons, through its Chamber and, to a lesser extent, its Committees, becomes the arena for the political battle between the ideologies of the principal political parties. The government presents its policies in as favourable a light as possible, but their presentation, and the criticism of the opposition, is directed towards the electorate outside the House. The policies of the competing parties are in this way constantly exposed to analysis – though the system gives different opportunities to the different parties, depending on whether they are the party of government, the main opposition party or one of the others.

In the Standing Orders and formal rules of the House political parties hardly figure, but party effectively governs many of the more domestic conventions of the House – for example, government supporters sit on the side of the House to the right of the Speaker, the official opposition sit opposite. Committees are selected 'to reflect the composition of the House', which means, in effect, that they have the same proportions of MPs from each party as exist in the House. There has also, since 1975, been limited official financing of opposition parties. The formula under which this is paid was revised in 1993. In the year ending 31 March 1995, parties will be paid on the basis of £3,521.67 for each MP elected from the party at the most recent general election, plus £7.04 for every 200 votes cast for the party. Both figures were based on ones set in 1993, and have been adjusted in line with inflation. Future figures will also be inflation-adjusted. Under the formula, the Labour Party will receive £1,439,803 in 1994–95, while, for example, the Scottish National Party, with 3 MPs and 629,552 votes, will receive £34,610.

The party whips

The term 'whip' is said to owe its origin to the whippers-in – people who keep the hounds in order at fox-hunting meets. Parliamentary whips are supposed to be similar disciplinarians controlling the pack of MPs in their party. There is a good dose of exaggeration in regarding whips in this way. Their modern job is more that of personnel manager. Every party at Westminster has found whips necessary. The Conservatives currently have fourteen and the Labour Party eleven, while the smaller parties have one or two. Government whips are all ministers of the Crown, and the three senior official opposition whips receive special salaries – the only members of the opposition, except its leader, to do so. Traditionally, neither government whips nor the opposition chief whip ever speak in debate in the Chamber or in any committee – though a whip of each major party is always present in the Chamber and in Standing Committee.

The principal task of the government chief whip is the arrangement of government business in the House. He must get the business through and must try to ensure that, in spite of the activities of the opposition, by the end of the session, Parliament has passed all the legislation and done all the other tasks which the government has planned for that period. To achieve this in a reasonable manner, he and all the other whips have to remain in touch with one another. Life would be intolerable unless there were cooperation between the parties to ensure that the opposition parties are given a reasonable chance to oppose the government and the government a reasonable opportunity to get its legislation through the House. Parliamentary procedures can always be used to disrupt parliamentary proceedings, but the opposition uses disruptive tactics only as a last resort. Cooperation generally brings better results. These day-to-day working arrangements and compromises are made through what are called the 'usual channels', a mysterious parliamentary phrase which covers the close working relationships between the whips of the different parties and their secretariats – principally those of the government and the official opposition. The 'usual channels' are sometimes criticised by backbenchers: the relationship between whips of different parties is seen as too cosy, and sometimes is used to prevent dissent within parties. For example, the 'usual channels' might arrange for a debate on European matters to take place 'on the adjournment' (see Chapter 9), so avoiding embarrassing anti-EU votes from 'Eurosceptics' in both main parties. But most people would accept this work of oiling the parliamentary machine as essential.

The second task of the whips is to ensure communication inside the party. Most obviously this involves sending to MPs 'the whip', a statement of the forthcoming business in the House, with items underlined once, twice or three times to indicate their importance to the party leadership. When a 'three-line whip' is issued, the leadership is telling MPs that it expects them to turn up and to vote on the matter under discussion. Normally most MPs will accept a three-line whip without question, but when they disagree with what they are being asked to do, the whips will act as the channel of communication from those MPs to the leadership. An MP who is not prepared to toe the party line is expected to go to see a whip and explain his or her views. The whip will probably arrange an interview for the MP with one of the party leaders who will explain why their vote is wanted and try to persuade the MP to change his or her mind. MPs who persistently disagree with the whip may well get into trouble with their local parties, as we explained earlier, and may (though this happens rarely) be disciplined by their Chief Whip – eight Conservative MPs who failed to vote with their party on an issue of confidence (where a lost vote would have meant a general election) had the whip withdrawn in late 1994, though many expect them to be returned to the party fold in 1995. The Labour Party's whips have no power by themselves to withdraw the whip from a Labour MP.

Whips in the two largest parties are organised by region and by subject. There will be a Home Affairs whip and one for the North-East of England, for example. These whips keep a watching brief on feeling inside the party on the issues they cover and among the MPs who sit for the geographical region for which they are responsible. Their analysis of these views is reported back to the leadership, and acts as an early-warning system allowing them to defuse any storm brewing on the backbenches. This is especially true when their party is in government and its leaders have the time-consuming job of being ministers, so taking them away from constant day-to-day contact with their backbench supporters.

Efficient communication of views should mean that the party is never embarrassed by unexpected votes in the House which go wrong. The first job of the government chief whip is to advise the Cabinet about the acceptability of its proposals to its backbench supporters. Once he has assessed backbench opinion, if he advises that the proposals are acceptable, he is expected to ensure business is arranged in such a way that his party members are present and voting in sufficient numbers in the House and in standing committee to give the government a majority. That means avoiding procedural obstacles, having a keen nose for any trouble which may flare up and being responsible for an efficient 'pairing' system so that every absence of one of his supporters is neutralised by an arrangement for an opposition supporter to be absent also.

Whips, then, are business managers for their parties, ensuring that the parliamentary party system is used to convert political aims into political achievements through the use of MPs' votes, cast on a party basis.

Party committees and groups

The whips do not spring political surprises on MPs. For MPs are themselves part of the decision-making process in their party, and their influence comes across in the committees and groups which each party organises. This organisation is obviously more complex in larger parties, but each party has a formal structure, is supported by a secretariat, and has special office accommodation.

The Conservative Party

Conservative MPs are responsible, after consultation with peers and the party outside Parliament, for the election of the leader of the Conservative Party, and a leader is subject to annual challenge if demanded. The leader is responsible for the party's policy, and so, ultimately, Conservative MPs, as the leader's electorate, make the final decision on the direction of party policy. The power of Conservative MPs to challenge their leader was strikingly shown to be more than nominal in 1989 and 1990 when the incumbent, Margaret Thatcher, was challenged and, ultimately, having failed to win on the first ballot in 1990, obliged to step down as party leader and Prime Minister. Subsequently the party's rules were altered to make a challenge more difficult – the nomination of an alternative candidate now needs to be supported by 10 per cent of the members of the parliamentary party – but the power of

Conservative MPs collectively to change their leader remains.

Clearly parties will only very unusually want to change leaders against the incumbent leader's will, and so Conservative back-benchers' formal day-to-day influence in policy making is usually channelled through the 1922 Committee and subject committees. The 1922 Committee (so called either because it was initially formed by MPs elected for the first time in 1922 or to commemorate a meeting of backbenchers which overthrew Lloyd George in 1922) consists of all Conservative backbenchers. It meets quite briefly every Thursday evening and is usually attended by fewer than 100 MPs. Part of its meeting is informative – a whip outlines the following week's business and there may be reports from committees, while part may be used to air topical issues suggested by the executive of the committee or ordinary backbenchers. Occasionally a minister is invited to speak and answer questions. The Chairman of the 1922 Committee is elected annually and has an understood right of access to the leader of the party.

A varying number of subject committees – around two dozen – meet weekly, at meetings open to all Conservative MPs. Attendance varies – it can go over 100 when a controversial issue is being discussed, but is usually under 20. The officers of these committees are elected annually and the important committees' keenly contested elections are used as an indicator of feeling inside the parliamentary party. Through these committees backbenchers can force the leadership to change its policy on particular issues – the then Education Secretary Sir Keith Joseph, for example, withdrew his 1984 proposals on parental contributions towards student grants after opposition in the backbench Conservative Education Committee. Many of the groups have regular meetings with ministers – the officers of the Foreign Affairs Group, for example, meet the Foreign Secretary each month.

As well as subject committees, the Conservatives have geo-graphical area committees meeting with varying regularity. Conservative MPs also organise together in other ways. There are groups with formal constitutions which MPs as well as other Conservative politicians join, like the Tory Reform Group and the Bow Group, and there are several semi-political and semi-social clubs, especially the dining clubs of like-minded MPs. In addition MPs who share a common political aim, for example those who are opposed to further European integration, have private meetings to discuss tactics.

The Labour Party

Since 1981 the Labour Party has given others, as well as MPs, a role in the election of its leader and deputy leader. At present, MPs (and members of the European Parliament) hold a third of the votes – though a candidate for leadership needs to be an MP and to be nominated by 30 other MPs. Party policies are formally determined by the party conference, rather than the leadership. When Labour is in opposition, its MPs elect the Shadow Cabinet, properly called the Parliamentary Committee. Individual members of the Shadow Cabinet are given areas of responsibility and the media usually turn to them for the 'Labour Party view', though strictly they only represent the Parliamentary Labour Party.

All Labour MPs, backbench and frontbench, are members of the Parliamentary Labour Party (the PLP). The PLP meets twice weekly – a short meeting on Thursday evening to hear the following week's business arrangements, and a longer meeting on Wednesday mornings (from 11.30 a.m. until 1 p.m. or so) when reports are made from the Shadow Cabinet, motions can be moved by individual Labour MPs and other items are placed on the agenda. There is usually a lengthy period devoted to topical issues raised under 'any other business'. The PLP has a number of departmental committees, each covering one government department with occasional sub-committees to cover particular topics like the arts or sport. These committees are attended by frontbenchers, and by Labour Party members of the equivalent select committees, both of whom may report on their work. The departmental committees have varying numbers of MPs attending, depending on the interest the subject generates in the party. Unlike the Conservatives, Labour MPs are limited to membership of three committees but can attend any committee in a non-voting capacity. The committees may advise on parliamentary tactics – for example, the tabling of motions and questions – and discuss the presentation of policy. There are also regional groups of Labour MPs.

The Labour Party has many different sources of power and influence – the trade unions and the constituency parties are at least equal to the parliamentary party – and there are groups which organise across the party like the Fabian Society, as well as groups of like-minded Labour MPs which have formal constitutions and meetings and are intended to influence the broad direction of party policy: the left-wing Tribune Group is probably the best known of these.

The Liberal Democrats

The Liberal Democrat party formally came into existence in March 1988 and had its first Assembly in September 1988. Although the Leader must be an MP, and must be nominated by two MPs, he is elected by a postal ballot of the party's total membership throughout the country. The party's policy Committee is also headed by an MP – at present the party Leader.

The Liberal Democrats have continued the previous Liberal

Party's practice of electing the Chief Whip from among MPs, and of meeting weekly on Wednesdays at 6.30 for an hour or more with representatives of Liberal Democrat peers and national officers and staff in attendance. Forthcoming business in both Houses is likely to be discussed first, followed by items submitted by the Members and lengthy 'any other business'. Occasional longer meetings also take place, including meetings lasting a couple of days away from Parliament during recesses.

Other parties

The three Scottish National Party and four Plaid Cymru MPs meet jointly on Wednesday afternoons. The chair alternates between the leaders of the two parties. A principal concern of these weekly meetings is to develop coherent tactics and to ensure a presence in debate. This is a particular problem for small third parties – business is principally arranged between the two major parties, and the Nationalists might find that they have to decide between support for the government and support for the opposition when they may agree wholly with neither. (The third option of abstention is not recorded officially – and an abstainer cannot be distinguished from an absentee.) The responsibilities for covering debates is divided up between the two parties.

The Ulster Unionist party, with nine MPs, holds weekly meetings – usually at noon on Wednesday. These meetings are held in Belfast when the House is not sitting. The meeting provides an opportunity for decisions to be taken on political tactics: for example, how to vote on a motion or what amendments to a Bill the party's MPs should table. The MPs' meeting complements the quarterly meeting of the party's policy committee which includes non-MPs among its members.

The Democratic Unionists and the Social Democratic and Labour Party have three and four MPs respectively. With such small numbers, the necessity to have formal arrangements for MPs' meetings is obviously less.

*   *   *   *   *

Political parties consist of much more than MPs, but MPs are the principal group of full-time political workers in the country, and consequently have an important role both in the determination of their parties' policies, and in the presentation of them. Each parliamentary party has different formal methods of involving MPs in the decision-making process, but underlying these are individual informal personal contacts and relationships – the newest back-bencher may spark off an important new idea with the leadership as a result of a three minute conversation in the dining room or the division lobby. Indeed, some MPs would argue that their influence is most effective when it is exerted in private, as far away as possible from party committee meetings, let alone the Chamber of the House.

Non-party influences on MPs

MPs are not automata, and their loyalty to their party is balanced by other pressures. A survey published in January 1985, based on the views of two-thirds of backbenchers, showed that MPs were prepared to rebel. Statements were put to MPs with which they were asked to agree or disagree. Three of the answers are particularly interesting.

	Agree	Disagree
I would never vote against my party on a three-line whip	8.4	83.6
My primary loyalty is to my party	51.1	37.8
My electors expect me to use my judgement on issues	87.6	4.6

We shall now try to analyse some of the influences on MPs which cause them to vote against the party line.

Personal influences

MPs are individuals. Their views are determined by the same factors that apply to other members of society – their family background, the part of the country – or the part of the world – in which they were brought up, and their education. Comparatively few enter full-time politics without work experience elsewhere, and they will bring to their work as MPs the views acquired in their jobs and professions, either formally – as union-sponsored MPs or members of professional associations – or informally. MPs have friends and families who influence their opinions, and experience events in their own lives which make them particularly interested in areas of political action – for example, the MPs of Afro-Caribbean origin are concerned with racial discrimination in Britain, and an MP who has seen disablement personally in his or her close family may have particular personal experience resulting in an interest in helping the disabled. MPs also react to news in the same way as other people: television pictures of famine in Africa or newspaper stories about baby-battering, for instance, will influence MPs just as they influence everyone else.

Personal financial interests come into a different category. The House of Commons has always forbidden MPs to vote on issues from which they gain personally. Since 1975 MPs have formally been required to register certain interests. Currently these include all paid directorships or jobs, all financial sponsorship, names of any clients an MP acquires as a result of his or her membership of the House, gifts of more than 0.5 per cent of salary (around £160 in 1994), any overseas visits not paid for personally or out of public funds, all payments from foreign Governments, organisations or individuals, any substantial interest in land and the names of any companies where the MP has more than 1 per cent of the shares or a nominal shareholding greater than £25,000. The purpose of registration is to help ensure that MPs' personal influences are open to scrutiny. However, registration has caused controversy. In the past, a very small number of MPs have refused to register, arguing that the House does not have the power to require them to do so. Other MPs believe that the formal registration requirements do not go far enough: for example, they do not cover financial interests of MPs' sons or daughters. In mid-1994 a series of revelations about payments which certain MPs had received (some of which were declarable but not declared, and some of which were not declarable under present rules) led to further controversy about the registration of MPs' interests. Part of the remit of the Nolan Committee on standards in public life, set up in October 1994 as part of the government's response to the controversy, is likely to be the proposing of new and clear standards in these areas for MPs and other public office holders.

The constituency

We referred earlier to Edmund Burke. While he believed that an MP owed a duty to his constituents, he wrote to them: 'You choose a Member indeed; but when you have chosen him, he is not the Member for Bristol, but he is a Member of Parliament.' Few MPs in the 1990s have such a detached public position about their constituencies. The growth of State intervention, media coverage of politics and Parliament and diminished respect for institutions has meant that MPs are exposed to increasing pressure from their constituents to act on their behalf. In consequence, MPs regard their roles as spokesmen and women for local interests, as local ombudsman and as constituency welfare officer as increasingly important.

Most MPs now operate a form of 'constituency surgery'. The word 'surgery' is appropriate because seeing one's MP is very much like seeing the doctor. Depending on the size of the constituency, the MP is available at one or more well-publicised locations, usually on Saturday mornings or Friday afternoons once a week or once a fortnight, to meet constituents for personal interviews. The MP's hours of attendance are advertised, and constituents simply arrive and wait until it is their turn to put their problem to their MP. He or she may be alone, or joined by constituency party activists or local councillors. The interview is much more likely to be concerned with a personal matter – especially housing or social security – than with questions of national importance. The MP is seen as a powerful ally who can act as an advocate for the constituent's case, not just with bodies which are responsible to Parliament (social security offices or job centres, for example) but with local authorities on housing matters and even with private firms from giants like British Telecom right down to small local employers. Most MPs will try to steer clear of disputes between neighbours, and all will avoid attempting to influence the courts, but with these exceptions they will normally involve themselves in the issues constituents bring to them, even when they are outside the MP's formal area of responsibility. MPs realise – as do the constituents – that views expressed on House of Commons writing-paper are likely to have a greater impact than the same views put by a private individual who may have a worthwhile cause but may not have the ability to express it properly.

Constituents themselves increasingly expect to see their MP, and an anecdote reported in the *Western Mail* shows how different the modern concept of constituency representative is from that of Edmund Burke: a new Labour MP for a Welsh valley constituency had previously been a local councillor. Within weeks of being elected to Westminster he was stopped in the street by a constituent he had known a long time. 'We don't see much of you now,' she said. He replied that he had been elected as an MP. 'Yes, I voted for you. But we still don't see much of you.' He explained that he was very busy in London from Monday to Friday. 'So,' she said, 'you aren't going to be here as much as you were?' 'No,' he said, 'I'm sorry, I'm not.' 'Oh well,' she said, 'if I'd known that, I'd never have voted for you.'

A large part of the MP's work in the constituency is almost formal but may occupy a great deal of time – opening a new Citizens' Advice Bureau, attending Remembrance Day parades, prodding the animals at the local agricultural show, or whatever is appropriate to his or her part of the country. As the MP Julian Critchley has written:

The MP must be available. He will be expected to respond to invitations to lunch, to dine and to speak, and to pay visits to local institutions, such as hospitals, police and fire stations.

Many of these events will, of course, be connected with the MP's local party. As Mr Critchley goes on to write:

The MP's relations with the local party are every bit as important [as surgeries]. This will mean that Fridays (when the House is sitting) and weekends (all the year, save for August during which politics takes a holiday) can be taken up with wine and cheese parties, fêtes and fayres, the annual general meetings of ward associations, and a plethora of Christmas parties. These can be tiresome, but are more often entertaining. I seem to have spent the best part of my life drawing the raffle.

Julian Critchley is the Conservative MP for Aldershot, and the events he describes should be seen in that context – but there are different sorts of party activities for all MPs from Democratic Unionists in Belfast to Labour MPs in the Welsh former mining valleys.

Of course, in addition to the social obligations to the local party, the MP has political obligations too. This is particularly obvious in the Labour Party where mandatory re-selection of candidates means that MPs must ensure that their relationship with their constituency party is good if they are to be sure of remaining their candidate at the next election. But it is also dangerous for MPs of other parties to run counter to the wishes of their constituency party activists.

To meet this demand, MPs estimate that they spend an increasing amount of time in their constituency. A January 1985 survey showed that only 7.1 per cent spent four or fewer days in their constituency per sitting month, 19.9 per cent spent five to seven days, 52.1 per cent eight to twelve days and no less than 20.9 per cent more than thirteen days. When we remember that in most sitting months, the House meets for more than twenty days, and that some constituencies are geographically remote or badly served by transport from London, these figures represent an enormous commitment – though, paradoxically, because of the availability of frequent flights, many constituencies in Scotland and Northern Ireland are more accessible than seats in the remoter parts of England and Wales.

As well as visits to his or her constituency, the MP is expected to receive constituents in London. Every morning sees large parties of constituents from schools, Women's Institutes, Rotary Clubs and so on in organised tours around the Palace of Westminster, many of them conducted by the MP in person. When the House is sitting, any constituent – or any other member of the public – has access to the central lobby of the palace, where they can fill in a 'green card' which a messenger will then take to their MP to let him or her know that their constituent is waiting to see them in the central lobby. The MP is not obliged to see the constituent, but most try to do so especially if the visitor has taken the trouble to travel to Westminster. Constituents also write letters: a 1993 survey found that over 40 per cent of MPs receive more than 100 such letters each week. Many receive a greater number.

There is a correlation between the strength of the MP's public profile and the demands constituents put on him or her, and there are other factors which mean that MPs do not all have the same workload: some areas of the country are more traditional and more respectful of institutions than others – for example, Conservative suburban constituencies in the South-East of England generate more constituency work than rural Conservative constituencies in East Anglia and Lincolnshire.

Finally, the local MP is expected always to defend constituency interests. Obviously an MP from a fishing constituency will be concerned about fisheries policy, and an inner-city MP about urban problems. When an MP changes constituency, interests must alter to suit the new area. The present MP for the rural Devon constituency of South Hams was previously a Liverpool MP. His parliamentary questions now cover areas like tourism and farming which are Devon rather than Liverpool preoccupations. He may still personally be concerned with inner-city problems, but they are not ones which are high on his constituents' agenda. In the last analysis, constituents expect important constituency matters to be paramount for the MP, even if that means rebellion from the party's line. For example, the otherwise loyal Conservative MPs who sit for seats in Cornwall where a substantial number of constituents are fishermen, have consistently expressed their willingness to vote against the government if they think that their constituents' interests are being affected unfairly in comparison with other fishermen in the European Union.

Lobby groups

In the campaign to protect fishermen's interests, the campaigners were not just individual constituents. There were also pressure groups (or interest groups or lobbying organisations) which worked on their behalf – the trade unions which were affected, for example, and the local councils. The campaign was not just directed at the local MPs – the media were used and the Ministry of Agriculture was approached directly. But the support of the MPs was important – they were able to spearhead the campaigners' work on the political front.

The word 'lobbying' originated in the United States, but soon crossed the Atlantic to be used about similar activities in the British Parliament. Constituents met their MPs in the Central Lobby, and their attempts to influence MPs came to be known as 'lobbying'. The modern practice of lobbying is not restricted to parliamentary activity or to MPs, but pressure groups generally think it important to find MPs who support their case and will use parliamentary means (such as questions or amendments to bills) to pursue it, so heightening its political visibility. Some believe that MPs are increasingly subject to pressure group lobbying. Sometimes this is indiscriminate and badly thought out. MPs are simply sent hard-to-digest documents about issues in which they are not interested or they are overwhelmed by centrally instigated letter writing campaigns. But the more effective lobbyists do not just approach MPs with a word-processor produced document which will in most cases go straight from its envelope to a waste paper bin. Instead they attempt to select and cultivate particular MPs who will be sympathetic to their cause.

There are several ways of doing this. As we said earlier, MPs do not get elected to Westminster with blank minds. They had views beforehand, and may well have been active in lobby groups themselves which they continue to support after their election – one current MP has been Director of the Child Poverty Action group, another Director of the Spastics Society, for example. In other cases, new MPs' views may not be known, and the lobby groups will study their speeches, their voting record and the House, party and all-party committees of which they become members. This will be particularly important when the pressure group is promoting a cross-party cause – all political parties are against cruelty to children or maritime fraud, for example, but not all MPs will be equally concerned about both.

When the lobby group has discovered which MPs are likely to be sympathetic to it, it goes to work to get its case over to them – to influence them so that they can influence others. If the MP is converted to their cause, he or she can be very useful – by asking parliamentary questions, tabling early day motions, writing to ministers, speaking to the media, debating in the House, moving amendments in standing committee, raising the topic in a select committee and introducing private member's legislation – all the normal activities of backbench MPs. All of these will raise the profile of the lobby group's cause, and may actually result in action, even legislation.

The Consumers' Association (CA), who publish the magazine *Which?* and work to promote consumer causes, have been one of the most effective lobby groups. Through their lobbying of backbench MPs, they have mounted three particularly successful campaigns which have resulted in changes to the law. The Unfair Contract Terms Act 1977 now gives consumers rights to disregard unfair 'small print' in contracts they are party to; the Unsolicited Goods and Services Acts regulate the nuisance caused by organisations which send things to people who haven't asked for them and then demand payment; and due to the CA's work, house conveyancing has been removed from the monopoly control of solicitors. Not all pressure groups are directed towards positive aims – it may be just as important to prevent the government from doing something. For example, there was a great deal of speculation before the 1985 and 1993 budgets that VAT on books would be introduced. No one will know whether this was *really* being considered. What is known is that a well-organised campaign against the tax by pressure groups representing authors and publishers was mounted involving MPs, and that neither budget subsequently contained any proposal to introduce VAT on books. We have mentioned several individual lobby groups. But is there a definition of what constitutes a lobby group or a pressure group? Some people would claim that Parliament itself is a special interest group – a set of people with its own interests to support. Certainly the civil service or the armed forces or the churches are sometimes described as pressure groups, though they are clearly far more complex organisations than just that. Trade unions, charities and professional associations, all with declared public aims, are obvious lobbying groups.

MPs are useful to the pressure groups, but so are the pressure groups to MPs. Most MPs depend upon the pressure groups which cover the areas in which they are interested for authoritative briefing. As explained earlier, MPs have very little research provision either personally or through the services of the library. Organisations varying from the CBI and the National Farmers' Union to the National Association for the Care and Resettlement of Offenders and the Campaign for Nuclear Disarmament often influence MPs not so much by persuasion as by providing them with information. The channelling of views through lobby groups is a useful way of influencing the political debate so long as the lobby group acts openly and is properly accountable to the people on whose behalf it claims to speak.

Lobbyists

Many organisations undertake lobbying on their own behalf, but there has been an increasing tendency over recent years to use the services of firms of professional lobbyists, some of whom style themselves as parliamentary or political or public affairs consultancies. Parliamentary consultants may simply monitor legislation or parliamentary questions on behalf of their clients, but most firms offer a wider service. This includes working inside Parliament and Whitehall to provide information to clients (including advance warning of government proposals), developing contacts with ministers, MPs, peers and civil servants, and proffering advice on the way to present a case to opinion-formers in Parliament and the media and decision-takers in the civil service and government. A typical assignment for a lobbying firm might be to attempt to head off a policy proposal which concerns their client. This will mean discussing the shortcomings of the proposal with many outside Parliament, such as journalists and civil servants, but may also typically involve contacts with MPs and peers and advice to those who are sympathetic to their client's views on the exploitation of available parliamentary opportunities to ask questions, move amendments and so on.

Anyone can engage the services of parliamentary consultancies, though the fees tend to be substantial. In principle there is nothing wrong with organisations set up to help commercial bodies which have little experience of the political world in their dealings with Whitehall and Westminster. They understand the process and can explain it – and save their clients unnecessary, unproductive effort. But concerns have been expressed by some MPs and others about some of the activities of lobbying firms. There have consequently been proposals to expose their activities to greater scrutiny so that, for example, there can be no question that any lobbying firm has achieved privileged access to parliamentary facilities by offering inducements to MPs or peers. Already parliamentary journalists and MPs' staff are obliged to record any work they do for, or payment they receive from, lobbying organisations. A number of leading consultancies came forward with proposals for self-regulation in May 1994, but it is possible that a wider code of conduct, or system of registration, will emerge in the future for parliamentary lobbyists – this was a matter under active consideration in 1994 by the responsible Commons committee.

All-party and backbench groups

To gauge cross-party opinion, lobbyists are greatly helped by the all-party backbench groups which organise at Westminster. There has been concern about the indiscriminate use of the label 'all-party group' and the House of Commons has decided that the term 'all-party group' should be restricted to groups which consist only of MPs or peers. Another term, 'registered groups' is used to cover groups which admit people other than MPs and peers to their meetings.

No one is certain how many of these two kinds of groups exist. The best developed are the country groups, formed of MPs and peers who are interested in the affairs of particular countries. Countries as remote as Mongolia and Paraguay, as well as better known places, have their own group. Most country groups receive briefing from the embassies of the countries which they study, and their members are sometimes invited to visit. Country group members do not normally see themselves as defenders of the governments of the countries concerned, but as people who know something of its politics, culture and history and so able to make some contribution to the formulation of British foreign policy.

The subject groups are more concerned with domestic matters. They are a focus for cross-party discussion and can help influence the government on particular issues by showing what the views of informed backbench MPs are. Not all the groups meet as frequently as others, and only a few of them have a well-developed support system. Some deal with comparatively minor areas of policy (anti-smoking, cycling, jazz) while others are far-ranging (human rights, information technology, overseas development). One of the most prestigious of the registered groups is the Parliamentary and Scientific Committee, formed in 1939 to liaise between parliamentarians, scientists and science-based industry. Particularly active has been the All-Party Penal Affairs Group which has brought MPs into contact with prison officers and governors, magistrates, probation officers and prisoners' organisations and has been in the forefront of discussion on penal reform. In a sense, groups like this could be seen as pressure groups themselves, with the pressure here being exerted by MPs as well as upon MPs.

How independent are MPs?

The previous two sections have looked at party and non-party influences on MPs. However, the independence from these influences which MPs display also needs to be emphasised.

The electoral system has made it just about impossible for an independent to be elected as such to Parliament. Those who have been elected as independents in recent years were MPs who had resigned from their party because of some disagreement and who were then re-elected by the same constituency on the basis of their personal prestige (Dick Taverne in Lincoln, Eddie Milne in Blyth and S. O. Davies in Merthyr Tydfil are examples from the last thirty years). MPs who are independent of party to all intents and purposes do not exist.

But political parties are broadly based. Inside each there are disagreements about most individual aspects of policy, though there may be agreement about the broad direction of economic and social thinking. Analysis of voting records in the House of Commons has shown that MPs have increasingly shown their disagreement with party policy by voting against their party's line – though there are many instances where MPs' attitudes prevent the government from proceeding with policy initiatives at an earlier stage. A good recent example was the decision in 1994 not to privatise the Post Office.

In the period of the minority Labour government between 1974 and 1979 dissenters on the government side effectively prevented devolution to Scotland and Wales – a major plank of the government's programme. Between 1983 and 1992, with government majorities of more than 100, dissenting votes were not likely to put the government's programme in jeopardy, though the number of them grew. On occasion, the government was defeated – for example, on the liberalisation of Sunday trading laws in 1985–86. But even when a defeat was not imminent, government MPs were not afraid to say that they disagreed with their government's policy, whether on the EC, child benefit, television licence fees, airport policy, local government reform, the possible sale of Austin Rover to Ford, farming quotas, fees for sight tests or dental examinations, the future of the post office or the coal industry or the Cornish tin industry, dog licences, the poll tax, protection of official information or the monitoring of the security services. Since 1992, with a much smaller majority, it has become more important for the government Chief Whip to secure each Conservative MP's vote in the division lobbies. Nonetheless, the 1992–93 session saw a succession of rebellions on the bill to implement the Maastricht Treaty, culminating in a government defeat on 22 July 1993 when 20 Conservatives voted with the opposition. Rebellion continued in late 1994 on legislation to increase the funding of the European Union, and on the proposal to impose VAT on domestic fuel – in the latter case the government was defeated, and forced to backtrack on its budget taxation proposals. Not all government supporters are free to vote against the party – many are ministers, whips or parliamentary private secretaries (the payroll vote) obliged by the conventions to support the government. These, no doubt, express their views privately. But the old argument that those who do rebel publicly are either former ministers who have been sacked or disappointed office-seekers does not hold water – for example, in the 1983–1987 Parliament, of the eleven rebels on television licence fees, six entered the House in 1983 as did almost half of the 60 or so rebels on airport policy. More recently, two of the poll tax rebels in 1988 were first elected in 1987 while a number of the most vocal rebels on the Maastricht Bill entered the Commons in 1992. Although more attention is naturally given to dissenting votes in the government party, opposition parties do not always agree internally, as their voting records also demonstrate.

Votes on the floor of the House are not the only way of registering independence. Work in select committees or all-party committees will often lead the MP to reach a consensus with political opponents which will make him or her depart from the orthodox party line. Speeches in debate, articles in newspapers, parliamentary questions and all their other political work will reflect MPs' individual approaches to politics. An MP's private dealings with his or her leaders can display independence at least as effectively as what is done publicly.

An MP's independence and individuality is given structure by party affiliation and governed by a natural wish to see the party which he or she supports in government and running the country. But inside those broad guidelines, what an MP does is influenced by personality, constituency and the issues which he or she as an individual feels strongly about. It is the MP's independence which is the best guarantee that Parliament will remain powerful, and that 'parliamentary sovereignty' will not become a synonym for 'government sovereignty'. As we will see in Chapters 6 to 10, Parliament has an ample reserve of powers. What it needs is the confidence to show it is prepared to exercise them, and that confidence will come from independent-minded MPs. That, of course, does not imply that Parliament is only powerful if it is busy defeating the government. The government can only exist because it is acceptable to a majority of the House of Commons, and the majority in the House naturally owes a debt of loyalty to the government they support in office. But the government is not omnipotent once it has achieved office – its first job of persuasion is in the House of Commons. It has to convince its own party's MPs to vote for the policies it puts forward while those policies are constantly being held up for examination by the opposition parties. Since an overwhelming majority of MPs believe that their electors expect them to use their judgement on issues, the government's job is no walk-over.

Controls and influences on the House of Lords

The principal constraint on the House of Lords is its unequal position in Parliament *vis-à-vis* the House of Commons. The limitations on Lords' powers to reject or amend bills are fully described later. But it is important to grasp at this stage that the Lords, by not being elected and therefore being unrepresentative, are put at considerable disadvantage in terms of power to the Commons. If the Lords always attempted to insist on its will against the will of the elected House of Commons, especially if the Commons were only giving effect to policies endorsed by the electorate, there would be a constitutional show-down between the two Houses. As a result the Lords would be likely to find themselves out of business or at least having their wings clipped, as they have in the past after similar resistance to the Commons. Because of this, the Lords tacitly recognise the right of the government to govern, and of the House of Commons to see its will prevail. They willingly sacrifice their power in the same sort of compromise as that made by MPs when they willingly accept the supremacy of the government in their House. That said, the House of Lords, like the House of Commons, is also subject to government, party and external pressures but these influences are perhaps less obtrusive in the upper House.

The government

The position of the government in the Lords is not as well entrenched as in the Commons. Following a general election the party with the majority of seats in the House of Commons forms the government and it is that party which occupies the government benches in the Lords too. The government frontbenchers in the Lords may contain two to four Cabinet Ministers and fewer than twenty other ministers, from junior whips to Ministers of State. Thus the government presence is, relatively speaking, much smaller in the Lords than in the Commons and promise of ministerial office accordingly holds much less sway. The government's influence over its own backbenchers and over other members of the House is, in the absence of a large 'payroll' membership, that much the weaker. And party discipline – including that of the government party – is weaker because peers do not have to submit themselves to the rigours of selection by the constituency parties.

There is an understanding that the government can expect to get its business through. As we will see on page 143, under the 'Salisbury convention' the Lords will not reject at Second Reading legislation relating to commitments contained in an election manifesto. But a more general understanding on business is indispensable for the proper functioning of the House as there are no procedural devices for curtailing debate on legislation, nor do the Lords' Standing Orders give government business precedence over other business. In the House of Commons, we have seen that a high proportion of sitting time is reserved for government business. In the Lords, anything up to 60 per cent of sitting time can be occupied with government business but none of it is formally reserved for government use. In the last resort a government might try to suspend Standing Orders in order to give its own business precedence, but fortunately this is rarely necessary. Provided the government business managers respect the conventions of the House, consult the opposition through the usual channels and do their best to accommodate the demands of the private member, the other parties and private members alike are content to leave the arrangement of business to the government chief whip.

Governments are able to get their business through because they make sure that they are seen to deal fairly with the other parties and interests in the House.

The political parties

Although the members of the House are not elected, many of them – but by no means all – belong to political parties. The most recent figures were given on page 17. Because Lords are not elected, it is important to remember that the political composition does not change after a general election.

Officially, the House scarcely recognises the existence of the political parties. They are nowhere referred to in Standing Orders and they are barely mentioned in the *Companion to Standing Orders* – the House's own procedural handbook. But the reality is very different. Each party has its leader and its whips and a small secretariat paid for from party funds. The government party has the advantage of an office manned by civil servants to organise its affairs. Committees of the House tend to reflect the composition of the House, as in the House of Commons, and the government party negotiates through the Whips' Offices of the other parties (the usual channels) and, where appropriate, with the Convenor nominated by the Cross Benches in the arrangement of business.

Like the Commons, the party whips send their members statements of forthcoming business in the House with items underlined to indicate their importance to the party leadership. But discipline is not as strong as in the House of Commons and there is no 'pairing' system. There are weekly party meetings – every Thursday afternoon – at which future business is discussed and there is, even in the Lords, a general predisposition to toe the party line. However, for many members of the House, their political careers are not their principal interest and the allure of office carries less weight. So there is often some cross-voting. And the crossbenchers – who profess no party line – are all, theoretically, floating voters.

The leader of the government party in the Lords is the Leader of the House and together with the government chief whip advises other ministerial colleagues on the problems that might be encountered in getting their business through the House.

Non-party influences

Personal

The composition of the House guarantees great diversity of interest. The non-political hereditary element provides a lay presence. Then there are the politicians – either those hereditary peers who have taken up political careers based in the Lords or those created peers who have formerly been MPs or prominent in local government. Finally there are those, mainly but not exclusively life peers, who are experts in their field. Very often they are retired or approaching retirement but their expertise still places them at an advantage where detailed scrutiny of policy is required – in debates on funding of scientific research or in scrutiny in committee of some abstruse piece of EU agricultural legislation, for example. The diversity of the members of the House ensures that personal interest and influences are very strong in the Lords.

However, unlike the Commons, there is no register of members' interests. It is a long-standing custom of the House that Lords speak always on their personal honour and if a Lord decides that it is proper to take part in a debate on a subject in which he or she has a direct pecuniary interest, or any kind of interest – whether pecuniary or not – of which his audience should be aware in order to form a balanced judgment of his argument, he or she is expected to declare it.

Although Lords may indicate that an outside body agrees with the substance of the views they are expressing, they speak for themselves and not on behalf of outside interests.

Subject to the observance of these conventions, the personal connections of individual members provide the House with a rich source of talent and expertise.

Territorial

Members of the House of Lords have no constituencies: they are not representatives. As Lord Birkenhead once remarked of a member of the House who had incurred his ire, 'The noble Lord represents no-one but himself and I don't think much of his constituency'.

But sometimes members of the House will be approached by interests in the locality in which they live or whose title they bear by reason of some long – and sometimes extinct – association, asking them to take up a particular stance on a public matter. Members are undoubtedly responsive to such approaches.

Lobby groups

All legislation has to be considered in the Lords as well as the Commons and some legislation begins its passage through Parliament in the House of Lords. Members of the House therefore find themselves courted in much the same way as members of the House of Commons by lobby groups either directly or through parliamentary consultants. The dramatic increase in lobbying since the end of the 1970s has been a conspicuous feature of the revival in the House of Lords' influence in recent years – part cause and part effect. Some lobbyists are skilful and selective in their targets. Others resort to an indiscriminate 'mail-drop'. These organisations will prepare evidence for committees, draft amendments to be moved to bills (over forty groups, for example, lobbied peers during the passage of the Criminal Justice and Public Order Bill in 1994, from the National Gypsy Council to the Prison Reform Trust and Save the Children), offer to take peers on visits, or arrange lectures at which their policies are expounded. As a result, some peers form potentially close associations with, for example, local authority organisations, the country landowners, the bankers, the major exporters, or libertarian groups. These contacts not only influence members of the House but help to provide briefing and a wide range of assistance to what is essentially still a part-time – even amateur – Chamber of the legislature. Like MPs, some peers also belong to the all-party and registered special interest and 'country' groups.

The independence of the Lords

Despite party and other influences, members of the House of Lords are rather more unpredictable in their allegiances and voting than MPs. This has manifested itself strongly under the successive Conservative administrations since 1979, with marked consequences for legislation, as we shall see in detail in Chapter 6.

CHAPTER 5

Day-to-day organisation of business

In this chapter, the day-to-day organisation of the House of Commons is described. We also look at some of the rules of procedure which Parliament, in particular the House of Commons, has imposed on itself to enable it to get through the business before it. Less fraught with party political tension, the House of Lords is, generally speaking, less rigid in its rules and method of operation but where appropriate we shall be looking at business in the Lords too.

The parliamentary day

MPs do not have a detailed job description. There are many different expectations of what they *should* do – individual constituents expect them to take up their grievances, party activists to support party policy, whips to turn up and vote. Among MPs there is a kaleidoscope of views of what the job entails which ranges from those who confine themselves to constituency issues through to those who aspire to become – or are – well-known world political leaders. MPs vary widely in age, experience, intellectual ability and certainty of purpose. There is no typical MP, and so, strictly speaking, no typical MP's job or MP's day.

Much of an MP's work – as we will see later – is done in the constituency, in select committees and standing committees and in a whole range of private meetings at Westminster. But at the core of each MP's life remains the Chamber: it is the place where they first join the Commons, the place where they vote and, even if they are among the least frequent attenders, the place where they come to witness – and perhaps try to take part in – the great set piece occasions from the budget to Prime Minister's question time.

The last chapter described the way in which the 'usual channels' (party whips and their staff) smooth the day-to-day running of both Houses. In the Commons, government business managers have particularly wide powers. This is because the government effectively controls the timetable through a combination of its powers under Standing Order (Standing Order No. 13 provides that government business normally has precedence) and its support from a majority of backbenchers. However, even government business managers cannot know for sure what each parliamentary day will bring. Both Houses are notoriously unpredictable, and quickly able to respond to political events outside. The way in which the day in the Chamber is organised is complicated. There is a carefully worked-out order in which events happen, but some of these events are relatively unimportant or infrequent. A complete list would be unnecessarily confusing, but some of the items which happen infrequently need to be mentioned because they can be of importance when they do occur. The more important events are described in more detail later in the book. To confuse matters further, the Commons will experiment with new sitting hours in 1995. These will involve sittings on Wednesday mornings and the elimination of ten Friday sittings in a normal session. We will therefore describe both the position which exists in Standing Orders and the likely course of events under the experiment. We also explain why the experiment has come about (see pages 75 to 77).

Every day begins with prayers. No members of the public are present during these few minutes when the Speaker and her chaplain kneel at the Table of the House, MPs who are present stand and face inward and the traditional prayers for Parliament are read. Prayers occur at 2.30 pm on Mondays to Thursdays, except during the experiment when they will occur at 10.00 am on Wednesdays. But even on experimental Wednesdays, events after 2.30 pm will take the same course as on Mondays, Tuesdays and Thursdays. On sitting Fridays the House's business begins at 9.30. Fridays are exceptional for other reasons also, so we shall begin with a description of what happens from 2.30 onwards on the first four days of the week.

Up to the end of question time

The first event is that the Speaker makes any formal communications necessary. The most frequent of these are announcements of the deaths or resignations of MPs. Deaths are announced by a simple and invariable formula. There is normally no opportunity for a eulogy – though the House adjourns upon the death of a Prime Minister, former Prime Minister or Leader of the Opposition after speeches in praise of the deceased have been made. A death gives rise to a vacancy, as does a resignation. Strictly, an MP cannot resign, so an MP who wishes to leave is appointed to a nominal office of profit under the Crown, which disqualifies the MP from membership. The two offices used are the stewardships of the Chiltern Hundreds and of the Manor of Northstead. No duties are involved with the appointments and no fees are received. When a seat is vacant, any MP can move a motion which, if carried, would give rise to a by-election. This motion is moved at the beginning of the day's business, after any formal announcements by the Speaker. Traditionally only the chief whip of the party to which the former MP belonged 'moves a writ', as the procedure is called, but a Labour backbencher did so in June 1985 when the Brecon and Radnor by-election, in a seat formerly held by a Conservative, was pending. Most of these by-election writs are not opposed, but, if they are, debate is deferred until later in the day. By convention, almost all vacancies are filled within three to four months, but there is no formal limit to the period during which a constituency remains unrepresented.

After these proceedings, which are uncommon, comes 'private business'. This consists of private legislation and related motions. More details of what private business entails will be found in Chapter 6. At this time in the sitting day, only private business which is not opposed by a single MP can pass. Much private business is totally uncontroversial, and it is not unusual for private bills to go through all their stages on different days at this time.

The items of business before questions normally take up no more than two or three minutes. Under the Standing Orders, oral questions must begin no later than 2.45 p.m., but they are usually under way by 2.40 at the latest. Question time then continues until 3.30 p.m., though it may be extended by a private notice question until 3.50 p.m. or so. More details of the questions procedure are given in Chapter 8.

After question time and before the main business of the day

The government is responsible to Parliament, and when a new policy initiative is announced or some important event occurs, from a High Court decision that the government has acted unlawfully to a major terrorist outrage, the government will want to present its views to Parliament at least as soon as it presents them to the media. To do this, ministers often make statements to the House. Formally they notify the Speaker of their intention to do so, but neither her permission nor that of the House is required. Statements come after question time and can last for anything from two or three, to twenty minutes or so. They are followed by a short riposte to the statement by the main opposition spokesman, ostensibly in the form of a question, and then by a question and answer session which lasts between 30 minutes and an hour, depending on the Speaker's judgement of the level of controversy the statement arouses and on its interest to the House. Statements are a very frequent occurrence, as the following table demonstrates:

Session	No. of days	No. of statements
1987–88	218	83
1988–89	176	77
1989–90	167	68
1990–91	160	89
1991–92	83	22
1992–93	240	95

Advance warning of statements is only given to MPs at 1 p.m. on the day they are made, and backbenchers frequently complain that they are given no advance access to the often complicated publications which are released at the same time as the statement is made. This means that their questions are not as well judged as they might be – for example, the statement on the government's review of social security in June 1985 was accompanied by the publication of documents 291 pages long.

After statements, any new MPs who have been elected at by-elections are introduced. They are sponsored by two existing MPs, and in a brief ceremony swear the oath of loyalty to the Queen (or make a similar affirmation if they do not wish to swear), sign the roll and shake the Speaker's hand. By-elections are hotly contested, and frequently result in upsets for the government party. The introduction of the new MP is often treated as the culmination of the campaign, and is usually greeted by cheering from the victorious party and good-natured heckling from everyone else.

After this, individual MPs have an opportunity to call for an emergency debate. More details of these debates are given in Chapter 9. Very few occur. However, requests for emergency debates are relatively frequent. To the MP who is passionately concerned about it, any matter – a big factory closure in his or her constituency, an idiosyncratic decision of the European Community affecting local fishermen or an allegation of police harassment – is worth raising under Standing Order No. 20, the Standing Order which governs emergency debates. The Speaker has to be more discerning, and will grant an emergency debate only when the matter raised is of national significance and not likely to be debated by other means. A proposal of a Procedure Committee that MPs should give notice in advance to the Speaker of their proposed topics for emergency debate and that only those which were going to be granted should be called did not meet with approval in the House. This is hardly surprising – in the 1991–92 and 1992–93 sessions 8 and 18 applications respectively for emergency debates were made. Only one was granted. MPs know perfectly well that most of their requests will not be granted. Informally, the Standing Order No. 20 procedure allows them to ventilate deeply held feelings about matters of current controversy, according to the judgment of the individual MP. They are, however, limited to a three-minute speech in putting their cases.

Other formal types of business may occur after statements. Two which should be mentioned are ballots to decide which backbenchers can choose the topic for debate on backbenchers' debate days (days which the 1995 experimental reforms would abolish) and personal explanations. These are statements made by ministers announcing their resignation, or by other members explaining their conduct in some way. These are understandably very unusual, though, when they occur, tension can be electric, as it was during the statements of Geoffrey Howe, Michael Mates or Norman Lamont following their resignations as ministers. Questions do not follow personal explanations.

Next comes business which is described on the Order Paper or agenda as 'at the commencement of public business'. There are four types. The first is the formal presentation and first reading of public bills – a formality, the significance of which will be explained in Chapter 6. Then come government motions to regulate the business of the House for the day – to suspend Standing Orders in some way or to allow some unusual procedure to take place. These motions can be debated, and a vote taken. To avoid this, motions of this type are frequently put at the end of the agenda on a day previous to the one which they regulate. Fewer MPs are present at that time, and the motion suspending Standing Orders can often be passed without debate or vote. Another type of motion taken 'at the commencement' allots tasks to standing committees. The fourth type consists of 'motions under Standing Order No. 19'. The only important type of motion under this Standing Order is the one which backbenchers can move on Tuesdays and Wednesdays from (usually) the seventh week of the session onwards. This is the so-called 'Ten Minute Rule Bill Motion' – a procedure described in Chapter 6. One MP each Tuesday and Wednesday has the chance to bring forward a proposal for new legislation and explain in ten minutes why he or she thinks the House should agree to it. After the explanation, an opponent can also speak for ten minutes against the proposal, and the issue can then be put to the vote. Ten Minute Rule Bills are very popular, not so much because they are actually likely to result in a change to the law, but because they allow backbenchers to ventilate their views and vote on an issue of controversy. Three weeks' notice are normally given of Ten Minute Rule Bills, and occasionally MPs queue all night to be first to give notice.

Privilege

Very occasionally, after the Ten Minute Rule Bill slot, the Commons debate a matter of privilege. Theoretically, these debates take precedence over any other business, but MPs have become increasingly wary about using this rather misunderstood and ill-defined power. The Bill of Rights of 1689 declares that 'freedom of speech and debates or proceedings in Parliament ought not to be impeached or questioned in any place or court outside Parliament'. This is one of the bases on which privilege is founded. Having privilege does, of course, mean having something which most people do not have, but MPs and peers have privilege only because they are members of assemblies which need to be able to meet together freely and debate freely without threats from people outside or interference with their work. MPs cannot be sued for libel for any statement they make during parliamentary proceedings. Successive Speakers have emphasised that this privilege should be exercised responsibly.

The detailed law of parliamentary privilege has been built up from individual cases where Parliament has decided that certain acts interfere with the essential rights of Members of Parliament or constitute improper conduct by Members themselves. These are called 'contempts'. Examples include deliberately lying to the House, giving false evidence to a committee or threatening an MP if he or she votes a particular way. Some would argue that the net of contempt has been drawn too wide – there are, for example, cases of newspapers being judged guilty of contempt for publishing stories which debunked the House of Commons, on the theory that by doing so they had diminished the respect in which it was held and so obstructed its work and committed a contempt. Modern MPs are unlikely to be so sensitive. As an illustration of this, in 1986 the House voted to take no action against a *Times* journalist who had published a leak from a select committee, though the Committee of Privileges had recommended that he should be banned from the precincts for six months.

When a contempt is committed, the House of Commons has the power to punish the offender. In the past, physical punishments were used, and imprisonment was frequent. Though the power to imprison still exists, it is doubtful whether it would ever be used. Punishments for persons outside the House now consist only of the power to reprimand or to ban from the House. In the law courts, contempt is normally punished by a substantial fine, and there have been several recommendations that the Commons should have the power to fine those who committed contempts of it. Legislation to do this has never been introduced. For those who are MPs, the powers of the House are more real – members can be expelled. Four MPs since 1945 have either been expelled or resigned before they were expelled after the House or its committees had decided they were guilty of dishonourable conduct.

When an MP believes that a breach of privilege has been committed, he or she first contacts the Speaker, as described in

Chapter 3. If the Speaker decides that a *prima facie* breach has occurred, she announces so in the Chamber. On the following day, after the Ten Minute Rule Bill slot, the MP who has complained can move a motion referring the issue to the Committee of Privileges, a very senior committee, chaired by the Leader of the House and containing the Attorney-General, senior frontbenchers and senior backbenchers. Debate follows, and a vote, if necessary. If the House decides to refer the issue to the committee, the committee will meet and probably take evidence. It will agree a report, which will normally contain recommendations on the particular issue and on any general matters which arise. This report is usually debated in the House, which can accept or reject the recommendations.

There is an enormous volume of case law relating to parliamentary privilege which the interested reader will find in the appropriate chapters of *Erskine May*.

Main business of the day

Although in theory a lot can go on before the Commons get down to their main business, it is unusual for the events already described to last much beyond 4.45 p.m. They can end as early as 3.30 p.m. – though at least one or two MPs will want to raise 'points of order' – more often an easy way to score a political point rather than raise a genuine issue about the rules of the House.

The main business of the day is described on the Order Paper as 'Orders of the Day and Notices of Motion'. The technical distinction between these two need not concern us. Two or three items are usually listed, though there may be many more or only one. Generally speaking, the first item listed will be the principal debating subject for the day and debate on it will continue until 10 p.m. Sometimes debate will finish earlier – by arrangement between the parties or because the Standing Orders say so or just because no one else wishes to speak. It is also likely that efforts will be made to end business early before non-sitting Fridays. There are also a number of days (until recently about ten or a dozen in an average length session) when debate is interrupted at 7 p.m. by 'opposed private business' – private legislation which a group of MPs wish to debate, and which they were not willing to see taken at the time for unopposed private business at the beginning of the sitting day. The day's business could also be interrupted by an emergency debate under Standing Order No. 20, but these normally take place the day after they are granted. Only three debates have taken place on the day they were granted since 1979. The main business of the day can either be debate on legislation, financial procedure or some general matter. Each of these is described in more detail later.

At 10 p.m. comes what is known as the 'moment of interruption'. This should be the signal that the day's proceedings are soon to come to an end. However, it has been comparatively unusual for the Commons' business to end this early. First of all, a motion can be moved to suspend the rules which are intended to prevent debates after ten o'clock. Motions of this type are moved at 10 p.m. by the government (who must give notice the previous day of their intention of doing so). Debate is not allowed. A vote can take place, but the government whips should ensure that the government wins. When carried, the motion, depending on its wording, allows named pieces of business – or government business in general – to continue until any time or a particular time. Secondly, there are certain types of business which are not affected by the moment of interruption anyway. These include proceedings on the annual Finance Bill (which can continue until any hour) or on statutory instruments (see page 145) or European Community documents.

Sometimes sittings have been deliberately prolonged by backbenchers or the opposition parties so that the following day's sitting is 'broken'. This occurs if one sitting continues until after the time when the House was due to meet on the following day. When this happens, the following day's business is lost. Usually the first day's business is controversial in any case – as in 1981 when the House debated the bill to privatise British Telecom in a sitting lasting 25 hours, or 1984 when a bill was debated which was part of the government's programme to abolish the Greater London Council and the sitting continued for over 32 hours. In 1986, the Labour MP Tam Dalyell was prevented from moving a motion highly critical of the then Prime Minister on a private members' Friday because government backbenchers had stretched Thursday's business on past 9.30 a.m. on the Friday morning.

Whatever time the House finishes its main business, it has one event still to follow – the adjournment debate. This in turn can be preceded by the presentation of public petitions. Public petitions are described further in Chapter 8, and the adjournment debate in Chapter 9. On the occasions when the House finishes its main business before 10 p.m., the adjournment debate may start then and continue until 10.30 p.m. More than one backbencher may speak. However, the majority of debates occur after 10 p.m., are limited to half an hour and consist only of contributions from the backbencher who has won the ballot and from the minister who replies.

Late sittings and the 1995 experiment

The pressure of business, and the way in which the rules have operated, have resulted in late sittings becoming a regular feature of the House of Commons. The average time the House rose in the decade to 1990–91 was well after midnight, with some sittings lasting much longer. These late hours are frequently condemned by MPs themselves, especially new MPs or those with family commitments, and they rarely seem sensible to the public – or to MPs' spouses.

There was an experiment with morning sittings in 1967, but it was abandoned later that year. Then, as now, many MPs wanted to have some part of the day free when they could do business away from Westminster, or attend Committees, without the fear of having to return to vote.

However, responding to the pressure for reform, the Government in 1991 proposed the establishment of a Select Committee on the Sittings of the House, under the Chairmanship of Michael Jopling, a former Conservative Chief Whip. The Committee reported just before the 1992 General Election. In essence, the Jopling Committee proposed that the House's main business should end by 10 p.m. on Mondays to Thursdays, followed by the half-hour adjournment debate. On ten Thursdays a year, business would finish three hours earlier, with the following Friday free. Much private members' business would be taken on Wednesday mornings. To compensate for these reduced hours, certain business would be taken without debate or be referred automatically to Standing Committee, second adjournment debates would be abolished and – most radically of all – all government bills would be timetabled after second reading.

Although enthusiastically received by many MPs, the Jopling report was not immediately implemented. Some opposition business managers were particularly concerned about the erosion of their ability to use delaying tactics which the Jopling package would entail. There is no easy answer to the dilemma of how to combine adequate opportunity for scrutiny with sensible hours, especially when non-cooperation with government business managers remains an opposition's final deterrent.

Nevertheless there was renewed pressure for change after the untimely death of the then Leader of the Opposition, John Smith, in May 1994, with the ideas behind the Jopling report being endorsed by the front benches of all three main parties in the months which followed. In December 1994 proposals were at last put before the House for an experiment during 1995 along the lines sought by Jopling. These proposals were endorsed in the House by fairly substantial majorities in a succession of votes.

Not all of Jopling's proposals are to be implemented. Timetabling of bills is to be achieved by co-operation not compulsion, and the government has simply promised to use its best endeavours to avoid late sittings. But a considerable amount of legislative business, especially on statutory instruments, will be taken in committee, while other business (like money and ways and means resolutions) will be taken without debate. Many of the traditional forms of backbenchers' business will be replaced by sittings on Wednesday mornings when a series of backbench proposed subjects will be debated on the adjournment between 10.00am and 2.30pm. Votes are unlikely. The Fridays which had formerly been private members' motion Fridays will become non-sitting days.

The advantages and disadvantages of the new system will only be apparent after it has been in operation for some time. While few will miss the late nights, the effect on government, opposition and backbenchers' perceptions of their opportunities will be interesting to observe.

Fridays and weekends

On sitting Fridays the Commons meets at 9.30 a.m. and the 'hour of interruption' is 2.30 p.m., with the half-hour adjournment debate following. Earlier Friday hours were introduced in 1980. They were designed to enable MPs to get away early to their constituencies, and the government undertook not to ask the House to sit beyond 3 p.m. except in special cases of urgency and importance. The way in which a Friday sitting is constructed is similar to the earlier days of the week, with some changes: there is no private business, no questions (except private notice questions) and no opportunity to apply for emergency debates. Petitions are taken at the beginning of the day instead of at the end (as a result, the majority of petitions are presented on Fridays) and, if a private notice question is allowed or a ministerial statement is to be made, business is interrupted for the purpose at 11 a.m. A number of Fridays are taken up with debates on backbenchers' proposals for legislation (private members' bills). Under the 1995 sittings experiment, the former backbenchers' debate Fridays have now become non-sitting days. The Fridays which are government days are generally not used for very controversial measures. In this way, Fridays have a very different feel from other days of the week.

The House does not normally meet on Saturdays or Sundays, but can do so in emergencies. Saturday sittings in the last 30 years have been used to debate the Suez crisis (1956) and the Falklands invasion (1982). The only Sunday sitting this century was on 3 September 1939 – the outbreak of the Second World War.

The parliamentary day in the House of Lords

The House of Lords usually sits from Monday to Thursday, and on Friday in the latter part of the session. In the 1988–89 session – a very busy session – it sat for 153 days, which averaged 7 hours 2 minutes each (the Commons sat for 175 days, averaging 9 hours

4 minutes). In 1990–91, by contrast, it sat for 137 days, which averaged 6 hours 28 minutes each. On Mondays, Tuesdays and Wednesdays the Lords meet at 2.30 p.m., on Thursdays at 3 p.m. and on Fridays at 11 a.m. As in the Commons, Saturday and Sunday sittings have taken place only at times of national crisis. The length of Lords' sittings has grown gradually – in the 1974–75 session the average sitting lasted under six hours.

As in the Commons, the day begins with prayers. In the Lords, prayers are read by a bishop and members kneel on the benches. Immediately after prayers new peers go through their ceremony of introduction, hereditary peers sitting first after the death of their forebears (usually their father) take their seat and peers who have not yet sat in the present Parliament take the oath. The business starts with a short question time. Only four questions – known as 'starred questions' because they are marked with a star on the order paper – are taken on any day, and they are not expected to take up more than half an hour in all. Private notice questions are very rarely allowed in the Lords but, when they are, they come immediately after starred questions. Business statements – indicating the limitations on speaking time to be observed in time limited debates, or the hour of adjournment for dinner during a particularly long piece of legislative business, for example – follow. Ministerial statements, in theory, come next but only if the minister making the statement is a Lord. Most statements are made in the Commons and repeated in the Lords. Occasionally statements to be made in the Commons are deemed by the usual channels not to be sufficiently important to the Lords to be repeated. When they are important, they are usually delivered in the Commons at 3.30 p.m. and in the Lords as soon after as convenient. In the Lords, brief comments and questions for clarification from the opposition frontbenches and from backbenchers of all parties are allowed. Members clearly value this opportunity to comment and probe the government further on statements, and an attempt by the Lords Procedure Committee to restrict comment to frontbench spokesmen of the main political parties received very short shrift from the House.

The substantive business then begins. Discussion of private legislation comes first, followed by Business of the House motions, usually moved by the Leader of the House and signifying a change in the order of business. Then, when necessary, comes Chairman of Committees's business. This usually relates to the discussion of any reports by committees for which the Chairman of Committees has responsibility – such as reports of the Committee on House of Lords Offices, or the Procedure Committee. Discussion of public bills, delegated legislation and reports from Select Committees comes next followed by other motions. At the end of business, any questions for debate which have been tabled for oral answer by the government may be taken. These are called 'unstarred questions' (to distinguish them from the questions put at the commencement of business, which do not give rise to debate, they are not prefixed by a star on the order paper). Proceedings on unstarred questions are very like adjournment debates in the Commons. Indeed, so popular have they become that, if time permits, they are now sometimes taken during the adjournment for dinner of proceedings on a major bill.

The order of business is slightly different on Wednesdays when motions have precedence over bills and other business. The practical effect of this is to make Wednesday a day of debates. Any other business has to come last.

It would be very unusual to find all the different kinds of business set down for any one day. A typical day might begin with prayers, followed by starred questions and business statements; proceedings on a private bill might come next but would usually be very brief; there may then come a business motion; then would follow the legislative stages of one or more bills. If the principal business consists of a lengthy stage of a major bill requiring constant attendance, then at 7 p.m. that stage may be adjourned for an hour in which time short items of business – like an uncontentious piece of delegated legislation or a private member's bill or, as has recently become the practice, an unstarred question – might be taken. The adjourned proceedings on the major bill will then be resumed and the House might adjourn at any time between about 9 p.m. and 11 p.m. If it is likely that business will finish earlier in the evening an unstarred question may have been set down as last business.

The sitting time of the House of Lords in the 1993–94 session broke down approximately as shown below.

	Percentage of time spent
Prayers	1.2
Introductions	0.3
Starred questions	7.0
Private bills	0.3
Statements	2.0
Public bills (government)	48.4
Public bills (private members)	4.6
Affirmative instruments	4.0
Debates	20.4
Unstarred questions	8.4

The parliamentary session

In Chapter 2, we saw that general elections must be called at least every five years, and that the period from one general election to the next is called a parliament. But as well as this election-to-election cycle, Parliament operates on an annual cycle called a 'session'. Typically, any one parliament is divided into four or five sessions – though when two general elections follow each other in rapid succession, as in 1974, there may be only one session in a parliament.

Parliament needs to meet annually to vote the money which the government needs to continue operating. It also needs annually to approve an order which has the effect of allowing the armed forces to remain in existence. But in themselves, these are not reasons for the sessional divisions. Their purpose is to allow Parliament to make a clean break. When a session ends, all outstanding business falls. The decks are cleared, and the new session can start afresh. As well as this clean-out, the sessional pattern means that there are obvious goals for government and opposition parties. The government has to restrict its programme to what can be done in one year, and the opposition parties know that the government may make concessions if its programme is running late as the year goes by. Time is a vital element in parliamentary tactics. The government's power is in essence its ability to control the agenda, but the opposition's tactics are to stall progress in completing the agenda.

People outside Parliament are sometimes critical of the cycle of sessions and parliaments. The speed which can be involved in completing all stages of a complex piece of legislation within one session can lead to badly drafted law, for instance. More generally, working within these sorts of time frames means that short-term goals can take the place of long-term objectives. For example, the Director General of the Confederation of British Industry has said that industrial decision makers regard even the five-year term of a parliament as too short. Obviously, any large industrial project takes much longer than this from conception to execution – a big power station, for example, would take from ten to fifteen years.

In modern times, the parliamentary session has usually begun in late October or early November, and lasted for just about twelve months. There is then an interruption of (usually) four or five days, and a new session begins. The interruption is called 'prorogation' and there is a small ceremony to mark the action, on behalf of the Queen, of proroguing Parliament. At the beginning of the century, the period of prorogation could continue for months – the session might last from February to July only. There is still no fixed time when sessions should begin or end, especially in general election years. For example, the 1991–2 session ended in March 1992 and the 1992–93 session began in late April 1992.

Even when there is no general election, the amount of time either House sits during a session can vary very substantially – the Commons sat for 191 days in 1975–76 but for 160 days in 1990–91, for example. The number of sitting days in an election year is, of course, usually even fewer. Variation is partly explained by differing lengths of holiday adjournments, often (though, strictly incorrectly) called 'recesses'. Each House decides on the length of its own holiday adjournment itself – or, more accurately, the government decides the length of the adjournment. This is then endorsed in the Commons' case by a vote. Each House is free to adjourn for different periods. Because the Lords need to sit longer than the Commons later in the session, and because they rarely sit on Fridays in the early part of the session, the Lords often sit for more weeks than the Commons but for fewer days. But a session is of the same length for each House – it is Parliament which is prorogued, not one or other House.

In the Commons, adjournments of three weeks for Christmas, a week at Easter, a week for the spring bank holiday and eleven or twelve weeks in the late summer and early autumn are usual. After the summer adjournment, the Commons generally meet again for two weeks or more and the Lords for three weeks or more (the 'spill-over') before prorogation marks the end of the session.

The new session always begins with the State Opening of Parliament. The Queen rides in her carriage from Buckingham Palace to the Palace of Westminster, and wearing her parliamentary robes and the Imperial State Crown, she delivers the Queen's Speech to both Houses of Parliament, assembled for the purpose in the House of Lords. This is a great State occasion. Peers wear their parliamentary robes of scarlet and ermine and a number of wives of peers, the diplomatic corps, and the judges are also present on the floor of the House. The Queen's Speech – written by the government – outlines in 1000 or so words the government's programme for the session ahead. The session then begins with a debate lasting six days in the Commons and four days in the Lords on that programme. This is known as the debate on the Address.

The main legislative proposals for the year are published as bills and mostly introduced in the Commons before Christmas and given their second reading debates. In the months after Christmas they are considered in standing committee, and then come back to the House for their report stage before being sent to the Lords. Less controversial bills generally begin their parliamentary passage in the Lords, and come to the Commons later in the year. There is a tendency for the Lords to have a shorter summer recess because controversial bills do not clear the Commons before the late spring, and must then be considered by the Lords. As well as legislation, the government has to ensure that its financial business is conducted on target. The estimates are presented and voted upon on three main occasions a year. They are given statutory authority by Consolidated Fund Bills. The Budget is now presented in November, and forms the basis of the Finance Bill.

All these procedures will be described at greater length in Chapters 6 and 7. The legislative programme announced in the Queen's Speech and financial business form the back-bone of each session. But because Parliament is responsive to political needs, many other events will happen which will be debated in the House, and which may even give rise to new legislation – an example is the legislation to ban alcohol at soccer grounds, introduced late in the 1984–85 session as part of the government's response to the deaths on the Brussels terraces at the Liverpool vs. Juventus game.

No two sessions are identical, and since the 1993 change in the Budget and Finance Bill timetable, only the 1993–94 session has given an illustration of the way a session is currently organised. 1993–94 is somewhat atypical because of its late start and lengthy adjournments. Nevertheless, the timetable below sets out the principal landmarks of that session and will give some indication of how a session usually runs. For illustration, the table also includes the main stages of three of the 41 public bills which passed into law in 1993–94. The Criminal Justice and Public Order Bill was a highly controversial (at least, in part) government bill, while the Local Government (Wales) Bill and the Sunday Trading Bill were also controversial government measures. A number of free votes were allowed on the latter, and the government was defeated in standing committee by backbench defections on one particular aspect of the former bill's contents. The table should be treated with caution: it should be remembered that well over 100 other bills all had their slots in this sessional timetable, and that they were joined by many hours given over to general debates, oral questions and the other activities of the two Chambers. Nor does the table include any reference to all the work which took place away from the Chamber in select and standing committees.

		Commons		Lords
1993				
November	18	State Opening of Parliament		
	18–25	Debate on Queen's Speech		
	19	Sunday Trading Bill presented		
	29	Sunday Trading – second reading		
	30	Budget Day	30	Local Government (Wales) Bill presented

		Commons		Lords
December	7	Budget debate ends and Finance Bill presented		
	13	Estimates voted		
	14	Consolidated Fund Bill	14	Local Government (Wales) – second reading
	16	Criminal Justice and Public Order Bill presented		
	17	*Christmas adjournment begins*	17	*Christmas adjournment begins*
January			10	*Christmas adjournment ends*
	11	*Christmas adjournment ends*		
	11	Criminal Justice and Public Order – second reading		
	13	Sunday Trading – standing committee begins		
			17 & 21	Local Government (Wales) – committee
	18	Crinmal Justice and Public Order – standing committee begins		
	25	Finance Bill – second reading Sunday Trading – standing committee ends (after six sittings)		
	31	Finance Bill – committee of whole house (first day)		
February	1	Finance Bill – committee of whole house (second day)		
	2	Criminal Justice and Public Order – committee of whole house		
	3	Finance Bill – standing committee begins		
	9	Sunday Trading – committee of whole house		
			10	Local Government (Wales) – report
	23	Sunday Trading – report and third reading		
			24	Sunday Trading Bill brought from Commons
			28	Local Government (Wales) – report
March	7	Local Government (Wales) Bill brought from Lords	7	Local Government (Wales) – third reading
			8	Sunday Trading – second reading
	14	Estimates voted		

		Commons		Lords
	15	Local Government (Wales) second reading		
		Criminal Justice and Public Order – standing committee ends (after 31 sittings)		
	17	Consolidated Fund Bill		
			24	Sunday Trading – committee (first day)
	28	Criminal Justice and Public Order – report (first day)		
		Finance Bill – standing committee ends (after 16 sittings)		
	31	*Easter adjournment begins*	31	*Easter adjournment begins*
April			11	*Easter adjournment ends*
	12	*Easter adjournment ends*		
		Local Government (Wales) – standing committee begins		
	12 & 13	Criminal Justice and Public Order – report (2nd and 3rd days) and		
		third reading	14	Sunday Trading – committee (second day)
			15	Criminal Justice and Public Order Bill brought from Commons
			18	Sunday Trading – committee (third day)
	19 & 20	Finance Bill – report and third reading		
			25	Criminal Justice and Public Order – second reading
May	5	Finance Bill – Royal Assent	5	Sunday Trading – report
			16	Criminal Justice and Public Order – committee begins
			19	Sunday Trading – third reading
	24	Local Government (Wales) – standing committee ends (after 17 sittings)		
	26	*Spring adjournment begins*	26	*Spring adjournment begins*
June	14	*Spring adjournment ends*	14	*Spring adjournment ends*
	15 & 16	Local Government (Wales) – report and third reading		

		Commons		Lords
	21	Sunday Trading – Lords Amendments considered	21	Criminal Justice and Public Order – committee ends (after 9 days)
July	5	Local Government (Wales) – Royal Assent Sunday Trading – Royal Assent	5, 7, 11, 12	Criminal Justice and Public Order – report
	18	Estimates voted		
			19	Criminal Justice and Public Order – third reading
	20	Consolidated Fund (Appropriation) Bill		
	21	*Summer adjournment begins*		
			26	*Summer adjournment begins*
August and September		Parliament does not meet		
October			10	*Summer adjournment ends*
	17	*Summer adjournment ends*		
	20	Criminal Justice and Public Order – Lords Amendments considered	25	Criminal Justice and Public Order – Commons Amendments considered
November	3	Criminal Justice and Public Order – Royal Assent *Parliament Prorogued*		

(Those interested in a more detailed portrait of an earlier session should turn to Appendix 1 of Dermot Englefield's book *Whitehall and Westminster*.)

One of the reforms which many newer MPs would like to see introduced is a fixed parliamentary year. For example, they argue that if Parliament was obliged to rise on 15 July for the summer adjournment, the government could not use the threat of keeping the House at work during August to ensure its legislation was passed. The Jopling Committee recommended that the House should normally rise by mid-July, though they made no recommendation about when any extra sitting days should be held to compensate for this loss of sitting time. Generally those who advocate a fixed year also favour a fixed time for rising in the evenings and the timetabling of bills. The pros and cons of timetabling will be discussed later. However, flexibility is not just an advantage for the government – it is a weapon which can be just as easily exploited by an opposition or even by individual backbenchers. The MPs who suffer most under the present system are Scots who are parents of children at school – Scottish school holidays end early in August, and Scottish MPs, who work furthest from home in any case, are usually very impatient by late July. That, in itself, is a worry for any chief whip!

Parliamentary papers

The parliamentary process generates a great deal of paper. Much of it is private and relevant only to individuals or groups, but there is also a central core of printed material, added to every day, which provides MPs with their bread-and-butter information – and which is also available to people outside Parliament.

The vote

Each MP receives a daily bundle of papers called 'the Vote'. The most important among these is the *Order Paper*. The order paper logs chronologically the various items which occur in the parliamentary day. It is, in effect, the agenda for the Chamber – although some types of business can take place without any prior notice on the order paper being given. Two important activities which occur away from the Chamber are also included – all committees due to meet that day with the place of meeting and subject of discussion (if the sessions are public) are listed, as are all the parliamentary questions due for written answer that day. Various other papers are produced from time to time in the same format as the order paper. These include notices of amendments due to be considered in committee and at the report stage of bills, notices relating to future private business and the texts of public petitions and of any government observations on them. As well as these occasional documents, there are three publications included with the order paper every day. The *Votes and Proceedings* is the official record of the things done and decided in the Chamber. It does not record the things said, but includes, for example, all votes taken, reports from committees, papers presented to Parliament and the resolutions and orders of the House. It makes interesting reading only for the initiated, but is a procedural record providing the basis for the sessional Journal, the legal record of the proceedings of the Commons. The *Notice Paper* contains notices of questions and motions tabled on the previous day and is the only place where early day motions (described in Chapter 9) are recorded. The *Remaining Orders* is effectively a list of some outstanding government business. A more comprehensive list of forthcoming business would be helpful for backbenchers.

Hansard

The proper title of *Hansard* is the Official Report. T. C. Hansard was a nineteenth-century printer and publisher whose daily record of the Commons was published privately. From 1909 staff of the House became responsible for recording debates, but the name 'Hansard' stuck, and was officially adopted in 1943. *Hansard* is the verbatim record of the words spoken in the Chamber. Editorial corrections are allowed, but corrections of substance are not. When the House is sitting, each morning sees a new printed volume of *Hansard* produced – and it usually contains words spoken up until at least 10 p.m. the previous night. Although written questions and their answers are recorded (including nowadays the texts of the letters written by the Chief Executives of Executive Agencies to whom Ministers have referred MPs' questions for reply), this is the only form of activity which does not take place in the Chamber which *Hansard* includes. Unlike the US Congress, it is not possible for a speech to be recorded which has not actually been delivered. *Hansard* reports of standing committee proceedings are also published. Verbatim accounts of the public evidence sessions of select committees are also produced, though usually not as rapidly as standing committee *Hansard* reports. This work is not done by *Hansard* staff, but by the shorthand writer to the House and her staff. The shorthand writer is not an employee of the House: the firm of W. G. Gurney & Co. has had the contract for over 150 years.

Papers presented to Parliament

Rather more than 2000 documents are 'presented' to Parliament each year. There are two main classes of these – 'Command Papers' and 'Act Papers'. All these documents are intended to inform Parliament. The Act Papers are those which are presented because an Act of Parliament says that they should be, and the Command Papers are those presented by the government 'at Her Majesty's command' because they are of sufficient public importance. Typical Command Papers are treaties and other agreements with foreign countries, reports of non-parliamentary committees of investigation or Royal Commissions, 'White Papers' (i.e. statements of government policy) and 'Green Papers' (consultative documents on government policy options). A large number of Act Papers are statutory instruments (described in Chapter 6). Others include annual reports and accounts of a whole range of public bodies, and many different sets of statistical tables. Many of the Act Papers are printed on the authority of the House of Commons, and join a sessional series of papers which contains the reports of select committees and the evidence presented to them as well.

The House of Lords

The House of Lords also has its working papers. The most important of these is the *Minute*. The Minute is broadly speaking the Lords' equivalent of the Commons' Order Paper, Votes and Proceedings and Notice Paper rolled into one. It is compiled each day and sent out to peers overnight. It begins with a formal record of the business conducted in the Chamber that day, including the judicial decisions of the House; next come the motions and orders of the day for the coming month in so far as business will have been set down (the next day's business is also printed separately as the *Order Paper* each day); and finally there are listed motions awaiting debate, questions for written answer, bills and orders of various kinds in progress, and forthcoming meetings of committees. There is a sessional Journal.

The House of Lords also has its own *Hansard*, just like the Commons. And nearly all the papers presented to the Commons are also laid before the House of Lords.

Public information

In general, the daily working papers of Parliament are not as informative to an outsider as they could be, and are costly to purchase. In France, parliamentary publications are subsidised, while in Germany, they are all published in a logical and straightforward series, and there is a great deal of glossy material produced for the general reader as well. In the USA, the internal working papers are also supplemented by publications such as the readable *Congressional Quarterly*. However, a weekly information bulletin is published by the Public Information Office in the House of Commons on business in both Houses. The Public Information Office in the House of Commons and the Information Office in the House of Lords also produce a series of information booklets on aspects of work in the two Houses. A commercial publication – the *House Magazine* – also circulates widely inside and outside Parliament which gives a certain amount of coverage to weekly business and contains useful summaries of committee reports and progress of legislation along with articles and features.

Procedures in the Chamber

Those who watch the proceedings in the Chamber from the public gallery or on television can often be bemused by what occurs. An elaborate dance seems to be acted out, quite as bewildering as any ballet – if rather less elegant. For this reason it is worth outlining some of the customary procedures in the Chamber.

Rules of debate

An MP is called to speak by the Speaker, who exercises her discretion as described in Chapter 3. Conventionally, preference is give to maiden speakers (i.e. newly elected MPs who have not spoken before) and to Privy Councillors (many senior MPs, including current and former Cabinet Ministers, belong to this body). MPs often notify the Speaker in advance of their wish to speak, but she does not issue any speaking list as happens in other Parliaments. The result is that many MPs bob up and down as other MPs finish their speeches. They are 'trying to catch the Speaker's eye'. When at last called, an MP stands to speak and addresses his or her speech to the Speaker.

If they talk about other MPs in debate, MPs must refer to them in the third person, and not use their names, but the constituency's name or the office which they hold. For example, the MP cannot talk about 'Mr Ashdown' or 'You in charge of the Liberal Democrat Party' but must refer to 'the leader of the Liberal Democrats' or 'the Right Honourable Member for Yeovil' (Mr Ashdown's constituency). Privy Councillors are called 'Right Honourable' and ordinary MPs are called 'Honourable', though MPs who are also Queen's Counsel are sometimes called 'Honourable and Learned'. If an MP is of the same party, he or she is called 'Honourable Friend'. So Liberal Democrat MPs would call their party leader 'my Right Honourable friend, the Member for Yeovil'. This form of circumlocution does give a breathing space for the MP speaking, and perhaps does something to avoid personal abuse.

For the most part, MPs may only speak once in any one debate, and that speech must not be read, though notes can be used. In the past, the length of speeches was unlimited, but there have been various experimental limits imposed in recent years. Since mid-1988, a Standing Order has allowed the Speaker to announce that no speech during a two-hour period in the evening, in the most popular debates, may last longer than ten minutes. A survey of MPs' attitudes published in early 1985 suggested that a ten-minute limit is popular and both the Procedure Committee and the Jopling Committee have recommended its wider use. As part of the 1995 experimental changes, the Speaker is to have wider discretion to limit speeches to 10 minutes, while frontbenchers have been encouraged to strive to limit their speeches to 20 minutes.

One effect a limit has is to diminish the number of 'interventions'. During a debate, an MP is often interrupted by calls of 'give way'. This is because another MP wishes to intervene in the speech to ask a question or to comment on what has just been said. The MP who is speaking decides whether to allow his or her speech to be interrupted, but the convention is to 'give way' and allow the interrupter to put a point across. This convention of interruption – which is not seen as often in European parliaments – does a great deal to keep debate alive.

Many other rules govern the content of speeches. One of the most important is the *sub-judice* rule. This is a limitation which MPs have imposed upon themselves to prevent any speech in the House prejudicing a pending British court trial. The rule is particularly strict in the case of criminal trials, and MPs are not allowed to refer to a case from the time when the individual concerned is charged with an offence. A second rule prevents MPs from making offensive personal allusions about other MPs or using 'unparliamentary language'. Lists of words banned in the past as 'unparliamentary' always make amusing reading: former Speakers have ruled that MPs cannot be any one of a menagerie of animals – jackasses, swine, stool-pigeons, rats, pups or dogs. But the serious point behind this is the one made by Speaker Weatherill in 1984 and emphasised again by Speaker Boothroyd ten years later – good temper and moderation are the characteristics of parliamentary language, and, in judging these, the context in which words are used is all important. Tempers do sometimes flare up – though not to the extent sometimes seen in volatile assemblies like those in Italy or Taiwan – but it is the Speaker's role to ensure that parliamentary disputes are conducted only verbally, and then with decorum. Finally all speeches must be relevant and not tediously repetitive, though a quick-thinking MP can make most things relevant and unrepetitive.

Those MPs who are not speaking must also obey rules. Barracking is not allowed. MPs cannot walk around the Chamber or in front of an MP who is addressing the House. All MPs have to bow to the Speaker's Chair on entering and leaving. Dress conventions – involving ties and jackets for men – are generally upheld. Eating, drinking, reading and smoking are forbidden – the House of Commons Chamber has been a no-smoking area since the resolution of 1696 'That no Member do presume to take tobacco in the gallery of the House or at a committee table'.

The rules of debate are a little different in the House of Lords, although many of the conventions of behaviour are very similar. The most important difference is that the Speaker (the Lord Chancellor or any Deputy Speaker) does not call peers to speak.

Members usually give advance notice to the Government Whips' Office of their intention to speak in debates and speakers' lists are prepared by the Leader of the House, in consultation with the usual channels and the mover of the motion, and published before the debate begins. Any Lord not on the list may speak but only after those already on the list and before the winding-up speeches. So there is no problem in the Lords of having to 'catch the Speaker's eye'. As we have already seen, preservation of order is the responsibility of all members present, though the Leader of the House will intervene when he thinks appropriate to assist.

As in the House of Commons there are conventions governing the way in which other members are addressed. The House does not shrink from mentioning members by name occasionally. Common styles of address might include 'The Noble Earl, Lord . . .' or, if a baron, 'The Noble Lord, Lord . . .', 'The Rt Reverend Prelate, the Bishop of . . .', 'The Noble and Learned Lord, Lord . . .' if a Law Lord or, where appropriate, 'The Noble Minister', 'My Noble Friend' or 'My Noble Kinsman'.

Generally speaking a Lord can speak only once in debate, except when the House is in committee on a bill, and must not read. Unless speaking from the frontbench, where Lords speak from a despatch box, members speak in their place. Speeches must be relevant, and indeed, in 1965 the House even resolved that they should be shorter. Members must refrain from 'asperity of speech', and they speak on their personal honour and must therefore declare any personal financial interest.

In addition to these rules of debate, various rules of conduct, along with the custom of 'making obeisance' to the Cloth of Estate behind the throne as members enter the Chamber, lend the Lords a veneer of good, and even courtly, manners as those who watch the House will already be aware.

Voting

One of the most bizarre rules in the Commons is the one which obliges MPs who wish to raise a point of order when a vote is taking place to wear a hat and to speak sitting down. Two collapsible top hats are kept by the Serjeant at Arms for the purpose. Over the years, many MPs have tried to have the rule changed, but the House has held on to its old custom. Being conspicuous is still an asset, as anyone who has witnessed what happens when the House votes will agree. When a vote takes place, MPs arrive at the Chamber from all over the building. They mill about and chatter, and people seem to walk off in all directions.

Votes are called 'divisions' because those who vote are asked to divide physically – the reason for all the milling around – into two groups – the 'ayes' and the 'noes' ('contents' and 'not contents' in the House of Lords). There is no opportunity to register an abstention in the British Parliament. Any vote must be either for or against. During the course of a sitting day, many opportunities for divisions occur. Relatively few actually result in votes taking place, though the House of Commons votes, on average, about twice every sitting day. When the opposition – or a group of MPs – wish to make trouble for the government, it is possible to force many more divisions, as happened regularly during the early months of 1994. Normally these votes occur at the end of a debate. The Speaker then 'puts the question', or tells the House what it is being asked to decide. For example, she says 'the question is, that this House has no confidence in Her Majesty's government' or 'the question is, that the amendment be made'. On an uncontroversial matter, the only response she will hear is a muffled 'aye' or 'no', as appropriate, from the government whips, and no division will take place. When there is more controversy, MPs on different sides of the House will shout out 'aye' or 'no', depending on the way they intend to vote. The Speaker judges the louder cry, and then says 'I think the noes/ayes have it'. If at this stage both sides shout out again, the Speaker says 'clear the lobby' – the signal that a division is to take place. Bells ring throughout the precincts – and in local pubs and restaurants and MPs' own homes within the Westminster area. Not more than two minutes later, the Speaker again puts the question, and, if both sides still wish to vote, she names tellers. Tellers are responsible for counting the MPs who vote. A division cannot take place unless there are two from the 'ayes' and two from the 'noes'. On official votes, they are normally whips, though any MP can act as a teller. The tellers take up position to count outside the division lobbies (one teller representing each side at each lobby). The MPs who are voting are by that time either inside the division lobbies or on their way there. They have physically divided into two groups. (The aye lobby is on the west side of the Chamber, the no lobby on the east, as can be seen on the plan on page 3.) They give their names to clerks as they pass out of the lobby, and are counted by the tellers. This is the act of voting. Only eight minutes are normally allowed from the time the bells first begin to ring before the entrances to the division lobbies are locked. No one who takes longer than this to arrive can vote. After the doors have been locked and all the MPs in the lobbies counted, the tellers return to the table and give the result to the Speaker. The whole process takes about twelve to fifteen minutes.

Why is this apparently cumbersome procedure used when other parliaments use electronic voting machines? When the atmosphere is tense and the opposition insists on a series of votes late at night, many backbenchers would approve of an electronic system. However, the present physical system does have the advantage of bringing backbench and frontbench MPs together at – usually – times well-known in advance. Junior backbenchers can meet and talk to their frontbench colleagues, and ordinary MPs use divisions as fixed points for meeting one another. The need to come physically to the Chamber also emphasises its central role in an MP's life.

By no means do all MPs vote on each occasion. The whips have the duty of warning their own sides about important votes, as described in Chapter 4. When a three-line whip has not been issued, MPs 'pair' with one another. This allows two MPs from the two different sides to be away from the vote without affecting the result. Normally pairs are long-standing and sought after arrangements. New backbenchers from the government side are not able to find pairs because, by definition, there are more of them than there are MPs on the other side. A weapon which the opposition can use, as it did in the winter of 1993–94, is to withdraw pairing arrangements. This means that government frontbenchers and backbenchers can be forced to remain in the precincts, perhaps until the early hours of the morning, in case of a surprise vote. Understandably this leads to frayed tempers. For critical divisions, sick MPs can have their votes recorded by being present in the precincts and then 'nodded through'. There were instances of MPs brought in ambulances to New Palace Yard to be nodded through on the critical divisions in the 1974–79 parliament. This practice was roundly condemned by the Jopling Committee in 1992, who were 'firmly of the opinion that the gruesome prospect of Members being taken to Westminster in ambulances to vote should never happen again'.

Voting is very similar in the Lords, the principal difference being one of terminology. Three minutes elapse before the question is put a second time and six minutes pass before the doors are locked. Generally speaking the numbers of members voting in divisions in the Lords are fewer than in the Commons but a vote can still take up to ten minutes from beginning to end.

Because party discipline is weaker in the Lords, there is no tradition of pairing. But the whips nevertheless try to keep their members in the House as long as they can when important divisions are likely. In a busy session this can be fatiguing: there were 250 divisions in 1985–86, compared with 165 in 1992–3.

The Commons can transact business without any minimum number present – it has no quorum. However, if fewer than 40 members (including the occupant of the Chair and the tellers) take part in a division, the business under consideration stands over until the next sitting of the House. The quorum of the House of Lords is generally three, though for legislation it is increased to 30 if a division takes place.

Closure and guillotine

In the Commons, some speeches are time-limited, and so are some debates. However, in most cases those MPs who oppose a particular bill, or less frequently, other types of parliamentary business may try to 'talk it out'. The opportunity of doing so is severely limited by two procedural devices – the closure and the guillotine. The guillotine is a time-tabling motion which is introduced by the government for its most controversial legislative proposals and ensures their progress through committee and in the Chamber. Since it is concerned with public legislation, it will be discussed at greater length in Chapter 6. The closure can be used to end debate on a particular stage of legislation or on any other matter which the House is considering. An MP who is in favour of the measure before the House or who wants to ensure a vote upon it and who is afraid that others are intent on talking it out, stands up in the Chamber and asks the Speaker to accept the motion 'That the question be now put'. The Speaker has discretion about accepting this closure motion, but if she feels the debate has continued for an appropriate length of time and that the rights of minorities in the House are not being infringed, she allows the closure to be put to the vote without debate.

The closure motion must be passed by a majority, and, as a further protection against its abuse, at least 100 MPs must vote for it if it is to be carried. If this happens, the House then immediately votes on the issue which was being discussed before the closure was moved (the so-called 'original question'). To take an example, the government bill allowing the fluoridation of the water supply caused a good deal of controversy in 1985. Many government backbenchers opposed the bill, and they tried to delay its progress by proposing numerous amendments and debating these at length. The Commons finally gave a third reading to the bill at a sitting lasting more than 30 hours. Debate began on one particular amendment at 11 p.m. At around 3 a.m., the government deputy chief whip moved the closure, which was carried by 120 votes to 49. Many MPs who were opposed to the bill still wanted to speak, but if they had been given the opportunity to do so, the bill would never have proceeded. The Deputy Speaker therefore allowed the closure in a sense to protect the rights of the majority. Straightaway after the closure had been carried, a vote was taken on the amendment ('the original question') and it was decisively defeated by 122 votes to 43. But the minority have rights also: later that night, a closure motion was moved after a debate had only lasted two and a half hours. The Deputy Speaker refused to accept the closure at that time, and debate was allowed to continue for a little longer.

The closure is used fairly frequently. For example, in the long 1992–93 session, it was carried on 47 occasions, and defeated twice

– on both of these occasions because fewer than 100 MPs voted in favour, despite there being more in favour than there were against. The Chair refused to accept the closure three times during that session.

The guillotine does not exist in the House of Lords and the closure is a most exceptional procedure. The greater spirit of cooperation and compromise – and the persuasive powers of the Leader of the House – militate against the use of delaying tactics there.

The press and broadcasting

The often strange procedures of Parliament are normally interpreted for the public by parliamentary journalists. A great deal of the coverage of the newspapers and broadcasting media is, of course, taken up by politics in its broadest sense and interviews with individual MPs, articles written by them and reports of their views form a substantial part of this coverage. But there are also special aspects of the coverage of Parliament which we need to look at.

Two hundred years ago, it was considered a contempt of Parliament to report its proceedings in the newspapers. Nowadays politicians need the media to give them and their ideas publicity. At Westminster, the special system known as the 'lobby' has grown up. The leading national and provincial papers and magazines and the broadcasting media each have a 'lobby correspondent' who has privileged access to the facilities of the Houses of Parliament. When the House is meeting, lobby journalists are to be seen talking to MPs in the members' lobby, and there is a bar ('Annie's Bar') to which only lobby journalists and MPs and senior officials of the House have access. More importantly, the lobby correspondents also have access to MPs and ministers in both Houses on special lobby terms: the journalists are told information on the basis that its source is not disclosed without specific permission. For example, a senior Cabinet Minister or opposition frontbencher who is dissatisfied with some aspect of his leader's policies could call lobby journalists together and tell them so. But, under the rules, the lobby correspondents' reports would read 'senior sources in the party say . . .' rather than 'Mr X says . . .'. There are also daily lobby briefings by senior government officials, and occasional briefings by ministers.

This form of unattributable briefing has come in for some criticism in recent years, and there are a number of journalists who are in favour of abandoning the lobby system particularly because of the way in which they believe it can be used to 'manage' the news. No doubt the confidentiality of the system can be misused, but the existence of a group of specialist parliamentary journalists with behind-the-scenes contacts is probably desirable for MPs. Select committees, for example, are often able to cooperate with lobby journalists to the mutual advantage of both: the press receive information, the committee receives publicity. Backbenchers too, are able to use the lobby to get their own ideas across, especially if those ideas are controversial. The local journalists who are members of the lobby are particularly useful when constituency issues arise.

As well as the private briefings which journalists receive, they also report the public events in Parliament – the debates in both Houses, and, increasingly, the hearings held by select committees. What goes on in Parliament is news in itself. Several of the daily papers include a parliamentary sketch – a facetious look at some part of the day's proceedings, not much use if one wants to understand what Parliament is doing, but part of the process of ensuring that politicians do not think too highly of themselves. 'Straight' reporting of debates is still carried in *The Financial Times, The Times, Telegraph, Independent* and *Guardian*, but fewer column-inches are given up to it. Indeed, a 1993 survey by the Labour MP Jack Straw suggested that this type of reporting, having been at a fairly constant level from 1933 to 1988, had declined by three quarters between 1988 and 1993.

Reporting of the day's events has become easier for radio journalists since 1978 when regular sound broadcasting of both Houses and their committees began. There are some restrictions on the use to which sound recordings can be put (e.g. they should not be used out of context in satirical programmes, although during the Falklands War recordings from the House were used in a protest song recorded by a rock group), but editorial control generally rests with the broadcasting authorities. Radio news and current affairs broadcasts now often contain excerpts from Parliament.

The Lords have been televised since 1984 and the Commons since 1988. Both Houses began with an experimental period. Indeed, the Commons had rejected television in 1966, 1971, 1975 and 1985, and the division of opinion remained close in 1988 – 320 MPs were in favour and 266 against.

Each House of Parliament now has a Broadcasting Committee, whose role it is to oversee the broadcasting arrangements in that House. Day-to-day monitoring of adherence to rules of coverage laid down by the two Committees is delegated to the Supervisor of Parliamentary Broadcasting. In response to recommendations made by the Broadcasting Committees, a company called PARBUL Ltd was set up in 1991. The board of directors of PARBUL Ltd is made up of representatives of various broadcasting companies, and members of the House of Commons and the House of Lords. PARBUL Ltd is wholly funded by the broadcasting companies.

PARBUL has contracted an independent company to record all proceedings on the floor of both Houses. Select and Standing Committee proceedings are also recorded if there is a demand from the broadcasters for the footage. The broadcasting companies who are shareholders of PARBUL are then able to use the recordings for broadcast use. At present, all the recordings are kept and archived.

The rules of coverage are different for the two Houses. In the Commons, a number of guidelines govern the types of shots that may be used in proceedings – notably, the prohibition of 'reaction shots' during debates of MPs who are neither speaking nor being referred to personally. In the Lords, as long as only proceedings on the floor are recorded, there are no particular rules.

Inevitably, more media interest is shown in Commons proceedings than in Lords proceedings. For example, in January and February 1994 the coverage of Lords proceedings in the BBC's radio programme *Today in Parliament* was only 21 per cent of programme time; in BBC's TV programme *Westminster Daily*, coverage was about 14 per cent. Channel 4's *A Week in Politics* devoted 15 per cent of its time to the Lords between October 1993 and February 1994. Recipients of cable television are able to watch the 'Parliamentary Channel', which shows both live and recorded highlights of proceedings in both Houses on sitting days.

Some feel that broadcasting, especially televising, trivialises parliamentary debates or gives excessive coverage to frontbenchers and 'colourful' MPs at the expense of diligent, ordinary backbenchers. And there has undoubtedly been a tendency to concentrate on the half hour a week devoted to Prime Minister's question time in the Commons – a sensational but rather untypical feature of the parliamentary week. But advocates of broadcasting believe that Parliament can only occupy the centre of the public stage if proceedings in the Chamber and in Committees appear regularly through the medium which gives the majority of people their news: 98 per cent of British households now have a television set. The use that is made of footage of parliamentary proceedings in news bulletins and specialist programmes is now a fact of life – even though people may not always like what they see when proceedings become raucous.

Away from the Chamber

We said at the beginning of this chapter that the Chamber was at the centre of parliamentary life. However, a very important part of every MP's life and work is conducted outside the Chamber or the committees of the House. There are no comprehensive statistics available about this side of parliamentary business, and, if there were, they would not tell us very much. The opportunity to interpret the job according to his or her individual judgement is one of the principal attractions of an MP's life.

Those who visit the Commons are sometimes surprised to see that only twenty or so MPs are in the Chamber, and many MPs are worried that the televising of the Commons has led to a lot of ill-informed criticism about attendance levels. There is, in fact, no official record of attendance in the Commons, and though the Lords have a record, it shows only if a peer attended on a particular day, not the length of time he or she stayed. Attendance in the Chamber naturally varies in accordance with the business under consideration. For the most part, a bill on oil policy will attract only MPs with interests in energy and one on agricultural diseases only those who are concerned with farming. Some policy areas – social and economic questions – attract wider interest, and, of course, the Chamber is packed for the twice-weekly Prime Minister's question time or for the great events of the parliamentary year, like the budget speech. MPs also respond to heightened political tension – as during the Gulf War, or during the to-ings and fro-ings in 1990 when Mrs Thatcher lost the Conservative party leadership – by coming to the Chamber, especially between 3.30 and 4 p.m., when points of order are raised, accusations traded across the floor of the House and the political tension can be relieved. This, of course, is the time sensationalist reporters find most interesting. It is also convenient for meeting the deadlines for morning papers.

Members of both Houses are kept informed of the business currently being conducted in their respective Chambers through closed circuit television systems with outlets throughout the building. The screens register the item being considered and the current speaker. Often one can see the Commons Chamber filling soon after the television has shown that a senior and respected MP is addressing the House. Over the next few years a video relay system will be provided throughout the Commons to allow MPs to see what is happening in the Chamber in their own offices. This happens in other Parliaments, but opinions had been divided at Westminster about its effect on attendance in the Chamber. The decision to go ahead with the relay system was taken in June 1994.

At some stage during most days, the majority of MPs who are not away from Westminster altogether at least look in at the Chamber, even if there is no particular political excitement or if they are not interested in the matters being discussed. The rest of their day depends on their tastes, but most will find that they have very similar tasks to fulfil.

The first of these is dealing with the post-bag. All MPs receive letters from national and local pressure groups and from their constituents – we will look at constituency work in a more general way later in this section. Most MPs would say that they spend two or three hours a day dealing with correspondence. Some of the busier MPs allow their secretary or research assistant to draft replies for them to sign, especially on routine matters, and response to a letter can result in no more than the MP signing an early day motion. At the other extreme, correspondence can cause a great deal of work, if, for example, the MP decides to pursue some individual's case by the full parliamentary means of correspondence with ministers, and debates. Statistics released in 1986 showed that ten and a half million pieces of mail are handled by the special House of Commons post office annually. Some, of course, are not for MPs, but the figure gives some idea of the magnitude of correspondence passing through Parliament.

Depending on the extent to which the individual MP is known to the public, he or she may receive much more correspondence than normal, but almost invariably MPs take up individual cases only on behalf of their constituents. If they are approached by a non-constituent, there is an unwritten rule that they should refer the case to the appropriate constituency MP.

Dealing with correspondence is, of course, just one of the MP's duties as a representative, and a part of most days will probably be taken up with more time-consuming representational activities. An MP may meet individually or take part in a delegation to see a minister or union or business leaders to advance some constituency or more general political case. Depending on their known interests, MPs will be asked to attend exhibitions, conferences, presentations and meetings – and perhaps to speak at them. Pressure groups and interests outside the House may invite MPs to lunch or dinner to put their case across and in the hope of gleaning political intelligence from the MP. MPs need to fit all these time-consuming – and often unrewarding – activities inside a timetable which requires them to be in the House if whips have demanded their presence with a three-line whip, or if they have to attend the meetings of standing committees or select committees – very few MPs, except the Speaker and her deputies and the Prime Minister, escape service on a standing committee or select committee during the course of a parliament. MPs notoriously find that they have to break engagements, but this is almost inevitable because of the varying pressures upon them and the unpredictability of the parliamentary timetable (MPs never know whether they will need to be in the Chamber at 3.30 on a Tuesday, for example, until 4 p.m. the previous Thursday following the business statement).

There are two or three areas in which a large proportion of MPs take part. Naturally the first of these involves party activities. In the Labour Party, several MPs from the front and backbenches are members of the party's National Executive, and several of the officers of the Conservative Party – normally including the

Chairman – are MPs. At a different level, most MPs will take part in the activities and meetings organised at a local and regional level by their parties.

Work in cooperation with outside pressure groups is another area which occupies many MPs' time. The Chairs of the Anti-Apartheid Movement, the British section of Amnesty International and of the Commonwealth Youth Exchange Council, among many others have been held by MPs in recent years, but the range of interest and activity is much wider and spreads into the area of consultancy. Many MPs are paid or unpaid consultants to outside organisations from the Police Federation through the Society of Civil and Public Servants to public or private companies such as British Airways. Depending on their level of commitment to these organisations, MPs find part of their day taken up in briefing them or writing for their house magazines or advancing their case in the House and with the government. In addition, some MPs carry on working in their professions or are paid as company directors. It was estimated in an independent report of 1971 that 70 per cent of all backbenchers had regular or occasional part-time occupations, and that 19 per cent of these MPs devoted more than twenty hours a week to these part-time occupations. A glance at any current biographical list of MPs or at the register of members' interests will show that outside interests remain strong. Government ministers are not permitted to hold part-time occupations, but one could see them as part-time MPs nonetheless – their main work in government is tied in with, but is different from, their work as MPs. A final area in which almost all MPs are pleased to be asked to participate is writing for newspapers and magazines and broadcasting. If one listens to the 'Today' programme on BBC Radio each morning, for example, it is very unusual not to hear three or four MPs being interviewed on different subjects, and most MPs will find themselves asked to contribute to the regional, if not the national, media from time to time.

If one takes into consideration reading, researching and chatting over political gossip with colleagues, one can see that there is no shortage of activity away from the Chamber to attract an MP. The extent to which he or she takes part in these activities, and the mix adopted, is a matter for individual decision. Also for individual decision is the level of intensity of such activity – there are lazy MPs and hyperactive MPs, just as there are lazy and hyperactive solicitors, teachers or clerks.

Many MPs enjoy the opportunity to be away altogether from the Westminster grind. Invitations are often forthcoming. An oil company, for example, might study MPs' interests and invite those who concern themselves with energy matters to visit a North Sea oil platform or the company's research and development facilities. Particularly prized by many MPs are the opportunities to travel abroad offered by organisations like the Commonwealth Parliamentary Association (an association of parliamentarians from Commonwealth countries) or the Inter-Parliamentary Union (an organisation with 129 member states, ranging from Cuba to South Korea). More usually, travelling away from Westminster means returning to the constituency. In past generations some MPs chose to have very little contact with their constituency except at election time, but constituents' expectations have grown since 1945, and MPs with marginal seats are well aware that academic studies of recent general elections appear to show that a good constituency record is worth between 1000 and 2000 votes. In addition to this pragmatic reason for maintaining good constituency relations, most MPs realise that they only hold their position because of their constituents and they feel obliged to repay those who have given them their ticket to political activity. We discussed this relationship with the constituency in Chapter 4.

Occasionally commentators criticise MPs for working only part-time, but, as we have seen, it is very difficult to define what their 'work' should be. It is certainly not limited to attendance in the Chamber, and MPs who undertake additional paid work – consultancy services or in their professions – argue that they are more effective and better informed as MPs because of it.

Peers, even more than MPs, may be expected to have life outside the Chamber, for the House of Lords is very largely a voluntary body. Its members, though summoned to attend Parliament by their Writs of Summons, are not paid a salary like MPs (although they do receive some allowances) and many members of the House also hold down full-time jobs. Being unelected, peers have no representative function in respect of a constituency, and so there is less of an obligation to attend the House. But nearly all those eligible to sit come at some time in the session and average daily attendance, at about 380, has risen steadily.

Lord Glenamara, a former MP, told the House in 1986 that he had a larger post-bag in the Lords than he had had in the Commons. The more active peers can receive considerable post-bags in spite of having no constituents – from pressure groups, or organisations in which the peer in question might have an interest. And peers, like MPs, are active in their respective parties, in other organisations which they espouse, or in writing and in media activities.

CHAPTER 6

Legislation

If asked 'who makes the law in Britain?', most people would instinctively reply 'Parliament'. It seems to be an obvious feature of our democratic country that the law under which it operates has been decided by popularly elected representatives in Parliament. And if we were asked 'where can one find the law?', we might point to the long series of volumes entitled 'Statutes' or 'Acts of Parliament'. Each of these Acts of Parliament begins with the formula

Be it enacted by the Queen's Most Excellent Majesty, by and with the consent of the Lords Spiritual and Temporal, and Commons in this present Parliament assembled, and by the authority of the same as follows . . .

This seems to prove Parliament's law-making responsibility. But if we look at any particular instance of the law in operation, we soon find that we need to qualify the statement that 'Parliament makes the law': the way the law works in practice may differ from the intentions of Parliament when the law was passed, law-making powers may be delegated or the application of the law may vary in different parts of the country.

For example, a driver of an antique fire-engine used in a fun-fair is stopped by the police as he drives the wrong way down a one-way street. The police find he has no tachograph in his cab. This is required by law to record his hours of work and mileage travelled. He is charged with driving the wrong way down the street and with not having the tachograph, and is convicted by the magistrates. He appeals on the grounds that tachographs are not required in fire-engines, and the appeal court finds in his favour because the appeal judges decide the law is not clear. Over a drink afterwards, the driver is able to tell his friends about his 'brush with the law'.

What has Parliament to do with this process? The enforcement of the law is the police's duty. The interpretation of the law has been the job of the courts. The street was not designated as one-way by Parliament but by the borough council. The law about tachographs was set out in regulations made by the Secretary of State for Transport, not by Parliament. And all the Secretary of State has done was to give effect to European Community legislation in this area.

However, all the actors in this drama have been operating within a framework which derives ultimately from the statute law as set out in Acts of Parliament. The borough council made the street one-way because an Act of Parliament gave it power to do so, and the European Communities were able to make regulations about tachographs because an Act of Parliament – in this case the European Communities Act 1972 – allows them to regulate, in certain areas, the internal affairs of the United Kingdom.

This chapter will look in some detail at these Acts of Parliament – the basic foundation blocks of the law – and explore the role which Parliament in practice plays in their making. It will also describe the parliamentary procedures which govern delegated legislation, that is legislation made directly by the government and other bodies who have been authorised by Acts of Parliament to do so.

First, a few basic definitions are needed. When a proposal for a law is being considered by Parliament, it is known as a bill. When the parliamentary process is complete, if the bill has been agreed to, or 'passed', the bill becomes an Act of Parliament and part of the statute law. It is always referred to by the year in which it was passed. Bills are made up of 'clauses', but when they become Acts the clauses become known as 'sections'.

Bills and Acts can be divided into two types – public and private. We will consider each separately, but by far the more important are public bills and Acts. These apply throughout the country (though some apply only to Scotland or only to England and Wales etc). Private bills and Acts have only a particular or local application and are subject to different procedures. For example, a private Act might allow a particular local authority to close a particular cemetery or regulations to be made for common land in a particular area of the country. If new requirements were to be applied to all cemeteries throughout the country or to all common land, these would be contained in public legislation.

Public legislation

Although public legislation applies generally throughout the country, some Acts of Parliament are of far greater importance than others. For example, the 1992–93 session saw proposals for public legislation which ranged from the European Communities (Amendment) Bill, which implemented the controversial Maastricht Treaty, and the Finance Bill, which gave effect to the budget proposals, to the Carrying of Knives etc. (Scotland) Bill, the Welsh Language Bill and the Tattooing (Insurance Cover) Bill (the last did not become law).

From this it will be obvious that statistics about the number of Acts of Parliament passed every session are not particularly meaningful. More interesting might be figures for the number of pages of legislation passed every year. Excluding Consolidation Acts (these are Acts which bring together old legislation in a more convenient way: they do not make new law), in 1990, 1707 pages of public Acts of Parliament were passed – an average of just under ten pages for every day the Commons sat. (Forty years previously only 430 were passed, a three page a day average – and the pages in those days were smaller!) A considerable amount of the time of Parliament is occupied in considering the bills which will ultimately become these Acts – in the 1992–93 session over a third of the Commons' time went in debates on public bills (694 hours out of 1984), and almost 50 per cent of the Lords' time was taken up in this way. The Commons figure for the session was fairly typical, but the Lords figure represents, for them, a light legislative session. Some other sessions have found the Lords devoting over 60 per cent of their time to public bills.

Public bills can be divided into two main categories – bills promoted by the government and bills promoted by backbench MPs or peers. These are known respectively as government bills and private members' bills. Private members' bills are public bills just in the same way as government bills are, and, if passed, become public Acts. However, there are differences in the procedures to which public bills promoted by private members and those promoted by the government are subject in the Commons, and we shall look at the two categories separately, noting here only that 90 per cent of the time taken up by public bills in the Commons is devoted to government bills, not because backbenchers are reticent about making legislative proposals, but because the time of the Commons is largely in the government's control.

Government bills

Sometimes it appears that governments feel themselves under a sort of obligation to keep Parliament busy with more and more new legislation. Some government bills are vital, especially those which authorise the raising of taxes and spending of public money by government departments. In times of crisis, too, legislation may be vital: at the beginning of the Second World War, a number of Acts of Parliament needed to be passed urgently to put the country on a war-time footing. Similarly, emergency government legislation has been necessary to deal with terrorism in Northern Ireland, Rhodesia's unilateral declaration of independence and similar crises. A more political sort of crisis may also arise – for example, the courts decided in 1985 that a direction which the Secretary of State for Transport had given to the Greater London Council had not been lawful. The government decided to introduce a new bill to remedy the defect in the existing law and give them beyond any doubt the power in law which they had thought they already had but which the courts had said that they did not. Later that year, a different sort of crisis arose when over 40 people were killed in a riot at a football stadium. Urgent legislation was introduced by the government to control the sale of alcohol at sports grounds.

Crisis legislation is, however, the exception. Normally, the government brings forward legislative proposals voluntarily for two main reasons: because of political pressures and as part of the business of keeping the running of the State in good working order. Political pressures arise from the party system. Each political party has a set of priorities for the country expressed as its policy. Policy is formulated in a variety of ways: strong individuals in the leadership have ideas, ordinary members of the party express their preferences through their constituency parties or at party conferences, and pressure groups inside and outside the party bring their influence to bear. At this stage no one is really concerned with detailed questions about whether the law will need to be changed to achieve particular policy goals, though such questions will always have to be addressed eventually if the policies are to be given effect. This can be particularly noticeable when a political party is newly elected to government. It may find that a change in the law is required to ensure that the policies it announced in its manifesto, and which the public voted for, are put into effect. For example, the Labour Party is in favour of comprehensive schools. Not all local authorities agreed with this policy, and the Labour government was obliged to introduce a bill which later became the Education Act 1976 to compel local education authorities to go comprehensive. The Conservatives are opposed to compulsory comprehensive schooling. When they were elected in 1979, they in turn could only achieve their ends by introducing legislation to remove the compulsion on local authorities which had been imposed as part of the 1976 Act.

But there is also pressure from inside government departments for new legislation. Part of the job of the civil servants in these departments is to maintain the running of the State in good order, and they will often discover that new legislation is necessary to do this. Old legislation may have been shown up as ineffective because of court decisions or administrative difficulties in enforcing it. Legislation or court decisions emanating from the EU or other international organisations will require changes in British law. And new problems arise which require the State to move into new areas of statutory provision – like human fertilisation and embryology, for example. Very often this kind of legislation will have been preceded by some kind of study conducted within, or commissioned by, the responsible government department. Judicial Inquiries, like the 1989 Taylor Inquiry into the safety of football grounds following the Hillsborough disaster, or Royal Commissions, like the Runciman Commission on criminal justice, also make recommendations for legislative action. On top of all that, ministers and civil servants will be swamped by the ideas of special interest groups – from the disabled to bee-keepers – who will suggest how changes in the law could be introduced to their benefit.

Political pressures and day-to-day departmental pressures between them ensure that no government department is ever short of ideas for legislation. When ideas have been formulated, a process of consultation begins, the length and complexity of which will depend on the legislation being considered and on the urgency with which it is needed. Inside Government, the Treasury will be consulted as well as other departments with interests in the subject matter. Outside Government the pressure groups, industries or trade unions affected will also be consulted informally and sometimes formally. In due course the sponsoring department will have proposals to put before a policy committee of the Cabinet. This will often be done by correspondence and only if disagreements arise or if major issues are at stake will the subject need to be discussed at a meeting of the committee itself. Thus an intention to change policy relating to a defendant's right to remain silent would be considered by the Home and Social Affairs Committee of the Cabinet; policy issues relating to the privatisation of the railways would be considered by the Industrial, Commercial and Consumer Affairs Committee and so on. The Government has acknowledged the existence of 17 such ministerial policy committees of the Cabinet and 10 sub-committees. Of these, five committees – on Economic and Domestic Policy, Industrial Commercial and Consumer Affairs, Environment, Home and Social Affairs, and Local Government – regularly consider policy leading to legislation. The policy committee may endorse the proposal or defer a final decision until the policy has been subjected to further, more public, consultation, perhaps by means of a Green Paper or published consultation document. Endorsement by the committee is the point at which a proposal for change can be said to have become government policy.

But endorsement as government policy does not necessarily carry with it the immediate prospect of legislation. A minor change may have to wait until a suitable legislative vehicle, that is a bill in the same subject area, can be found for it to be included. A major policy development or series of developments may require a whole bill and hence a place of its own in the Government's legislative programme. Parliamentary time is scarce, so further decisions need to be taken centrally about priorities between competing legislative proposals and about balancing the programme of bills for each session of Parliament. This is the job of the special Cabinet committee which considers all future legislation – the Queen's

Speeches and Future Legislation Committee. The membership
of this committee includes the Leaders of, and government chief
whips in, both Houses of Parliament. It recommends to the Cabinet
which departmental legislative proposals will actually be mentioned
in the Queen's Speech at the beginning of the new session and be
presented to Parliament as bills.

Lawyers will have been involved from an early stage in the
discussion of the proposed legislation, but turning ideas into
draft laws is a highly skilled business, and is the responsibility
of the élite group of lawyers known as parliamentary draftsmen,
or parliamentary counsel. These are experienced barristers or
solicitors who are employed as civil servants by government in
a central service available to all government departments (there
are separate services for Scotland and Northern Ireland, for which
separate legislation is often required). Initially they receive a
memorandum of instruction from the sponsoring government
department which they will convert into a draft bill. If the matter
is complex, there will be several drafts before a final version is
approved for presentation to Parliament. It is this final product
which, just before its introduction into Parliament, is presented to
yet another committee of the Cabinet, the Legislation Committee.
The membership of this Committee again includes the Leaders and
government chief whips of both Houses (the business managers).
Their job is to try to ensure that bills presented to Parliament
are acceptable to a majority there, and that they will be passed
during the course of the session. Some critics of the quality of
draft legislation in recent years have looked to the Legislation
Committee to keep departments and parliamentary counsel on
their toes. But this is probably an unrealistic expectation, given
the Committee's membership and the late stage and short notice
at which it is shown the bills. With the approval of the Legislation
Committee, the bill may be introduced into one or other of the two
Houses.

To arrive at this stage of presentation, the whole process usually
takes many months. The government will be presenting a bill to
which it has given a great deal of thought, which it will naturally
think it has 'got right' and which it will hope to see pass into law
unaltered. The system of settling policy and preparing legislation
is, as we have seen, a sophisticated one and ought to have just that
result. It ensures that policies to be legislated upon are coherent and
acceptable throughout Government; it allows for wide consultation
for getting things right; it enables priorities to be set in a rational
manner; it limits the volume of legislation to what can reasonably
be got through Parliament in one session; and it ensures that the
skills of parliamentary counsel – whose drafting lends coherence
to the statute book – are focussed only on those bills which have
a place in the legislative programme.

In a perfect world this would, no doubt, be the effect of the system. In practice however, the machinery for preparing legislation is frequently overloaded. Too many large and complex bills are attempted in a session; policy is sometimes not settled sufficiently well in advance of the time when drafting and, on occasion, even introduction of the bills becomes necessary; and instructions from government departments to parliamentary counsel are sometimes late. The consultation process may be rushed or circumvented altogether. Such bills often have a difficult passage through the two Houses of Parliament and have to be heavily amended – as much by the Government itself as by, or in response to, the opposition parties or backbenchers. Parliamentary counsel, who retain a responsibility for the drafting of their bills throughout their passage, are thus frequently diverted from getting on with preparing the bills for the next session's legislative programme. Some of these difficulties were highlighted in a recent report of the Hansard Society (*Making the Law: the Report of the Hansard Society Commission on the Legislative Process*, November 1992).

Notwithstanding these criticisms, Parliament does not see a rough draft but what the sponsoring department and parliamentary counsel hope will serve as a finished product. Understandably, the sponsoring department hopes that the parliamentary stage of the legislation will be limited to what is called 'legitimation', in other words the democratic endorsement of the government's will.

From what has already been said, it will be readily apparent that in the majority of legislation with which it deals – government legislation – Parliament is certainly not the initiating or moving force. However, as we will see later, it would be inaccurate to describe the parliamentary processes to which the government bills are subject as a mere rubber stamp 'legitimation' exercise. It is important to remember how much MPs and peers have either been directly involved or considered in the internal process which leads up to the presentation of a bill to Parliament. As professional politicians, MPs are involved in the determination of their parties' policies. MPs and peers often act as spokespersons for the pressure groups which try to influence the form of proposed legislation. Debates in the House, select committee inquiries and parliamentary questions can all be used to canvass ideas for legislation or warn the government off legislation by exposing inconsistencies and problems to which it will give rise.

Furthermore, the Cabinet is made up of MPs and peers who have direct contact with their non-ministerial colleagues. For civil servants, Parliament is a little remote, but it is not so for most ministers who will always be testing legislative ideas against the criteria of acceptability to the public, their party and to Parliament. Especially sensitive to parliamentary pressures are the Queen's Speeches and Future Legislation Committee of the Cabinet. These sensitivities appear to have asserted themselves particularly strongly in the 1994 discussions of the legislative programme for 1994–95 when, it was reported, business managers and other powerful members of the Cabinet sought to curb the legislative bids of some of their colleagues. They felt that parliamentary and public opinion at large called for a period of consolidation of such extensive legislative changes as had already been effected.

When the statistics about government bills are examined, it is sometimes claimed that Parliament is ineffective just because almost all government bills are passed (all of the bills introduced in the Commons in the 1992–93 session, for example). But this may be no more than an indication that the government had done its homework properly and assessed parliamentary opinion in advance. Certainly there are cases where important legislative ideas have been dropped because it has become apparent that they would be unacceptable to Parliament – the Labour government in 1969 decided not to proceed with reform of industrial relations law, successive governments are known to have been studying reform of the House of Lords but have made no legislative proposals, and the problems of steering the necessary bill through Parliament was one of the reasons why water privatisation was not attempted before the 1987 election or why full post office privatisation will not be attempted in the 1992 Parliament. Indeed, since the 1992 election, the government, with its much reduced parliamentary majority, has been particularly sensitive to the need for legislative proposals to command support from a majority in the House of Commons – and not to antagonise a House of Lords which has increasingly shown its willingness to vote against details of bills.

Private members' bills

On the surface at least, there seems to be one area of legislation for which the government is not responsible – private members' bills. Ordinary backbenchers can think up desirable legislative reforms, and with luck and perseverance see them become law. However, if it is wrong to think that government bills are processed without any concern for opinion amongst backbenchers in Parliament, it is also wrong to believe that government has no influence over private members' bills. The government's chief weapon is time: private members' bills are always running against the clock. Only the government can extend the limits to which they are subject, and active government hostility to a bill can result in tactics by government supporters which use up the limited time available before the bill can be properly considered.

In past centuries government bills had no special status in the House of Commons, and, in the Lords, they still formally do not. However, the priority which government business now enjoys in the Commons (Standing Order No. 13 – as we saw – begins 'save as provided in this Order, government business shall have precedence at every sitting') means that private members' bills have an equal footing with government bills only in the very earliest stage of their parliamentary progress – their printing and presentation.

Backbenchers can present as many bills as they like as often as they like. The fact that in the 1992–93 session only 168 private members' bills came before the Commons in any form indicates how limited the opportunities of progress are after the bill has been introduced. Theoretically backbenchers can introduce ambitious and complex bills – though any bills which involve spending money or imposing taxes will require government approval if they are to proceed (and, indeed, bills whose primary purpose is a financial one may not be introduced by private members). However, the majority of private members' bills are short and limited in extent. In that way they have a better chance of making progress.

At the beginning of each session, certain Fridays are set aside for private members' non-legislative motions (which will be described in Chapter 9) and for private members' bills. The Standing Order provides for ten Fridays for motions and ten for bills. In the late 1960s the Order was varied to allow sixteen bill Fridays and four motion Fridays, but since 1970, in normal length sessions, the Order has been varied to allow twelve bill Fridays. In 1993–94 and 1994–95, thirteen were allowed. If a private member's bill is to succeed, it must pass all the stages taken in the Commons Chamber on these days. Under the experimental sitting arrangements in 1995, private members' motion Fridays will be abolished. The effect this will have on the number of bill Fridays, and on the progress of private members' bills generally, remains to be seen.

With time in such short supply, a rationing system is vital. Its principal tool is the ballot. At the beginning of each session the majority of backbenchers enter their names in a sort of legislative prize draw. This is held in one of the large committee rooms where, under the supervision of the Chairman of Ways and Means, twenty slips of paper are drawn from a black leather box. The MPs who have the numbers on these slips have priority in introducing private members' bills in the order in which their names came out. However, being drawn in the ballot is no guarantee that one's bill will be passed, even if a majority in the House are in favour of it.

In the next section of this chapter, the various stages through which a bill goes in the Commons will be described. However, to emphasise the time difficulties private members' bills encounter, some reference needs to be made here to two stages – 'second reading' and 'report stage'. Second reading is a debate on the principle of a bill. Out of the twelve private members' bill Fridays, six are intended for second reading debates. By convention, a debate on a second reading may take up the whole day before it can be brought to an end by means of the closure. This means that, out of the twenty MPs successful in the ballot, only the first six can introduce bills which are in any way controversial if they want to be sure that their bill has a chance of clearing the second reading hurdle. The first six MPs put their bills down for one of the six second reading days and the remaining fourteen MPs add their bills as second, third or fourth bills on one of these days depending on their judgment about how controversial the earlier bills on that particular day are. A non-controversial bill, introduced by the MP who came nineteenth, may be unopposed at the second reading and be passed even if it is fourth on a day when there are three private members' bills higher in the queue. But the MP who came seventh, if introducing a controversial bill – or one opposed by the government – and who puts it down second to what seems to be the most uncontroversial bill in the top six, will suddenly discover that his or her opponents find a lot to talk about in the previous, apparently non-controversial, bill so that there is no time left to consider the second proposal.

Even the top six bills are not certain of passing the second reading stage. Naturally, they need the support of a majority of MPs, but, even if they receive this, they can be 'talked out' unless debate on them is brought to an end by means of the closure. As we saw in Chapter 5, at least 100 MPs must vote in favour of the closure of debate for the motion to be successful. So a backbencher who introduces a mildly controversial private members' bill not only needs to be in the first six out of some 400 but must ensure that at least 100 supporters of the cause are present in the House on a Friday afternoon. Most MPs return to their constituencies on a Friday, and although public opinion will expect them to be back in Westminster for a vote on a very controversial measure, there may well be difficulties in mustering 100 MPs in favour of a bill which arouses opposition among a vociferous minority but which is not particularly controversial throughout the country at large – say divorce reform in Scotland or stricter controls on game shooting.

After second reading, private members' bills are considered in committee. Controversial bills may be opposed vigorously here, or simply allowed to pass on to their next stage because their principal obstacle comes when they are next seen on the floor of the House at report stage – the second six private members' Fridays are principally taken up with this stage. This is an opportunity for further detailed amendments to be discussed. Here each bill normally has only one opportunity. It is not difficult for opponents to think up amendments and to protract debate so that the whole day passes before the consideration of the bill can be completed. The partially considered bill then drops to the end of the queue, and its chances are lost unless the Government decides to give it some of their own parliamentary time. This is most unusual – it has not happened since 1979 – and normally occurs because the bill reflects government thinking, rather than because of its support by a majority in the Commons whose will is being frustrated (an argument always put forward by the bill's supporters).

For example, the Sexual Offences Bill 1976 which provided for anonymity in rape cases received extra government time, having been warmly endorsed by government ministers. By contrast, the Unborn Children (Protection) Bill 1985 to limit research on embryos was approved by 238 votes to 66 on second reading, but was not supported by Department of Health ministers and was not provided with any extra government time. The history of the passage of the Civil Rights (Disabled Persons) Bill is a good example of the problems which a controversial bill can encounter. Its sponsor was drawn seventh in the ballot in the 1993–94 session, when seven second reading Fridays were allowed. He entered the bill for second reading on the seventh bill day, and it was necessary to move the closure at 2.29 p.m. The closure was carried and the bill was given a second reading by 231 votes to nil. When the bill emerged from its committee stage, it failed to clear its report stage in one day – only two groups of amendments were considered and there were still others waiting to be discussed when time ran out – and despite some clever procedural manoeuvres and attempts to secure government time, the bill was lost.

Despite all these handicaps, a good number of private members' bills do become law – almost 200 Acts of Parliament passed between the 1979 General Election and autumn 1993 were sponsored by backbenchers. It is difficult to categorise these laws precisely. Many are minor pieces of tidying up of the statute book to remove generally recognised anomalies and a number of these will have been suggested to sympathetic private members by government departments. Other Acts deal with small social reforms, particularly in areas affecting the rights of the disabled; marriage, children and the family; gaming and alcohol; care and control of animals, or the environment. In fact, a very wide range of matters have been the subject of successful private members' bills. Examples include the British Nationality (Falkland Islands) Act 1983 giving British nationality to Falkland Islanders; the Pet Animals Act 1951 (Amendment) Act 1983 making illegal the sale of pets at market barrows; the Access to Health Records Act 1990 allowing patients to see many of the records relating to them kept by doctors; the Football (Offences) Act 1991 introducing new criminal offences of pitch invasion, racist chanting or missile throwing at main soccer matches; the Bingo Act 1992 dealing with the advertising of bingo or the Race Relations (Remedies) Act 1994, giving industrial tribunals new powers in cases of racial discrimination. Although many of these reforms may have been relatively trivial, they will have had important consequences for particular groups of citizens.

Some private members' Acts have a wider application: out-standing Acts in the last twenty years include the Video Recordings Act 1984 which regulated the sale of 'video nasties', the National Audit Act 1983 which established the National Audit Office and introduced important reforms to make government more account-able to Parliament, the Housing (Homeless Persons) Act 1977 with its requirements upon local authorities to house the homeless and the Unsolicited Goods and Services (Amendment) Act 1975 which regulates the sending of unsolicited material to private individuals. In earlier years, private members' Acts brought about the abolition of the death penalty, the legalisation of abortion and homosexuality and the end of theatre censorship.

The figure of 168 bills introduced by backbenchers in the 1992–93 session was mentioned earlier. Yet only twenty MPs were successful in the ballot. Where did the other bills come from? There are two other ways in which private members' bills come before the House. Most straightforwardly, they are introduced without debate on any sitting day after the fifth Wednesday of the session (the day on which balloted bills are presented). All sponsors do is give notice of their intention on or before the previous day and then nod to the Speaker when their name is called and hand the title of the bill to the Clerk who reads this out. Except for the non-controversial, bills introduced by this method stand no chance of becoming law, but the method is regularly used to give currency to ideas by expressing them in the form of legislation. One of the 62 bills introduced by this method in 1992–93, for example, was Tony Benn's legislative proposal for radical constitutional reform, the Commonwealth of Britain Bill. This bill obviously had no chance of proceeding any further in the House of Commons. A number of bills introduced by this method do become law – the Act which makes the practice of circumcising women illegal was introduced as a 'presentation' bill by a backbencher.

A better known method is the so-called 'ten minute rule bill'. Beginning in the seventh week of the session, on every Tuesday and Wednesday before the main business of the day, one MP is called to make a ten-minute speech setting out a case for a bill which he or she wishes to introduce. Other MPs are alerted to the subject matter of the bill by a brief description on their Order Papers of its main purposes. If there is objection to the proposal, one opponent can speak against the motion in another ten-minute speech. The House then votes on the proposal. If the proposer is successful, the bill is introduced in a little ceremony which involves the MP walking from the bar of the House to the Table, bowing three times en route. However, despite success in introducing the bill, it is unlikely, unless the proposal is uncontroversial, that the MP will see it progress any further than other private members' bills which were not in the first six of the ballot. Ten minute rule bills which became law include the Solvent Abuse (Scotland) Act 1983 which was originally introduced by an opposition backbencher, and which was an attempt to deal with glue-sniffing in Scotland, and the Bail (Amendment) Act 1993, which tightened up rules on the granting of bail.

Ten-minute rule bills are very popular with MPs and the right to introduce them is allocated on a first come first served basis. Still occasionally an MP camps out all night to be first in the queue to give notice of a ten-minute rule bill at 10 a.m. on the first day when this is possible, usually three weeks in advance. It is easy to understand this popularity. Ten minute rule bills are discussed in prime parliamentary time – the early afternoon – when the gallery is full of journalists. The idea behind the bill and the publicity it receives are often more important than any intention of actually changing the law during that session, although by canvassing his or her ideas the sponsor hopes to work up some of the support which will eventually result in the idea bearing fruit. Ten-minute rule bills can often cover vast subjects – devolution to Scotland, reform of the House of Lords – or subjects which are not really suitable for legislation but are matters of controversy. For the public outside Parliament, it would be wrong to have too great an expectation of what ten-minute rule bills can actually achieve.

At the very least, private members' bills are an opportunity for non-government ideas to be publicised through Parliament. At most, a winner in the ballot can bring about a change in the law. Outside interest groups have seized on the value of the private members' bills and encourage MPs to introduce their own pet bills. Organisations like the Consumers Association or the RSPCA have been particularly effective in this field, suggesting ideas and helping in the drafting of the legislation (only limited financial help – at present £200: a sum not increased since 1971 – is available to the top ten ballot-winning MPs in the complex business of drafting).

The government also sees the value of private members' bills: backbenchers who are successful in the ballot are approached by government whips with suggested bills, just as they are by pressure groups. Often the government-suggested bill will be attractive, not just to a government but to an opposition backbencher who has no particularly burning issue about which he or she wishes to see legislation introduced. Governments have also assisted private members promoting bills on issues to which the government is sympathetic, but which are very sensitive – for example, abortion and homosexuality. Successful and diligent sponsorship of a private member's bill results in some credit in the party and publicity outside, both of which most MPs like.

Because of the control over the time of the House which the

government has, some commentators have come to see private members' bills as a sub-species of government bill. This is too cynical a view: at the bill stage, backbenchers use the private members' mechanisms to bring many ideas to public attention without support from the government. Turning the bill into an Act of Parliament is more difficult and is helped by tacit, if not overt, government support. But even here, an MP who is lucky in the ballot, who chooses a subject which has popular support outside the House, preferably with an effective pressure group channelling that support, who can enthrall fellow backbenchers with the cause and who is prepared to work hard drafting the bill and then as a whip and publicist for it, can see the idea bear legislative fruit, despite initial reservations from ministers and civil servants.

If a private member's bill clears the Commons, it usually faces no particular difficulties in the Lords, though it may well be amended there. Private members' bills may also be introduced in the House of Lords and generous provision is made for debating them. As in the Commons, they cover a wide variety of subject matter and many are introduced with a view to initiating debate rather than with any serious intention of becoming law. Even if a Lords private member's bill survives all stages in the House of Lords (by no means all do), it has a hard time in the Commons where it has no special status and no special time allotted. But a few Lords private members' bills (especially those drafted with government help) do become law each session nonetheless. It is sometimes said that Lords private members' bills are not given a fair hearing in the Commons. However, worthy bills which have government support (or its benign neutrality) and are uncontroversial in a party political sense have as much chance in the Commons as any un-balloted Commons bill, provided they reach that House in sufficient time. And persistence pays, as it does for proponents of private members' bills in the Commons.

Opposition parties rarely sponsor bills officially in the same way as the government does. Examples are the Labour Party's Scotland Bill 1987 or its 1992 Right to Information Bill. However, there is no special facility for these bills, which must proceed as ordinary private members' bills.

How a bill becomes an Act

General principles

A great deal of the time of Parliament is taken up with its legislative work. In the 1992–93 session, almost 700 hours in the Commons Chamber and 246 sittings of standing committees were occupied with discussion of legislation. This part of the chapter will describe what happens during those hours in the Commons, and also, more briefly, the procedures in the Lords.

Bills may be introduced in either House. If they pass in the one House they are then sent to the other House to be considered. Generally speaking, a bill must pass in both the House of Commons and the House of Lords before it can become law. There are no strict rules about what sort of bill should originate in which House, but so far as bills introduced by the government are concerned, Finance Bills, other taxing and financial legislation and the most politically controversial bills are almost invariably started in the Commons. Controversial bills *do* sometimes begin their passage in the Lords: the Shops Bill in 1985–86 (a Bill eventually defeated in the Commons) and the Police and Magistrates' Courts Bill and the Education Bill in 1993–94 are examples. Because of the changes in the Finance Bill timetable in the Commons, it is likely that more controversial bills will in future start in the upper House so that the government's legislative programme may be achieved within the constraints of the parliamentary session. However, in the meantime it is generally true to say that it is tidying-up legislation or reforming legislation of a relatively non-controversial nature which tends to originate in the Lords.

In each House, bills normally have five stages: first reading, second reading, consideration by committee, consideration by the House on report from committee, and third reading. The term 'reading' is taken literally in some countries – for example, in Peru each bill was until recently literally read out from beginning to end in the Chamber. In Britain in modern times nothing of this type happens, but the term recalls a time when fewer people were literate, and the Clerk of the House's special skill was his ability to read and write. There is nothing in statute law, or even in the Standing Orders of the two Houses which requires that these should be the stages through which a bill is taken but the current practice has existed for several hundred years and is normally accepted without question even by those who wish to reform other aspects of parliamentary procedure.

All public bills go through the same principal stages irrespective of whether they are government or backbench sponsored. The amount of time they take to clear the process depends on their complexity and on the amount of controversy they arouse.

Introduction and first reading in the Chamber

The principal MP who sponsors a bill is known as the 'member in charge'. For the Finance Bill, this will be the Chancellor of the Exchequer; for other major government legislation, the minister in charge of the department behind it. The member in charge of a private member's bill is the MP who introduces it.

The most normal method of introducing a bill is by the member in charge giving notice of the bill's 'long' and 'short' titles and of the intention to introduce it on a future day, and then being called by the Speaker at the commencement of public business on that day to do so. The member brings the so-called 'dummy bill' – a piece of paper which records the long and short titles of the bill and up to twelve named MPs who back the proposal – to the Table of the House and the Clerk reads out the bill's short title. The bill is then said to have been read the first time, and it is ordered to be printed, and to be read the second time on a specified future day. Bills can also be introduced by Order of the House. This is strictly what happens when a backbench ten-minute rule motion is agreed to, and this procedure is in modern times almost invariably confined to this type of private member's bill and to the government bills which authorise the imposition of taxes. The third method of introduction is that for bills which have passed the Lords. As long as these are 'taken up' by an MP, they are given a first reading without any public activity in the Chamber.

At this stage, except in the case of bills coming from the Lords, a final version of the bill need not be available. The long title contained in the dummy bill is merely a brief statement of the bill's purpose. However, before the bill can proceed any further, it must be printed in full, and in the case of government bills this is normally done within a day of its introduction. The Finance Bill takes longer.

A short explanatory memorandum is added to all government bills, and some private members' bills. This explains in non-technical language the bill's purposes, and its implications for expenditure by the public sector and by business and for the level of public service manpower. Any clause or sub-clause of the bill which will give rise to public expenditure is printed in italics.

A typical (if short) bill – the Intoxicating Substances (Supply) Bill which was intended to control glue-sniffing – is set out in full on pages 118 to 120.

Second reading in the Commons

The first important discussion to which a bill is subject is its second reading debate. It is considered good practice for this to be delayed until at least two weekends have passed since the bill's introduction, though the government does not always comply with this, nor, less importantly, do backbenchers.

On a really important bill, debate on second reading can take several days – the 1972 bill to enable the United Kingdom to join the European Community was debated over three days on

Intoxicating Substances (Supply) Bill

EXPLANATORY MEMORANDUM

This Bill creates a new offence in respect of supplying to children under 18 a substance (other than a controlled drug within the meaning of the Misuse of Drugs Act 1971) which is likely to be inhaled to cause intoxication.

Clause 1 makes it an offence to supply or offer to supply such a substance to a person under the age of 18 or to a person acting on behalf of such a person. The supplier will have committed the offence only if he knows, or has reasonable cause to believe, both that the supply or offer is made to, or to a person acting on behalf of, a person under 18 and that the substance is, or its fumes are, likely to be inhaled by that person to cause intoxication. It will be a defence for a person under the age of 18 to show he was not supplying or offering to supply the substance in the course of furtherance of a business. The maximum penalty on summary conviction of the offence will be 6 months' imprisonment or a level 5 fine (current maximum £20,000).

Finance and public service manpower effects of the Bill
The Bill is not expected to have any significant financial implications and will have no effect on public service manpower.

[Bill 19]   49/2

A

B I L L

TO

Prohibit the supply to persons under the age of eighteen of certain substances which may cause intoxication if inhaled.

B E IT ENACTED by the Queen's most Excellent Majesty, by and with the advice and consent of the Lords Spiritual and Temporal, and Commons, in this present Parliament assembled, and by the authority of the same, as follows:-

5   **1.**—(1) It is an offence for a person to supply or offer to supply a substance other than a controlled drug—

    (a) to a person under the age of eighteen whom he knows, or has reasonable cause to believe, to be under the age;

    or

10   *(b)* to a person—

        (i) who is acting on behalf of a person under that age; and

        (ii) whom he knows, or has reasonable cause to believe, to be so acting.

15 if he knows or has reasonable cause to believe that the substance is, or its fumes are, likely to be inhaled by the person under the age of eighteen for the purpose of causing intoxication.

(2) In proceedings against any person for an offence under subsection (1) above it is a defence for him to show that at 20 the time he made the supply or offer he was under the age of eighteen and was acting otherwise than in the course of furtherance of a business.

Offence of supply of intoxicating substance.

[Bill 19]   49/2

Example of a bill

2   *Intoxicating Substances (Supply)*

(3) A person guilty of an offence under this section shall be liable on summary conviction to imprisonment for a term not exceeding six months or to a fine not exceeding level 5 on the standard scale (as defined in section 75 of the Criminal Justice Act 1982), or to both.

1982 c. 48.

5

(4) In this section 'controlled drug' has the same meaning as in the Misuse of Drugs Act 1971.

1971 c. 38.

Short title, commencement and extent

2.—(1) This Act may be cited as the Intoxicating Substances (Supply) Act 1985.

(2) This Act shall come into force at the end of the period of two months beginning with the day on which it was passed.

10

(3) This Act extends to Northern Ireland but not to Scotland.

Intoxicating Substances (Supply)

A
B I L L

To prohibit the supply to persons under the age of eighteen of certain substances which may cause intoxication if inhaled.

Presented by Mr. Neville Trotter
supported by
Mr. Alex Carlile, Mr. Geoffrey Finsberg,
Mr. Marcus Fox, Mr. Roy Galley,
Mr. Harry Greenway, Mr. Michael Hirst,
Mr. Charles Kennedy, Mr. Ron Lewis,
Mr. Christopher Murphy, Mr. Reg Prentice
and Mr. Tom Torney

Ordered, by The House of Commons,
to be Printed, 5 December 1984

LONDON
Printed and published by
Her Majesty's Stationery Office
Printed in England at St Stephen's
Parliamentary Press
75p net

[Bill 19]   (301950)   49/2

ISBN 0 10 301985 5

second reading, and the 1976 bill to give devolution to Scotland and Wales for 32 hours over four sitting days. Normally major bills are debated for one day from about 4 p.m. to 10 p.m. (or 9.30 a.m. to 2.30 p.m. on Fridays for private members' bills). Less important bills receive correspondingly shorter second reading debates, and wholly uncontroversial measures (including some private members' bills) can receive their second reading 'on the nod', that is without any debate taking place at all . It is also possible for non-controversial bills to be given their second reading debate in a standing committee – either a 'second reading committee', or for bills relating wholly to Scotland or Wales, a committee wholly or partly made up of Scottish or Welsh MPs – before receiving a formal second reading in the Chamber. These committees are set up *ad hoc*. As part of the experimental reform of sitting hours in 1995, it was agreed that greater use should be made of second reading committees, and, in particular, that non-controversial bills implementing Law Commission proposals for law reform should be referred to them automatically.

The debate on second reading is wide-ranging. It is the first public hurdle which legislation must clear and is an opportunity to discuss the principle behind the bill as well as the details of the actual bill before the House. For this reason, MPs often raise at second reading alternative means of dealing with the problem to those set out in the bill, as well as the extension of the bill to other areas.

On bills which arouse opposition, a vote normally takes place at the end of the second reading debate. If the vote is lost, the bill can go no further. This is most unusual in the case of government bills, because rebellion by government supporters at this stage is not usually so serious as to defeat a bill. However, it happened in 1986 in the case of the Shops Bill which had been intended to de-restrict Sunday trading. This bill was defeated in the Commons on second reading by a majority of fourteen. The Redundancy Rebates Bill was also defeated at second reading in 1977, but this was during the period of the minority Labour government. Controversial private members' bills are, however, fairly frequently defeated on second reading, as the Protection of Official Information Bill (to reform the Official Secrets Act) was in 1988. Abstention or voting against a government bill at second reading are powerful weapons for government backbenchers, and, since the 1950s, there has been an increasing tendency for this to happen in the case of those bills which are not universally supported in the government party. For example, 17 Conservative MPs voted against the second reading of the Local Government Finance Bill in 1987 which eventually led to the imposition of the 'poll tax' in England and Wales.

Committee

If a bill passes its second reading, it has next to be considered, ideally after an interval of not less than ten days, by a committee which has the responsibility of examining the text clause by clause and, where it seems it could be improved, of amending the bill. This stage of detailed scrutiny has received a great deal of critical examination.

At one time, almost all bills were considered in Committee of the Whole House. A Committee of the Whole House, as the name suggests, consists of all the members of the House. The only differences are that they are presided over by the Chairman of Ways and Means rather than the Speaker, and that there are certain minor changes in the procedures followed in debate. The committee meets in the Commons Chamber, during normal sitting hours and so takes the place of part of the House's daily sitting. The only difference apparent to the outside observer is that the presiding officer sits at the table beside the clerk and the mace is put under the table rather than on it.

In recent years, Committees of the Whole House have been confined to three types of bill. For convenience, straightforward and uncontroversial bills are considered in this way to save time: their committee stage can pass in a matter of minutes, and the preponderance of bills committed to a Committee of the Whole House are of this type. A second type of bill dealt with in Committee of the Whole House are those of extreme urgency which need to pass into law very swiftly. The Prevention of Terrorism Act 1974 for which the government saw an urgent need in the aftermath of serious bombing incidents in Birmingham was considered in this way.

The third type of bill which is committed to a Committee of the Whole House consists of major bills of 'first class constitutional importance'. Since 1945 governments have been committed to having such bills dealt with in this way, but there is no ready definition of 'first class constitutional importance'. Certainly the bills to allow Britain to join the EEC, to implement the Maastricht Treaty, to give devolution to Scotland and to Wales or to reform the House of Lords were considered in Committee of the Whole House, but claims are often made that other bills should be so considered. For example, the opposition parties argued successfully in 1984–85 that the proposal to abolish the metropolitan counties and the Greater London Council was constitutional. The precedents for committee stages of constitutional bills are not happy memories for government business managers: the Parliament (No. 2) Bill to reform the House of Lords was considered for twelve days in committee in 1969 before it was dropped, and devolution to Scotland and Wales took up 34 days in committee in the 1976–77 and 1977–78 sessions. The European Communities (Amendment) Bill, which implemented the Maastricht Treaty, took up 23 days in committee in 1992–93. It is not surprising that there is little enthusiasm by governments to concede that a bill is constitutional, though an argument in favour of Committees of the Whole House from the government's point of view is that they may be easier for the whips to control than a standing committee where one or two government supporters voting against the government can result in government defeats.

It is possible to consider only part of a bill in Committee of the Whole House and the rest in standing committee. This procedure was adopted in 1994 for the Criminal Justice and Public Order Bill where clauses dealing with capital punishment and the age of consent for homosexual men were committed to a Committee of the Whole House and the remainder of the bill to standing committee. The procedure is regularly used for the more important parts of the annual Finance Bill.

As well as Committee of the Whole House, bills may be considered in select committee. This is exceptional, and only used in recent years for the special five-yearly Armed Forces Bill which deals with discipline in the navy, army and air force.

Normally all routine government and private members' bills are committed to standing committees which meet away from the Chamber. It is there that their committee stages will be taken.

The term 'standing committee' is misleading because it implies a permanence which this type of committee does not have. New members are appointed for each new bill and when a standing committee has reported a bill to the House, it is effectively dissolved. For example, in 1992–93 Standing Committee D (each committee is designated by a letter of the alphabet) considered the Sea Fish (Conservation) Bill, the Judicial Pensions and Retirement Bill, the Merchant Shipping (Registration etc.) Bill and the Welsh Language Bill. But an entirely new set of MPs made up Standing Committee D each time – all that linked them was the name of the committee. There is no limit to the number of standing committees which can operate at any one time, though most sessions have seven or eight at maximum, with additional committees to consider Scottish legislation. One standing committee (C) is reserved for private members' bills. This means that only one such bill can normally progress through committee at any one time – a considerable bottle-neck for backbench legislation. (Standing committees do not only consider bills: their other uses are described on pages 147, 198 and 231. However, these other types of standing committee are generally set up under the rules operated for bill standing committees which apply to size, chairmanship*, nomination and place of meeting.)

Most other countries have permanent groups of specialised MPs to consider legislation, and a bill dealing with transport is considered by the Transport Committee, or one dealing with oil by the Energy Committee. While this practice does not occur in Britain, our *ad hoc* system nevertheless permits knowledgeable MPs to be appointed to a standing committee.

The committees are chosen by the Committee of Selection, a committee of senior MPs including whips from the major parties, who are responsible for deciding the membership of most committees in the House. The Committee of Selection's first job is to match the membership of each standing committee to the bill it is considering, paying particular regard to the qualifications of the MPs nominated and the composition of the House. This means that the committees – which must be between 16 and 50 in size, but which tend to be at the lower end of this range – should have the same proportions of government and opposition supporters as the House itself. Where there has been a free vote on second reading, for example on Abortion Bills in 1967 and 1988 or the Unborn Children (Protection) Bill 1985, the membership should also represent roughly the number of cross-party supporters and opponents of the legislation. At least one government minister will always be a member of the committee, including committees on private members' bills, and frontbenchers from the other parties are also appointed. The government and main opposition party have a whip as member. The remaining backbench members are a combination of those interested in the subject and those who are willing to serve on the committee and loyally support their party's line on the subject. Obviously the strength of the second group becomes more important when very contentious legislation is being considered, but the Committee of Selection has generally appointed a spread of MPs to standing committees and not tried to silence dissenting minorities inside the parties.

Each standing committee is chaired by a senior MP appointed by the Speaker from her panel of potential Chairmen. The occupant of the chair has similar powers to control the proceedings of the committee as the Speaker has in the House, including the power to select amendments for debate. He or she does not vote except when there is a tie, and then normally in accordance with well-known precedents so that the result of a tie can be predicted in advance.

---

*Both Houses use the word 'chairman' in their standing orders. Of course, female members may occupy the Chair, but the words 'chairwoman' and 'chairperson' or 'chair' when referring to a person are not at present used formally in Parliament. Because of this, these terms are not used in this book.

Standing committees meet in the suite of committee rooms on the riverside first floor of the Palace of Westminster, and for this reason bills committed to them are sometimes referred to as being 'sent upstairs'. The rooms are laid out in a similar way to the Chamber, with two sides facing one another and the Chairman in the position of Speaker. Meetings are open to the public, and a verbatim report of their proceedings is published. Committees start at 10.30 a.m. and, with the exception of the period from 1 p.m. until 3.30 p.m., they can in theory meet at all hours on days on which the House itself sits. However, typically, standing committees on bread-and-butter bills meet on Tuesdays and Thursdays from 10.30 a.m. to 1 p.m. and, for more controversial bills, again on those days from 4.30 p.m. Standing Committee C traditionally meets on Wednesdays. Sittings of the committee on the Finance Bill and other very contentious legislation can last into the early hours of the morning – and even until 1 p.m. the next day, when they must finish. On a controversial measure like the Transport Bill of 1984–85, the standing committee held 34 sittings. Long and contentious bills regularly spend well over 100 hours in standing committee in total. On the other hand, very straightforward bills can pass their committee stage in one short standing committee sitting. A Procedure Committee recommended in 1985 that standing committees should not sit after 10 p.m., but this recommendation has not been implemented, though late sittings are likely to become rarer as the spirit of the Jopling reforms permeates the House.

Whether it takes place in Committee of the Whole House or standing committee, the committee stage of a bill is discussed in a debate form. The clauses of the bill are looked at one by one. Any member of the committee is free to suggest amendments to the clause under discussion as well as entirely new clauses. The Chairman selects which amendments or new clauses are to be debated. In doing this, he or she first rules out any amendments or new clauses which are out of order. Not all amendments or new clauses are admissible under the rules of order. For example, they must be relevant, they must not attempt to wreck the bill or be inconsistent with previous decisions of the committee, or be outside the scope of the bill as indicated by its long title. They cannot be too vague or make the bill unintelligible. They cannot create a public charge if such a charge has not specifically been permitted in advance by the House in a special resolution (either a 'money resolution' or a 'ways and means resolution') which can only be moved by a government minister. In addition to these rules, Chairmen will normally only select amendments of which two days' notice has been given. Moreover, they have a wider discretion to select amendments (or not select amendments) as they think appropriate after weighing up the interests of the committee and the need to make progress in the bill. In the interest of progress, amendments are also grouped by the Chair so that joint debates are held on amendments which deal with related topics.

The committee considers each amendment before it in turn in the classic manner, having an MP propose the amendment, other MPs speaking alternately for and against it, the question put from the Chair and finally, if necessary, a vote taking place. When all the amendments to a clause have been dealt with (or if there are no amendments), there can then follow a debate – and vote – on the motion 'that the clause stand part of the bill'. When this has been completed, the committee goes on to debate the next clause, and so on. After the existing clauses have been considered, new clauses may be proposed, and amendments to these discussed.

Amendments can serve a variety of purposes. If the bill is highly contentious in political terms, many amendments will be pegs for debate to give publicity to government and opposition viewpoints. The opposition particularly will try to embarrass the government by exposing inadequacies in the legislation. Backbenchers frequently propose amendments after being briefed by outside pressure groups who are concerned with the bill, but many have their own ideas which they express in amendment form. Some of these amendments may be designed merely to make the bill more intelligible or improve its drafting, and the large number of amendments which the government itself proposes are predominantly intended to improve the drafting of the legislation, although they also reflect changes in the government's view of what the bill should contain which came too late to be included in the bill as first presented.

In general terms, the government wants to resist amendments which will alter the shape of the bill as it originally introduced it, and figures have been produced to suggest that very few indeed of the amendments to government bills proposed by backbenchers in standing committees are actually passed. For example, of the almost 800 amendments and new clauses tabled to the Criminal Justice and Public Order Bill in 1994, only 150 were made, and, of these, 145 were government amendments or new clauses. Despite this, a lot of backbenchers' time is taken up in the committees, which met in no fewer than 246 sittings in the 1992–93 session, for example. For these long hours ordinary MPs have few resources to back them – their research assistant and the library, and perhaps help from an outside pressure group with whom they are in sympathy and whose cause they are willing to promote. In many cases, voluminous briefing material from outside sources is sent to members of standing committees, but volume is not necessarily helpful. In contrast, the opposition frontbench spokesmen have their party organisation, and the government is in the best position of all with the resources of the whole civil service to back it. The process can be dispiriting for ordinary backbench MPs: many feel that they do not have the resources to scrutinise legislation properly, and that the debate format of committee meetings is in any case inappropriate for this to be done adequately. Moreover, as we shall see when we discuss the guillotine, the most controversial bills can often receive only truncated discussion in committee: the early stages are spun out by the opposition, the government then introduces a guillotine motion which the House passes and the committee has to speed through the rest of the bill in just a couple of sittings.

The Labour Cabinet Minister of the 1960s, Richard Crossman, wrote 'The whole procedure of standing committees is insane . . . Under the present system there is no genuine committee work, just formal speech-making, mostly from written briefs.' Other commentators have contrasted the British system with what they see as better scrutiny of legislation by foreign Parliaments like the Bundestag.

Standing committee are, of course, not always the sort of farce which Crossman implied, especially on social legislation and it may be useful to make a broad distinction between two types of bill which come before the Commons: the highly controversial, party-political bill and the bread-and-butter 'good administration' bill, though many bills will contain elements of both. The political debating formula of existing standing committees may be the only real option for politically charged bills, but some have argued that a formula akin to select committees is more appropriate for less controversial legislation – in other words, the committee members would regard themselves as having a common purpose in cooperating to improve the bill rather than in acting as political antagonists.

From time to time since 1981, a few bills have been considered by committees constituted along these lines and known as 'special standing committees'. These committees go through bills in the same way as ordinary standing committees, but, before they do so, for a maximum of four sessions, they are chaired by the expert chairman of the appropriate departmental select committee (the specialist Commons committees which will be described in Chapter 10) or some other specialist MP. Under the Chairman's guidance, the special standing committee takes evidence on the bill's provisions from government witnesses and other experts at three of these sessions. The fourth is deliberative. Once the four sessions are over (normally within 28 days), the committee begins the clause by clause examination in the normal way – but better informed and more used to working cooperatively together on the subject. A survey of MPs' attitudes in January 1985 found them broadly in favour of the special standing committee procedure, but its use has so far been confined to just five bills. Some of the most interesting comments about the committees have come from Sir Patrick Mayhew who, as a then Law Officer, was a minister with special interest in the quality of the law. He was also in charge of two of the bills which went through special standing committee procedure, and he spoke of the 'salutary' experience and commented:

It is very remarkable how the operation of the special procedure stimulates the interest of members of the committee, and brings them together even though their respective opinions may remain sharply divided. In my opinion it engenders the feeling, both among members and among witnesses, that here at least the House of Commons is permitting itself to do important work in a mature manner, and doing it well.

Special standing committees were originally experimental, but since 1986 the possibility that they may be used for the committee stage of bills has been recognised in Standing Orders. Despite this, the procedure was not used between 1984 and 1994. The government has taken the view that it is only suitable for specialist, highly technical, non-party-political measures. Most government bills do not fall into this category. It is, however, expected that the Children (Scotland) Bill – a government measure implementing reforms which partly stem from the judicial inquiry into alleged child abuse in Orkney – will be considered in 1995 by a special standing committee. The Labour Party has called for much more use of the procedure – for example, for the technical parts of the annual Finance Bill.

Report stage

Except for bills which are considered in Committee of the Whole House and are not amended there, all bills come back to the floor of the Commons for report stage, properly called 'consideration stage'. (A procedure exists to take report stage in a committee, but this is not used). The bill returns in the form in which it left committee, and report stage is a further opportunity for changes to be made. The important difference is that all MPs have the opportunity to contribute by speaking to amendments on report. Report stages of important legislation tend to occupy the period after Easter in the Commons, and although the report stage of a bill does not normally take up more than two sittings, these sittings can go on into the early hours of the morning because of the large number of amendments being discussed, much to the exasperation of those MPs not interested in the bill who have nevertheless to remain on hand to vote. Between five and ten per cent of the whole time on the floor of the House is taken up with report stages of government bills alone.

However, the opportunity in the passage of all bills for every MP to contribute amendments, whether or not he or she is selected as a member of the standing committee, is generally highly valued. Sometimes report stage is an opportunity for government backbenchers to register dissent on particular aspects of a bill, and, when cross party support is achieved, changes can be secured. For example in 1994, backbench amendments at report stage on the Criminal Justice and Public Order Bill led to restrictions on the use of eggs from foetuses for experimental purposes and on the availability of violent videos.

At report the Speaker exercises the power of selection with respect to the new clauses and amendments which are tabled. The rules which apply in Committee are once again enforced, if anything more strictly. The Speaker is also unlikely to select a topic which has been fully debated at Committee stage, unless undertakings were made by the government to come forward with changes at report. Backbenchers cannot be certain that the Speaker will select their amendments, and they occasionally feel aggrieved that government and official opposition amendments receive what they regard as preferential treatment. Fairly strict rules are necessary if report stage is not to last an inordinate amount of time.

Procedure on report is somewhat different from Committee of the Whole House. The Speaker is in the chair and the mace on the table. The bill is not considered clause by clause (and so there is no debate on 'clause stand part') and amendments are set out in a different way because the House is revising the bill as a whole rather than going through it clause by clause as it was at committee stage. Again, the vast bulk of the amendments carried are those initiated by the government – 211 out of 212 amendments made at the report to the Criminal Justice and Public Order Bill in 1994 were government amendments, as were 7 out of the 10 new clauses.

Third reading

A debate on the bill in its finally amended form is the last stage before it is said to have passed the Commons. This is its 'third reading'. In 1967 a reform was introduced which was intended to dispense with third reading debates for the majority of bills, but this was not successful and was abandoned. Generally a short debate takes place in which those MPs who have been most active in the bill's earlier progress look rather sentimentally back on their work in standing committee. On a controversial bill, the debate may be longer and more acrimonious, and a vote taken. A bill defeated on third reading is lost, though this is most unusual – the last occasion was in 1977 when the Local Authority Works (Scotland) Bill was defeated at this stage. Some indication of the relative unimportance of the third reading stage is given by the amount of time spent on it in the Commons: in the 1992–93 session just under 29 hours were spent discussing the third reading of government bills, with only one bill (the European Communities (Amendment) Bill) receiving a third reading debate which lasted for a whole day.

The timetable of a bill

In the Lords the intervals between the different stages through which a bill passes are prescribed by a recommendation of the Procedure Committee in 1977: two weekends between introduction of a bill and second reading, fourteen days between second reading and committee, fourteen days between committee and report where the bill is of considerable length and complexity, and three sitting days between report and third reading. Intervals in the Commons are governed by convention, and backbenchers and opposition parties sometimes feel that governments take advantage of this by pushing legislation through more quickly than necessary and so preventing proper scrutiny. The 1985 Procedure Committee recommended a new Commons Standing Order prescribing two weekends between first and second reading, and ten days both between second reading and committee and between committee and report. This recommendation has not been adopted. Both Houses however, recognise that many bills are required more urgently than this and there are always provisions allowing the normal intervals to be set aside. In extreme circumstances of national emergency a bill can pass in a single day's sitting. For example, the Gold Standard (Amendment) Bill in 1931 was introduced in the Commons after question time on a Monday, and had passed both Houses and received Royal Assent by soon after 11 p.m. the same day. Other urgently required bills can also pass in just a few days – the Northern Ireland (Temporary Provisions) Act 1972, which brought direct rule to Northern Ireland, was introduced on a Monday and became law on the Wednesday, and the Sporting Events (Control of Alcohol etc.) Act 1985, which was of a different order of urgency, took less than a month between introduction and Royal Assent. In 1994 the Transport Police (Jurisdiction) Act (which cleared up an oversight on the previous session's Railways Act relating to the jurisdiction of the British Transport Police) received Royal Assent three days after its introduction in the Commons.

The length of time taken by the various stages of run-of-the-mill bills differs greatly depending on the complexity, controversy and urgency of the legislation. Wholly uncontroversial bills can pass with just a few minutes debate at each stage – or even with none at all. The Race Relations (Remedies) Bill (which was referred to on page 112) was passed by the Commons with no debate at all. It was debated for just 21 minutes in the House of Lords.

When there is any substance to a bill, debate will occur at each stage of its passage. If there is no urgent need for the bill to be passed, its various stages will usually spread over several months in each House, as it jostles for a place in the timetable for the stages taken on the floor of the House or plods through standing committee. A major and controversial bill can take the best part of a year (or even longer in a long session) to pass all its parliamentary stages. Even a mildly controversial measure can take months to become law. Of course, the whole process of drafting legislation, steering it through Parliament and bringing it into effect may take years. A diagram on pages 132 to 133 shows the stages of the legislation privatising the gas industry.

Sensitive and controversial bills are debated at length, partly because MPs have strong opinions which they want to express and, if possible, include in the bill, and partly because the opponents of the legislation realise that lengthy debates delay the bill. In each session, it is part of the tactics of the opposition to delay as much as possible those parts of the government's legislative programme with which they disagree. The government, however, has remedies against this. The first of these is the use of the majority to force the closure of debate in the House and in committee – a procedure which was described in Chapter 5.

A more draconian power known as the allocation of time order or, more commonly, the guillotine, also exists in the Commons. In the late nineteenth century, a vociferous group of Irish MPs succeeded in disrupting parliamentary proceedings over several sessions as part of their campaign for Irish Home Rule. It was generally recognised that the rights of the majority needed to be preserved and, despite reservations, a procedure to limit debate – the guillotine – was introduced. The system was modified over the years, and at present allows the House to agree, at any stage during a bill's proceedings, strict time limits for the remainder of its progress. A timetable is set out in a motion put to the House and debated for three hours. If the timetable is agreed to, delaying tactics are of no further use – committee and report stages come to an end after a fixed period whether or not all amendments have been considered, and sometimes with many clauses of the bill not having received any consideration at all.

At one time, the introduction of a guillotine motion by the government was considered wholly exceptional and could arouse positive outrage inside and outside the House. Very few bills were therefore subjected to a guillotine – just over 70 between 1881 and 1970. However, between 1970 and 1994 well over this number of guillotine motions were put to the House, with an average of three or four bills guillotined each session in recent years. In a

1948: Gas is nationalised

1973: The British Gas Corporation is established –
a nationalised industry, responsible for finding,
distributing and selling gas

May 1979: Conservative Government elected

1981: British Telecom successfully privatised

1982: Ministers begin to think of future
privatisation plans

June 1983: Conservative Government re-elected

September 1983: Department of Energy civil
servants begin work on plans to privatise gas
industry

April 1985: Cabinet agrees that gas should be
privatised in the next parliamentary session

Chronology of the Gas Bill

November 1986: Shares in British Gas launched on the stock market

24 August 1986: The State-owned British Gas Corporation ceases to exist, and British Gas Plc established

18 August 1986: The Office of Gas Supply – the regulator of the industry – established

During first half of 1986: Government makes a series of announcements about the brokers who will handle the sale

25 July 1986: Bill receives Royal Assent

21 July 1986: Commons consider, and agree, Lords' amendments to bill

17 July 1986: Third reading of bill in Lords

24 April – 9 July 1986: Bill considered in committee and then on report, over ten days

10 April 1986: Lords second reading

26 March 1986: Bill arrives in the Lords

25 March 1986: Third reading of bill in Chamber

17 March 1986: Report stage of bill

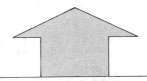

17 December 1985 – 6 March 1986: Bill considered in standing committee, over 32 sittings

10 December 1985: Commons second reading

28 November 1985: Formal publication of Gas Bill – first reading in the Commons

May–November 1985: The bill is drafted

7 May 1985: Plans announced publicly by a statement to the House of Commons

sense, the guillotine is a negation of the principle of parliamentary debate, and it could be a dangerous weapon in the hands of a government determined to stifle opposition. There has been some disquiet about the way in which controversial bills are guillotined in standing committee after only the first few clauses have been discussed, and its use early in a number of bills' passage led to a souring of relations between the two front benches in 1993–94. However, the disquiet has been not only with the truncation of debate caused by the imposition of a guillotine but with the delaying and time-wasting tactics adopted by a bill's opponents which can be involved in the present process. On the other hand, there is some evidence that guillotines can be successful in making debate more sensible. They do not need to be oppressive. For example, in introducing a guillotine motion in 1990 on the Human Fertilisation and Embryology Bill, the Leader of the House said that his proposal was 'designed to enable the House to debate the Bill in a structured and reasonable way. In no sense is it designed to curtail debate'. Similar points were made in 1994 when the Finance Bill was guillotined.

Some MPs have called for a procedure where bills are timetabled at an early stage, and this was recommended by the 1985 Procedure Committee. The essence of their argument was that, while the present guillotine procedure exists, it is doubtful whether the weapon of delay does anything to change the government's mind and may result only in uneven consideration of legislation by the Commons. For controversial bills, they recommended a timetable agreed by a committee on which all parties were to be represented, which would make a reasonable allocation of time for debate on the clauses of the bill in committee and on report. Although many MPs agreed with the committee and argued that this would do a good deal to improve the quality of scrutiny in the Commons of controversial legislation, the recommendation was not favoured by the government or the opposition frontbenches, and was rejected in February 1986 by 231 votes to 166 when the issue was put to the House for decision. Following this setback, the Procedure Committee recommended a modified form of timetabling which would apply to standing committee proceedings only.

The Jopling Committee returned to this question in 1992. It found that most MPs were in favour of timetabling of bills, and endorsed the earlier proposals of the Procedure Committee, recommending that all government bills should be subject to timetables. In the event, this part of Jopling's proposals is to be implemented in an informal way during the 1995 experiment with sitting hours. Part of the agreement involves the voluntary timetabling of bills through agreement between the usual channels, with guillotines avoided wherever possible. Like other aspects of the package, it remains to be seen how this will operate in practice: dissident groups and minority parties, for example, may not wish to abide by timetabling arrangements to which they were not party. Nevertheless, the *de facto* timetabling of government bills appears to be a likely feature of Commons proceedings in the 1990s, whatever happens to other aspects of the 1995 experiment.

The House of Lords

Bills can begin the parliamentary process in either House, and have to pass through both Houses before they can be presented for Royal Assent. A bill introduced in the Commons, and passed by that House after it has completed the various stages just described, is sent to the Lords. A bill introduced in the Lords (as we saw on page 116) will, after going through its stages in that House, be sent to the Commons for similar treatment. Consideration by the two Houses is – unlike the practice in the United States – never simultaneous, though on very rare occasions, to save time, identical bills are introduced in both Houses. One is later dropped, but the other then can proceed more quickly because its main points have been discussed already.

The Lords spend a great deal of their sitting time discussing bills. All stages are normally taken on the floor of the House. Indeed, a greater proportion of time is spent in this way in the Lords than in the Commons – just over half the total sitting hours as opposed to one-third.

Bills in the Lords go through the same stages as in the Commons – a formal first reading, a substantial debate on second reading, detailed amendments at committee stage and report, and further consideration (and in the Lords only, amendments) at third reading. But outward appearances hide substantial differences in procedure, many of which reflect the more flexible and less constrained procedures which have survived in the Lords long after their demise in the late nineteenth-century House of Commons.

The principal difference of this kind is that bills are almost always considered at committee stage by a Committee of the Whole House. The Lords have a procedure known as public bill committees which are roughly equivalent to Commons standing committees but they have seldom been a success except for considering uncontentious bills. Although the scope for using public bill committees as a means of saving time on the floor of the House is probably limited, they are occasionally set up.

Recent developments indicate that in future more bills may undergo their committee stage off the floor of the House in a new form of Committee of the Whole House. In 1994, a working group was set up by the then Leader of the House, Lord Wakeham, to consider the pattern of sittings in the House. In the wake of the Jopling Committee on sittings of the House in the Commons, and given that the House of Lords sits for more hours each year than any other parliamentary chamber in the world apart from the House of Commons, it is hardly surprising that such a review should have been commissioned. One of the group's recommendations was that some bills should be committed to a Committee of the Whole House off the floor. The committee would not have a fixed membership (any Lord might attend and participate) and no voting would take place. While the Committee would operate procedurally very like a public bill committee it would thus avoid many of the latter's drawbacks. Detailed scrutiny by interested peers could take place while major issues could be further considered and voted on at report stage on the floor. The Government are content for the procedure to be tried on an experimental basis, and it is to be tested in the 1994–95 session. If a few major bills are, by inter-party agreement, handled in this way, some of the pressures which sitting hours currently impose on members of the House may be reduced.

In addition, in 1992 the House approved the establishment of special public bill committees on an experimental basis, particularly to consider and facilitate the passage of Law Commission bills. Such a committee would take written and oral evidence within a 28-day period after second reading, whereupon it would become a public bill committee to consider the bill clause by clause. In 1994 the Law of Property (Miscellaneous Provisions) Bill became the first bill to be so considered. Nevertheless, the norm is for committee stage to be taken in Committee of the Whole House.

A second difference between the Lords and Commons legislative procedures is that there is no selection by a Chairman of amendments to be discussed. All the amendments that have been tabled may be considered. Thirdly, there is no guillotine procedure and so in theory proceedings could be very protracted indeed. Fortunately, filibustering is rare. Most members – and especially the party whips – realise that the excellent opportunities that arise in the Lords to consider all clauses and to take all amendments could not long survive persistent abuse by any one member or any one party.

Another substantial difference is that in the Lords it is possible to move amendments at third reading. The principal purposes of amendments at this stage are to clarify remaining uncertainties, to improve drafting and to enable the government to fulfil undertakings given at earlier stages of the bill. It is not permissible to raise an issue which has been fully debated and decided upon at a previous stage. If amendments have been tabled then third reading is taken formally and the general debate takes place on the motion 'that the bill do now pass', after the amendments have been considered.

Since 1992 all government and some private members' bills

are considered by a Lords Select Committee on the Scrutiny of Delegated Powers, which reports to the House whether the provisions of any bill inappropriately delegate legislative powers to ministers using statutory instruments; or whether they subject the use of any delegated powers to insufficient parliamentary scrutiny. All bills are considered – usually on the basis of memoranda supplied by the government – after Lords first reading; and the committee reports quickly so that its findings can if necessary be acted upon by the House at committee stage (see also page 150). There is no equivalent committee in the House of Commons.

It is worth noting that the government has no formal priority over other peers in introducing or debating legislation. In practice, government business is recognised to take priority but at the same time – possibly as a *quid pro quo* – generous provision is made for private members' bills in the Lords. Because there is no limitation on the number of days on which they can be considered, the government has little control on the number of these bills that will actually be considered on the floor of the House. Ultimately this does not cause any trouble for the government since a private member's bill, to which the government is opposed and which survives in the Lords, can always be blocked in the Commons.

House of Lords procedure gives a persistent backbench (or opposition frontbench) peer a far better chance of getting a point of view across than the equivalent MP in the House of Commons. And these procedural advantages, when combined with the comparative political independence of members of the House of Lords, can result in the acceptance by the House of amendments to bills even in the face of opposition from the government. It is the emergence of the Lords since 1979 as the principal forum in which changes can be made to legislation in the teeth of government opposition – in other words as the place where the government can actually be defeated on a vote – which is one of the most interesting recent developments in the ever changing parliamentary scene. This increasing influence on legislation is illustrated by the fact that during the administration of 1970–74 there were 26 government defeats in the Lords. In the 1979–83 sessions, the government experienced 45 defeats on votes in the Lords; in 1983–87, they experienced 62 defeats; and in 1987–92, they experienced 72 defeats. The trend has continued since the 1992 election. Most of these amendments have been accepted by the government either as they stand or with modification when the bills have returned to the Commons. But if they have been reversed, the Lords have only rarely insisted upon their disagreement. In the 1984–85 session, for example, the government suffered seventeen defeats in the Lords. Of these, sixteen related to amendments to bills; only two were reversed by the government in the Commons. (See next section for description of procedure when the two Houses disagree.)

Some of these amendments made substantial dents in government policy. In the 1984–85 session, one amendment limited the Secretary of State for Education's power to alter the arrangements for education in inner London following abolition of the GLC; another abolished corporal punishment in schools and so killed the Education (Corporal Punishment) Bill which had sought to make corporal punishment subject to parental consent. Other sessions have seen major reversals. In 1983–84 property owned by charities, or specially adapted for the disabled or old people, was excluded from the right to buy provisions of the Housing and Building Control Bill. Indeed, the amendment on housing for the elderly was actually successfully insisted upon following a reversal by the Commons and if the government had not conceded, the Bill would have been lost. In the same session an amendment to the Trade Union Bill required postal ballots to be held for union elections. In the 1987–88 session, a number of amendments relating to 'academic freedom' were written into the Education Reform Bill. A requirement was written into the British Technology Group Bill in 1990–91 which required privatised BTG to consult the universities before disposing of its patents; an important amendment to the Education (Schools) Bill in 1991–92 required the Chief Inspector of Schools to be responsible for choosing who will inspect schools; an amendment to the Railways Bill in 1992–93 allowed British Rail to bid for passenger rail franchises in competition with private sector bidders, though the impact of this was subsequently modified when the bill returned to the Commons; and in the same session numerous amendments excluded sheltered housing and various kinds of heritage properties from the franchisement provisions of the Housing and Urban Development Bill.

Bills are also amended in the Lords to stave off the prospect of almost certain defeat in the lobbies during later stages. Recent much publicised examples include the Police and Magistrates' Courts Bill in the 1993–94 session. Major provisions on the appointment of Chief Constables, the appointment of local Police Authorities and introduction of fixed-term contracts for magistrates' clerks were virtually rewritten by the government after scathing criticism from all sides of the House at second reading. Provisions on student unions in the Education Bill of that session received similar treatment.

How do the Lords pull it off and why does the government not always use its Commons majority to reverse the changes the Lords have made? To answer the first part of this question we have to remind ourselves of the composition of the House of Lords.

As we saw, in November 1994, the party allegiances were as shown below:

Conservative	456
Labour	109
Liberal Democrats	54
Crossbench	
including bishops and Lords of	
Appeal in Ordinary	293

Although the House is a predominantly Conservative body, not even a Conservative government can expect to have a majority on every issue. This is confirmed by a recent analysis (Shell and Beamish 1993) by political affiliation and peerage category of members attending on an 'average day' of the 1988–89 session (in fact, the total attendances divided by the number of sitting days). Only 46.1 per cent were hereditary peers, the remainder being life peers or created peers; and only 46.6 per cent were Conservatives, the remainder being Labour (22.1 per cent), Liberal Democrat and the then Social Democrats (11.7 per cent), Cross-Bench (18 per cent) and others (1.7 per cent).

Thus, were it not for the fact that many independent members on the crossbenches are conservative in their voting habits, even a Conservative government, despite even a large Commons majority, would find it difficult to command a majority in the Lords. On some issues, when opposition parties unite and win the support of the crossbenches, the Conservatives are in a minority. Furthermore, party discipline is weaker in the Lords than in the Commons and backbench rebellion more frequent. There are a number of reasons for this. First, the peers are not elected and so they are not directly accountable, as are members of the House of Commons, to an electorate and a party manifesto. Moreover professional politicians or former politicians are in a minority and even they may on occasions be out of sympathy with certain aspects of their party's policy. Furthermore the payroll vote (of office-holders) is very small in the Lords – there are usually only about twenty ministers, junior ministers and whips in receipt of a salary in the Lords. Finally the prospect of government office – and hence the need for circumspection in voting – holds less sway over peers, many of them in the twilight years of their political careers, than it does over the aspiring MP.

Why then, does the government not reverse every Lords amendment with which it disagrees, in the Commons? In point of fact most Labour governments do just that. But it is not so easy for a Conservative government for a variety of reasons. Some of the defeats have been on matters of principle which have commanded widespread support from the ranks of Conservative backbenchers in the Commons and from the country at large. So the government has accepted amendments of this kind graciously rather than risk unnecessary unpopularity for itself amongst its own supporters both inside and outside Parliament. As in the Commons, compromise amendments will be accepted by the government to expedite a bill's progress, and the government may even admit defeat on part of its bill in order to get the other provisions through on time. For example, in 1985–86 the government reluctantly agreed to Lords amendments to the Local Government Bill which considerably weakened its effect on local authorities' publications on party-political matters, so that the other provisions of the bill could receive Royal Assent before the Easter adjournment.

But amendments to bills following the defeat of the government on a vote are a very small element in the total number of amendments made in a session, for the fact remains that most of the Lords' work is of a revising character. In recent heavy legislative sessions between 2000 and 3000 amendments have been made to bills in any one session. The majority of them are drafting amendments of no real significance, and amendments introduced by the government either to meet points made in the Commons as well as in the Lords, or to introduce new provisions of its own into bills. And so far as the amendments carried in the teeth of government opposition are concerned, it will be interesting to see whether a future Labour administration would allow the Lords the leeway they have undoubtedly enjoyed in recent years – often to the undisguised delight and benefit of the opposition parties.

A recent study (Shell and Beamish 1993) analysed proceedings in the Lords on eight bills in the 1988–89 session. It traced the origins of the amendments made and showed that the vast majority were made by the government itself, with, relatively speaking, a few more being made with government approval but on the initiative of others. Thus, of the 1164 amendments moved by the government, 1161 (99.7 per cent) were accepted: of the 1047 moved by non-government members, only 65 (6.2 per cent) were accepted. A further look showed that, of these 65, only four followed defeats in the lobbies (in fact two of these were later reversed in the Commons). Of the remaining 61, 39 were consequential or drafting amendments and only some 22 involved matters of substance which the government accepted without a vote. Of the amendments moved by the government, about 35 were identified as arising out of ministerial undertakings to look again at aspects of the bills following criticisms in the Lords in the early stages.

Disagreement between the Houses: the balance of power

In the previous section we saw that on occasion there is disagreement between the two Houses on a bill. We now explore this more fully. We also consider constraints on the Lords' powers to amend bills. A bill which passes without amendment through the second House to consider it then needs only the Royal Assent – or formal approval by the Queen – before it becomes law. It does not go back to the House where its progress began. However, if the second House makes amendments to a bill, those amendments (but no other part of the bill) must be considered by the first House. If they are agreed, the bill is ready to become law. If they are not, the second House looks at the matter again and can either insist upon its amendments or attempt compromise proposals. Theoretically alternative compromises can be shuttled between the two Houses indefinitely. Each time, messages are exchanged between the two Houses. These can become fiendishly complicated. For example, in the final stages of the controversial Housing and Building Control Bill 1984, the Commons received the following message from the Lords:

The Lords do not insist on their Amendment to the Housing and Building Control Bill to which the Commons have disagreed; they agree without Amendment to the Commons Amendments in lieu thereof; they agree without Amendment to the Commons Amendment to a Lords Amendment and to the Commons consequential Amendments to the Bill; and they do not insist on their disagreement to a Commons Amendment to a Lords Amendment and they agree to the Commons Amendments to that Lords Amendment.

Eventually disagreements are ironed out – and the bill goes forward for Royal Assent in the form in which it was agreed by both Houses. If a compromise were not reached, the bill would be lost, as happened with the contentious bill to nationalise the aircraft and shipbuilding industries in 1976. This point is normally thought to have been reached when each House has taken up its position and insisted upon it. However, as we will see later, the Lords are playing a dangerous game if they try to insist on their will against that of the Commons.

The Lords do not have free rein in amending certain types of Commons bills. By ancient practice, they may not amend bills 'of aids and supplies' – a type of bill including the annual Finance Bill which implements the tax proposals made by the Chancellor of the Exchequer in his budget. However, if the Lords insist on their amendments to any other public bill in a manner which renders the bill wholly unacceptable to the majority in the Commons and to the point that the bill is lost by the close of the session, or if they reject altogether a bill passed by the Commons, the procedures of the Parliament Acts 1911 and 1949 may be invoked. These Acts were passed to ensure that important reforming legislation introduced by the Liberal and Labour governments of the time was not frustrated by the Conservative majority in the Lords.

The severest restrictions in the Parliament Acts apply to 'money bills'. These are bills which deal only with certain specified central government finance matters. The most important of them are pure taxation bills or the Consolidated Fund Bills which formally vote money to the government. These will be described in more detail in Chapter 7. (The annual Finance Bill, which implements the budget proposals, is not normally a 'money bill' because it contains wider provisions than those defined in the Parliament Act. This is somewhat paradoxical since the 1911 Parliament Act was passed as a reaction to the Lords' rejection of the 1909 Finance Bill.) Under the Parliament Acts, money bills passed by the Commons are allowed one month to pass through the Lords. If the Lords do not give them a third reading within a month, they can be sent for Royal Assent without the Lords' approval. All other public bills passed by the Commons may be delayed for a minimum effective period of thirteen months by the Lords. The rule is strictly as follows: any bill (except one to extend the life of a parliament, i.e. to postpone a general election) which passes the Commons in two successive sessions (whether or not a general election intervenes) can be presented for Royal Assent without the agreement of the Lords, provided (a) that there has been a minimum period of one year between the Commons giving it a second reading for the first time and a third reading for the second time, and (b) that the Lords have received the bill at least one month before the end of each of the two sessions.

The rigours of this legislation have only once been taken to their final stage since the 1949 Act (which reduced by one year the delaying time of the 1911 Act) was itself passed without the agreement of the Lords. In 1991 the War Crimes Act received Royal Assent under these provisions after the bill had been passed by the Commons and rejected by the Lords at second reading in two successive sessions. This bill sought, retrospectively, to create a new criminal offence so as to enable charges to be brought against alleged perpetrators of atrocities, chiefly against Jews, in Continental Europe during the Second World War. Many Lords felt that such prosecutions would be difficult to secure and that too many legal principles were offended by the proposed legislation. As the bill was not a manifesto commitment by the government, they felt entitled to reject it.

The Parliament Act procedures are the fundamental limitation on the legislative power of the Lords. When a general election is pending, the Lords may be able to use their delaying powers to kill Commons legislation if the election results in a change of government. But when the elected government which enjoys a majority in the Commons is in its first few years of office, it is ultimately able to exert its will on public bills irrespective of the will of the unelected House of Lords. However, for practical reasons, on many occasions, as we saw in the last section, the government's business managers find it easier to accept Lords' amendments than to attempt to overturn them every time, let alone threaten the use of the Parliament Acts.

Members of the House of Lords accept that the government of the day must be allowed to get its business through. The nearest that this has come to formal expression is in the Salisbury convention. This was an understanding reached between the Conservative opposition in the House of Lords (led by the Marquis of Salisbury) and the Labour government immediately after the Second World War in 1945. The convention is that the Lords should not reject at Second Reading any government legislation which has been passed by the House of Commons and which carries out a manifesto commitment – that is to say, a commitment made to the electorate in the government party's election manifesto. But this convention does not extend to the amendment of bills nor can it be held, strictly, to apply to government bills which do not reflect a manifesto commitment. So even this self-denying ordinance leaves the Lords with considerable room for manoeuvre.

In spite of the Parliament Acts, or historical conventions on matters of supply, or more recent conventions on manifesto commitments, in practice – and under certain conditions – the Lords' powers to amend bills other than money bills in the face of Commons (that is to say government) opposition are real and influential.

Royal Assent and implementation

A bill passed by both Houses of Parliament needs the Royal Assent before it becomes law. Queen Anne, in 1707, was the last monarch to refuse to accept a bill passed by both Houses, and nowadays the Queen's agreement is automatic. Although in theory Royal Assent can be given by the sovereign in person, this was last done in 1854, and in 1967 it was decided to stop even the quaint ceremony of the Commons' proceedings being interrupted by Black Rod summoning the Commons to the Lords' Chamber to hear commissioners announcing the Royal Assent. This now occurs only at prorogation. At other times the Speaker in the Commons and the Lord Chancellor in the Lords announce the Royal Assent at convenient breaks in each House's proceedings.

Although Royal Assent to a bill turns it into an Act and makes it law, the law does not necessarily enter into force immediately. The Act may contain what is known as a 'commencement clause'. Typically, this allows the Secretary of State to make an order at some future date to bring part or all of the Act into force. Sometimes the appropriate date never comes: the Employment of Children Act 1973 has never been brought fully into effect, nor even has the Easter Act 1928 which provided a fixed date for Easter Sunday.

As we saw when we discussed parliamentary sovereignty, it is not possible in Britain to ask courts of law to declare Acts of Parliament invalid. However, under the terms of Britain's membership of the European Union and of the Council of Europe, the European Court of Justice and the European Court of Human Rights respectively can find that Acts of Parliament conflict with treaty obligations. This does not in itself invalidate the legislation, but the government of the day needs to introduce new legislation amending the offending law if it is to keep its treaty obligation. Domestic courts are also able to take notice of European legislation and to rule against Acts of Parliament where they find them incompatible with European law. In March 1994, for example, the House of Lords sitting in its judicial capacity found against certain provisions of the Employment Protection (Consolidation) Act 1978 which seemed to them to restrict part-time workers' rights in a way which European law did not permit.

Secondary legislation

At the end of the last section, we saw that an Act of Parliament could sometimes be brought into effect by an order made by the Secretary of State. Commencement orders are one of a very large group of orders, rules and regulations which are made each year, mainly by government ministers but also by other authorised persons such as local authorities or nationalised industries, and which are as much part of the law of the land as Acts of Parliament. Parliament either considers them very perfunctorily or, more usually, not at all. This type of legislation is known as 'secondary' or 'delegated' legislation because the authority to make it is ultimately derived from an Act of Parliament – the 'primary legislation'.

The secondary legislation of 1985 included the Pushchairs (Safety) Regulations 1985, the Motor Cycles (Eye Protectors) Regulations 1985, the Gipsy Encampment (Designation of the Borough of Ipswich) Order 1985, the Warble Fly (Infected Areas) Order 1985, and even the Baking and Sausage Making (Christmas and New Year) Regulations 1985. The explanatory note attached to the last of these reads:

These regulations provide a temporary exemption from statutory restrictions to enable women who have reached the age of eighteen to be employed on specific Saturday afternoons and Sundays in December 1985 in the manufacture of meat pies, sausages or cooked meats, or in the pre-packing of bacon, and in the manufacture of bread or flour confectionery (including fruit pies but not biscuits) or in work incidental or ancillary to such work.

Parliament would hardly be regarded as spending its time sensibly if it debated at length the issues raised in these regulations, and most people would agree that detailed law-making at this level is best left in the hands of the experts in the Health and Safety Executive where working conditions are concerned or in the Ministry of Agriculture in the case of suppression of warble flies.

All these orders and regulations are statutory instruments, colloquially known as SIs. SIs are made under the authority of many different pieces of primary legislation (their 'parent Acts'). The Christmas sausages regulations were made nominally by the Secretary of State for Employment under authority given to him by the Health and Safety at Work etc. Act 1974. SIs cover the whole range of government, but common procedures are laid down for them all in the Statutory Instruments Act 1946. SIs are not the only form of secondary legislation: there are various other special types of secondary legislation subject to individually tailored parliamentary controls – for example, the Highway Code and Immigration Rules – and there is also a decreasing amount of secondary legislation made under old Acts of Parliament which pre-date the Statutory Instruments Act. Nor are all SIs matters for Parliament: about half of each year's SIs have only local effect, and are not subject to any parliamentary control. However, there are well over 1000 SIs a year which are brought before Parliament. Figures per session and per day over a recent six-year period are as shown below. The trend is clearly upwards.

Session	Total number of days	Total number of SIs	Number per day
1987–88	218	1567	7.2
1988–89	175	1117	6.4
1989-90	167	1199	7.2
1990-91	160	1324	8.3
1991-92	83	719	8.7
1992–93	240	2064	8.6

This daily weight of SIs forms the vast majority of the secondary legislation which passes through Parliament, and the rest of this section will deal with them exclusively.

. The first stage in the parliamentary process for an SI is for it to be 'laid', that is, presented officially to both Houses. A small proportion of SIs (general instruments) are subject to no further parliamentary procedure, and are laid before Parliament for information and nothing more. Typically, commencement orders bringing an Act of Parliament into force fall into this category. The other SIs laid before Parliament are of two types depending on the provisions of the parent Act – the primary legislation – under which they were made. The most important require the positive approval of both Houses (or, in the case of some financial instruments, the Commons alone), but the majority have the force of law unless one or other House votes against them. The two procedures are known as the 'affirmative procedure' and the 'negative procedure' and the instruments which are subject to them are called affirmative instruments and negative instruments respectively. As the three most recent sessions for which figures are available show, the bulk of SIs are subject to the negative procedure:

Session	SIs subject to (a) affirmative procedure	(b) negative procedure	SIs laid but subject to no parliamentary procedure
1990–91	201	1072	45
1991–92	95	611	10
1992–93	277	1723	55

Generally speaking, the negative procedure means that an SI has the force of law unless either House within 40 days of the instrument being laid passes a motion to the effect that the SI should be 'annulled' or, in other words, cancelled. These motions are known as 'prayers' because of the rather antique language in which they are drawn up. For example, if a group of MPs objected to the Lawnmowers (Harmonisation of Noise Emission Standards) Regulations, the form of the motion they would table would be:

That an humble address be presented to Her Majesty, praying that the Lawnmowers (Harmonisation of Noise Emission Standards) Regulations 1986, a copy of which was laid before this House on 28th October, be annulled.

In the Commons, prayers can be debated until 11.30 p.m., although debate rarely begins before 10 p.m. or 10.30 p.m. and the discussion is therefore a short one. Until the 1995 sitting hours experiment, debate on prayers will be limited to one and a half hours and the 11.30 pm cut-off, whatever time debate began, will remain. However, the principal disadvantage of the negative procedure in the Commons is that there is absolutely no requirement for prayers to be debated at all. The decision whether or not they will be is made by the government who, of course, are responsible for the legislation in the first place and are not keen to see it attacked by MPs who oppose it. Generally, the government feel obliged to find time for prayers tabled by the principal opposition parties, but backbench prayers are debated only rarely. The total number of hours spent in debating prayers in the sessions from

1990–91 to 1992–93 was just under 29 – and the total number of SIs subject to negative procedure was 3406. In other words, very few of this type of SI receives any debate in the Commons. Time is always found for prayers to be debated in the Lords, but very few are tabled. It is possible in the Commons for debates on SIs subject to negative procedure to take place in standing committees. These committees are constituted *ad hoc*, as they are on public bills, but they meet only once, and have a maximum of one and a half hours to consider the instrument. They cannot reject the instrument. From 1990–91 to 1992-93, around 70 SIs subject to negative procedure were considered by committees.

The most important SIs are subject to affirmative procedure. In the case of very urgent legislation, they may come into force immediately with the stipulation that they will cease to have effect within a specific period – normally 28 or 40 days – unless approved by Parliament. Regulations under the Emergency Powers Act 1920 need to be approved within seven days. These are very exceptional. More commonly, draft SIs are laid before both Houses, and have legal effect only after being approved. In the Commons, the most important of these SIs can be debated on the floor of the House, normally for one and a half hours late at night, but occasionally as the main business of the day. For example, important regulations relating to legal aid were debated for over three hours in 1993, the debate beginning at 4 p.m. Increasingly, however, the debates have taken place in standing committees (constituted like those which consider negative instruments) with the possibility of a vote, without debate, being taken on the SI on the floor of the House after it has been considered by the committee. However, Standing Orders provide that if at least twenty backbenchers object to the debate on an SI being held in standing committee, they can block the referral to the committee and ensure a full one and a half hour debate on the floor of the House. During the 1993–94 session when good relations between the front benches had broken down, many affirmative instruments were considered on the floor for this reason. Part of the package of experimental measures introduced for 1995 include the automatic reference of affirmative SIs to standing committee, with the understanding that the government will accede to any reasonable opposition request for de-referral of important instruments. Debate on any SI so 'de-referred' will be limited to one and a half hours. Very substantial areas of public concern can be contained in SIs subject to affirmative procedure. For example, statutory instruments set speed limits on roads, allow non-jury trials to continue in Northern Ireland and are responsible for the current levels of many social security benefits.

Although delegated legislation is not subject to the Parliament Acts, the House of Lords rarely opposes negative or affirmative instruments. As we will see, they are unamendable and so, if the

House pressed its opposition to a division, the result could be the wholesale rejection of the instrument. As the Lords usually consider instruments after they have been taken in the House of Commons, this constrains the opposition from pressing their disagreement with them. And, of course, the opposition is always mindful of the fact that it too will, when in government, benefit from such a convention. This convention of not opposing SIs, is not always observed. The Conservative opposition divided the House against the Southern Rhodesia (United Nations Sanctions) Order 1968, and defeated the government, so provoking a constitutional furore. Although this was the last time an affirmative order was defeated, between 1968 and March 1994, there were 29 divisions on such orders, 20 of which were on the motion to approve the order and 9 on amendments critical of the motion. On one further occasion an order was withdrawn following debate. Over the same period, there were six divisions on negative instruments. One of these was on a motion inviting the government to withdraw an instrument. This motion was carried and the Town and Country Planning General Development (Amendment) Order 1977 was not proceeded with in consequence. More recently, in July 1992, the government lost a vote on a motion moved by Lord Henderson of Brompton – a former Clerk of the Parliaments – asking them to amend the Income Support (General) Regulations 1987. On this occasion, however, the government did not respond positively and refused to amend the Regulations. The House uses its powers sparingly but there have been enough instances in recent years when it has flexed its muscles to indicate that the convention not to oppose affirmative and negative instruments is by no means a hard and fast rule. This uncertainty can be exploited to great effect. Even though the opposition may only rarely divide the House on motions concerning SIs, by opposing orders or tabling critical amendments, they are able to engineer a debate on the floor and tease out concessions. Thus the tabling by the opposition of a motion to withdraw the Hong Kong (British Nationality) Order 1986, an affirmative instrument, elicited some important concessions from the government. In the event, the motion was not pressed and the order was approved.

All SIs laid before Parliament are subject to another form of control – they are considered by a committee known as the Joint Committee on Statutory Instruments. This is a committee made up of members of both Houses, and it is usually chaired by an opposition MP. It is not responsible for looking at the merits of secondary legislation, but at specified and important technical matters. It conducts its proceedings informally and in private, and there is no party-political debate on an SI as there is usually in standing committee. For example, it considers whether the minister who made the order was acting within his or her powers, or whether the drafting of the SI is defective. The Counsel to the Speaker and to the Lord Chairman of Committees assist the Joint Committee. The Joint Committee's work is laborious and not very glamorous. Despite this, when it discovers a fault in an SI, it is not even rewarded by being able to prevent the government from pressing ahead with the instrument if they wish. In the Lords, an SI cannot be approved until the Joint Committee have reported, but an adverse report can be ignored. In the Commons, SIs are quite often debated even before the Joint Committee has had time to consider them properly. Sometimes the government will meet points made by the Committee, but this is always a concession rather than an obligation. For example, on 29 October 1985, the government had intended that the Commons should discuss controversial regulations concerning social security board and lodging payments. The Joint Committee was concerned that the Department concerned had exceeded its powers in making these regulations. It reported so, and the Leader of the House withdrew the regulations. But the number of SIs withdrawn each session is only a handful.

The ease with which the Joint Committee's work can be overridden is only one of the criticisms made of the inadequacy of parliamentary control of secondary legislation. The fact that SIs are subject to very little debate is another cause for concern, as is the inability of either House or of committees to amend an SI. They must either be rejected or accepted as a whole. A minister may withdraw an SI, one of whose parts came in for criticism in Parliament, and re-submit a new SI which is less objectionable, but this does not amount to a formal parliamentary power to amend secondary legislation.

When circumstances are changing rapidly and no fundamental political principles are at stake, primary legislation can be too cumbersome. Secondary legislation which fills in the details and which can easily be adjusted to all eventualities has what *Erskine May* describes as 'speed, flexibility and adaptability', precisely because it is subject to minimal parliamentary control compared with primary legislation. However there is no fundamental constitutional rule which determines the limit beyond which secondary legislation may not go, and there is a natural tendency by government to replace the inconvenience of primary legislation by secondary legislation precisely because of these attributes of speed, flexibility and adaptability. There have even been proposals that primary legislation should consist of 'framework Acts' with the details filled out by secondary legislation. In 1990, 2574 instruments taking up 6550 A4 pages of text were produced. Scrutiny of them is, as we have seen, rather sketchy, and any further moves to make greater use of secondary legislation might diminish Parliament's role in law-making very substantially.

In recent years members of both Houses have expressed unease at certain features of primary legislation which, in their view, have already given inappropriate powers to ministers with regard to secondary legislation. There are three principal sources of complaint. First, the inclusion in bills of so-called 'Henry VIII' clauses. These are provisions to enable primary legislation to be amended or repealed by secondary legislation with or without further parliamentary scrutiny. In certain cases – like amending lists or uprating figures – the practice is unexceptional. But many were alarmed to find provisions in the Criminal Justice Bill 1990, for example, for certain criminal offences to be added or removed by order. Secondly, the introduction of so-called 'Skeleton Bills' where the use of delegated powers is so extreme that the real operation of the bill would be entirely by the regulations made under it. The Child Support Bill 1991 and the Education (Student Loans) Bill 1990 attracted heavy criticism because of this. And finally, a general downgrading of parliamentary control so that orders and regulations which should, by virtue of their subject matter, be approved by the affirmative resolution procedure, are instead accorded the weaker negative resolution procedure; and orders which one might expect to be laid under negative resolution are instead laid as general instruments affording no parliamentary control.

Such tendencies are by no means unique to Westminster. The Australian parliament set up a select committee on Scrutiny of Bills partly in order to check such tendencies in that country. And in 1993 the House of Lords set up its select committee on Delegated Powers Scrutiny to perform that task. It remains to be seen whether the very existence of the Committee will result in greater moderation on the part of the Executive (see also page 137).

The government is clearly already sensitive to the issue of 'Henry VIII' clauses. In the Deregulation and Contracting Out Act 1994, ministers are given power by order subject to affirmative instrument procedure to amend or repeal primary legislation which imposes a burden affecting any person carrying on a trade, business or profession. Unusually, the Act provides for a 60 day period supplementary to the normal affirmative instrument procedure during which each House may have an opportunity to scrutinise in draft an order to be made under the power and to report on its merits. The Commons have decided to set up a Deregulation Committee for this purpose while the Lords will use its existing Delegated Powers Scrutiny Committee. It will be the task of these committees to consider these proposals for instruments, to take evidence if necessary, and to report whether or not the orders should be made, or amended before laying. Instruments laid following this pre-legislative scrutiny by the Select Committees are then reconsidered by them (along with a government statement setting out any changes which they have made) and not referred to the Joint Committee on Statutory Instruments. They remain, of course, subject to the approval of both Houses. In the Commons, this will involve a debate of up to 90 minutes or, if the government seeks to overturn a recommendation from the Deregulation Committee that an order should not be made, three hours. At the time of going to press, these committees had not begun this work. Their effect thus remains to be judged.

There are two particular areas which need a brief mention. Since direct rule was introduced in Northern Ireland in 1972, the majority of legislation for the province has been in the form of Orders in Council, a type of SI. Northern Ireland SIs are usually debated at greater length in the House or standing committee, and they are generally preceded by published consultation documents. However, MPs do not have the opportunity to propose amendments to these Orders in Council which cover all aspects of Northern Ireland life excepting security, taxation and constitutional matters. Some have been very contentious. For example, the Homosexual Offences Order 1982, which legalised homosexuality in the province, was approved in the early hours of the morning in the Commons after just one and a half hours of debate. The Unionist parties in particular have criticised the inadequacy of the scrutiny of Northern Ireland legislation.

A second type of legislation analogous to delegated legislation can also be contentious on occasion: the Church of England cannot make its own rules without securing parliamentary approval. When the domestic church bodies have agreed a new piece of church law (called a Measure), the Measure must be presented to Parliament and agreed by both Houses. In 1989, a Measure dealing with the ordination of divorced men was rejected by the Commons, though several MPs voting were not members of the Church of England. There was also concern about the vote on the later Measure allowing for the ordination of women to the priesthood, but this eventually passed successfully. Some clergy and others in the Church of England believe that any parliamentary control over their internal affairs is an anachronism.

European legislation is dealt with in Chapter 11.

Private legislation

The reader of the House of Commons Order Paper will often see at the beginning of the day's agenda on Mondays to Thursdays mysterious references to 'private business'. Occasionally the words 'At seven o'clock. Private business set down under Standing Order No. 16' can also be seen. The 'private business' is not private in the sense of being confidential or related to the internal affairs of the Commons. It is, in fact, business related to private legislation.

It is worth emphasising again that private legislation is nothing to do with private members' legislation. The names 'private bills' and 'private members' bills' are confusingly similar, but they are quite distinct. In essence, private legislation is legislation which brings particular benefits to an individual, or group of individuals or a corporate body but which does not bring the same benefits to all other individuals, groups or bodies. Its effect is private and particular rather than public and general. Typical private bills allow local authorities to make by-laws, public companies to alter their articles of association or individuals to become naturalised as British citizens. An important pre-requisite of a private bill is that what it seeks to do can be achieved only by legislation, not by other means. To take some examples of recent years: the Birmingham City Council Act 1985 allows motor racing on public roads in Birmingham; the Alcoholics Anonymous (Dispositions) Act 1986 allows the charity to decline to accept gifts – it wished to remain a self-help group; the Dartmoor Commons Act 1985 was promoted by Dartmoor farmers to provide means of arresting the over-grazing of the moors; the Dawat-e-Hadiyah (England) Act 1993 gives certain legal powers (for example, to acquire land) to a religious group, while the Woodgrange Park Cemetery and Crematorium Act 1993 allowed development of part of a cemetery although other provisions, notably allowing the construction of a crematorium, were rejected.

The first step in private legislation is for the person or group who wants the legislation to petition for the bill. Private bills are not presented by MPs or peers but by these 'promoters' of the legislation, who are represented by special lawyers known as parliamentary agents. Throughout the bill's passage – and, more especially, before it is introduced – the promoters will be working to ensure that the bill receives as little opposition as possible. Promoters need to comply with an elaborate set of Standing Orders which try to ensure that interested parties – who may know nothing of the promoters' intentions – are given notice of the bill. When this has been done, the bill is allocated to one of the two Houses for first consideration, and, after second reading, it is sent to special committees.

Anyone who is aggrieved by the bill's provisions has the right to petition against it but only those petitioners directly affected by the bill have the right to be heard. If the bill is not opposed by petitions or if all petitions are withdrawn after the petitioners' wishes have been met by the promoters, the bill is considered by a committee on unopposed bills, through which it usually passes swiftly after an explanation of its purposes by its promoters. Opposed private bills are considered much more elaborately over many days by a committee of four MPs (or five peers) who must have no personal interest in the matter. This committee acts in a semi-judicial capacity, examining witnesses and hearing barristers who appear for and against the bill. The fundamental duties of the committee are to decide whether the promoters have made out a proper case for the bill being necessary, whether those affected by it have been treated justly, and whether there is any objection to it on public policy grounds. They have the power to make amendments, or even to recommend that the bill should not proceed.

After their committee stage, private bills are considered on report (in the Commons, but not the Lords), read a third time and passed to the other House for similar stages to be taken. Unlike public bills, it is quite common for private bills not to complete all their stages in one session, and special orders are usually then made which allow them to be taken up again in the following session at the stage which they have reached. The restrictions which the Parliament Acts place on the power of the House of Lords to delay public legislation do not apply to private legislation.

Most private bills do not receive sustained opposition from MPs or peers, but the opportunity for any MP who is not on the bill committee to delay the bill is nevertheless huge. Each stage of the bill's progress is advertised on the order paper at the time of unopposed private business, and so long as just one MP objects in person on the first occasion when the bill appears, it cannot proceed without a full debate unless the MP withdraws the objection. The Chairman of Ways and Means is responsible for deciding the days on which these debates may occur (they can take place on any day from Monday to Thursday, from 7 p.m. until 10 p.m.), but the government business managers are anxious to avoid too much parliamentary time being taken up with opposed private business. The MP who objects to an aspect of a private bill therefore has a strong bargaining counter with the promoters: unless they go some way to meeting the MP's wishes, the MP can delay their bill by insisting on a full debate at each stage. In this way, the bill could well be lost.

The amount of private legislation has greatly diminished in recent years following important procedural changes in 1992. These changes stemmed from discontent among a sizeable number of MPs about private bill procedures and from the report of a joint committee of both Houses. The most important procedural change was made in the Transport and Works Act 1992, passed just before the General Election that year. That Act had the effect of removing from the parliamentary process private bills dealing with such matters as railway, tramway or harbour building or development. These were often the most controversial private bills. Nowadays the only parliamentary involvement in such projects will occur when a transport or works project is deemed by the government to have national significance, when a single debate on its desirability will take place on the floor of the House.

Figures for the numbers of bills introduced and, more importantly, the number which are petitioned against, demonstrate clearly the change in the amount (and level of controversy) of private business.

Session	Number of new private bills	Number petitioned against
1988–89	39	12
1989–90	32	12
1990–91	28	11
1991–92	24	10
1992–93	10	1
1993–94	4	2

Transport and works bills which had begun their parliamentary life before the 1992 changes continued to occupy part of the parliamentary agenda for some time after 1992: the highly controversial Crossrail Bill, for example, which provided for a rail link in central London from Paddington to Liverpool Street stations, and against which there were no fewer than 314 petitions, was considered – and rejected – by an Opposed Bill Committee in 1993–94. There will no doubt be private bills in the future which do not deal with transport or works but which will still prove controversial, as, for example, did the spate of bills promoted by local authorities in the 1980s which caused concern to civil libertarians because of the powers they introduced to restrict public processions. And any private bill may be a matter of crucial, even overwhelming, importance for the people who want to see it passed. But it is likely that private bills will become a parliamentary backwater, certainly compared with their nineteenth-century heyday.

Hybrid bills

Some bills have some of the characteristics of a private bill and some of a public bill. Strictly, they are public bills which contain some clauses of a private bill nature. Not surprisingly, they are called hybrid bills. Bills of a wholly private character which are introduced by the government are also hybrid bills. Examples of hybrid bills of recent years include the Channel Tunnel Bill (enacted in 1987) and the Cardiff Bay Barrage Bill (first presented to Parliament in 1988 as a private bill but not receiving Royal

Assent until 5 November 1993 after being re-introduced as a government bill). A hybrid bill dealing with the Channel Tunnel rail link – again likely to be bitterly opposed by those affected – was presented in late 1994. In the slightly more distant past, one of the best known examples of a hybrid bill was the Aircraft and Shipbuilding Industries Bill of 1976 which was intended to nationalise the two industries. It was discovered that the bill did not apply to one shipbuilding company which otherwise fulfilled the bill's criteria for nationalisation. Because this company was being treated differently from all other companies in the same class, the bill was declared hybrid. Hybrid bills are considered as public bills, except that they are examined to see whether they comply with the Standing Orders which relate to private bills, and there is an additional stage – they are referred to a select committee in each House which can hear petitions from those affected by the bill. The committee on the Channel Tunnel Bill received several thousand of these petitions. There is, however, no need for the promoters to prove the need for the bill in the same way as promoters of private bills. That need is deemed to have been proved by the approval of the bill at second reading in the House in which it was introduced. In the case of the Aircraft and Shipbuilding Industries Bill, the discovery that the bill was hybrid was made only at a late stage, and the government persuaded the Commons to carry a motion exempting the bill from usual procedures which apply to hybrid bills. The Lords did not follow suit and in that House the bill was committed to a select committee. The Commons' decision is a good illustration of how flexible parliamentary procedure can be on this and other issues.

CHAPTER 7

Financial control and accountability

At the centre of political controversy always lies the nation's financial balance sheet. Are the economic prospects good? Is government money being spent in the appropriate way? How is the money being raised? A very large part of Parliament's work is broadly concerned with questions such as these. There are underlying constitutional principles. The money the government needs to conduct its programmes must be raised by taxes which must be approved by Parliament. So, in theory, must most areas of government spending. Government must inform Parliament before approval can be given. Finally, government is accountable to Parliament for the good management of its funds.

The first part of this chapter will describe the main sources of information which Parliament receives to enable it to conduct its debates on these issues. Secondly we will look at the areas where Parliament and especially, as a result of custom and the Parliament Acts, the House of Commons have a formal control over financial matters. We will describe the complicated procedures, but also ask with what aims MPs actually exercise their powers. Finally the chapter will suggest that MPs are more concerned with exposing general trends in economic policy to debate than with attempting detailed financial scrutiny of government actions. The work of the Comptroller and Auditor General, National Audit Office and Committee of Public Accounts, which is the final stage when government accounts to Parliament for the way the money has been spent, is described elsewhere.

What information does Parliament receive?

We begin by describing the financial documents presented to Parliament. Recent years have seen considerable changes in these, and more are in the offing. There is no longer a Public Expenditure White Paper, while the introduction in November 1993 of a unified Budget containing taxation and spending proposals has altered the timetable of the financial year and led to the demise of the Autumn Statement.

The first financial document published in the normal session is now the *Financial Statement and Budget Report – the FSBR,* also known as the Red Book. This is presented to Parliament on budget day, as soon as the Chancellor of the Exchequer sits down after delivering the budget speech. It is supplemented by a whole raft of press releases which spell out the implications of the changes announced – no fewer than 90 in 1993. The FSBR deals with the Budget proposals, as well as setting out much of the material which was formerly contained in the Autumn Statement. In 1993 it ran to 143 pages and contained chapters on the medium-term financial strategy; recent developments and prospects for the economy; public spending and the public sector finances as well as chapters dealing with the budget measures themselves.

A substantial improvement in the financial information Parliament receives has come about through the publication since 1991 of *Departmental Reports*. Reports are now laid before Parliament by each government department in February or March each year. They are free-standing documents which vary in appearance and style between different departments. For example, in 1994, the Scottish Office's Report was 214 pages long and cost over £20, while the Ministry of Defence's Report was a modest 52 pages, and cost just £8. Certain core information must, however, be included by all departments in their Reports. First of all, departments are expected to publish tables giving financial information relating to their own spending and their support to local authorities and nationalised industries over the previous five years (in terms of outturn), the current year (estimated outturn) and the three subsequent years (plans). This financial information must be broken down in such a way that comparisons can be made with the Estimates (see below). Tables setting out the running costs and staffing of the department and, where appropriate, local authority expenditure are also compulsory. Much other information of financial importance must also be included in the reports. There must be a statement of aims and objectives, and a description of how the department's activities related to its aims. Achievements and targets must be described, with information on effectiveness and efficiency. Commentary on the financial tables must include explanations of the importance and context of the spending, as well as of any changes which have been made to previously published plans and of any failure to achieve planned targets. Any initiatives for achieving greater value for money must be set out. A description of the department's work in such areas as the Citizen's Charter and environmental protection is also obligatory. Reports do not make exciting reading, but they are valuable quarries of information for MPs and for departmental select committees in particular.

At the same time as the departmental reports are published, the Treasury publishes a statistical supplement to the FSBR which sets out more detail on the public expenditure plans announced in the previous November's Budget, and draws together and summarises a great deal of the information contained in the individual departmental reports. The supplement thus allows trends in spending across government as a whole to be analysed.

The *Supply Estimates* form the most detailed financial information presented to the Commons, though they are sometimes criticised for being the least helpful. 'Estimates' are the estimated totals of the part of public expenditure known as supply expenditure. This expenditure can be incurred only with parliamentary authority.

The concept of supply dates from an era when the monarchs needed to spend money which the Crown did not have, usually on wars. They were obliged to ask Parliament to be supplied with funds to do so. Nowadays, State expenditure is much larger and much more regular. However, each year the sovereign's government must still ask the Commons for a supply of money to allow all that expenditure to take place.

Expenditure for which supply is voted, while a major part of government spending, is not the whole story. There are very large areas of public expenditure which supply estimates do not cover – these include national insurance, expenditure by nationalised industries and local authorities, and net payments to the European Communities. In 1994–95, for example, the total of general government expenditure was £292 billion, and the supply estimates totalled £208 billion.

For those areas which are covered, a great deal of information appears to be provided in the supply estimates. These are divided up into classes which broadly reflect the different government departments (19 in 1994–95) and subdivided into what are known as 'votes' (163 of these in 1994–95). The votes are further divided into 'sub-heads'. However, across the estimates we find votes and sub-heads of very different sizes. For example, in 1994–95, Class XIII, Vote 1 (centrally administered social security benefits) amounted to £32,006 million, while Class XVII, Vote 14 (Government Actuary's Department) was for just £1 million. Some details which can be extracted from the sub-heads are relatively trivial (for example, the Royal Navy and Royal Marine Sports Control Board received a £52,000 grant in 1994–95, while £13,000 of supply expenditure was devoted to the detection, eradication and control of harmful botanical pests and diseases), while other sub-heads are vast – for example, £329,433,000 was to be spent in grants towards capital expenditure by highways authorities while the cost of council tax benefit was £1,900,050,000.

For illustration, one of the smallest votes (Class XIXA, Vote 1) in respect of House of Commons Administration is reproduced on pages 159–162. This vote is somewhat unusual, but the way it is set out and the detail it contains is fairly typical. The information it contains is, of course, of interest in other sections of this book.

CLASS XIX, A, VOTE 1

HOUSE OF COMMONS: ADMINISTRATION

Introduction

1. Expenditure borne on this Vote is not subject to a cash limit and is treated as a net Vote.

2. This Vote covers the main salary costs of the staff of the House of Commons and the costs of the associated general expenses including stationery and printing costs. Some travel costs of Members of Parliament in connection with Select Committees, and delegations to International Parliamentary Assemblies are borne on this Vote, but the main costs of Members' salaries and allowances are borne on Class XIX, Vote 7. Further details of the expenses in each subhead

will be given in the Annual Report of the House of Commons Commission, which is published in the summer, normally in July.

3. The forecast outturn for the Vote as a whole in 1993–94 is £66,750,000.

4. The Estimate for 1994–95 is some £661,000 below the figure agreed in the 1993 Public Expenditure Survey after taking account of revised share of security costs which is increased from 50 per cent to 60 per cent.

5. The provision of £69,041,000 for 1994–95 is £2,291,000 above the forecast outturn for Class XIX, A, Vote 1 for 1993–94.

Part I

£69,041,000

Amount required in the year ending 31 March 1995 for expenditure by the House of Commons Commission on administration; including security, broadcasting, publicity, stationery and printing.

The **House of Commons Commission** will account for this vote.

	£
Net total	69,041,000
Allocated in the Vote on Account (HC 4)	31,200,000
Balance to complete	37,841,000

SUMMARY AND SUBHEAD DETAIL

Part II

SUMMARY

	1992-93 Net outturn £'000	1993-94 Total net provision £'000	1993-94 Forecast Outturn £'000	1994-95 Gross Provision £'000	1994-95 Appropriations in aid £'000	1994-95 Net provision £'000
House of Commons Commission	**61,556**	**69,334**	**66,750**	**71,631**	**2,590**	**69,041**

SUBHEAD DETAIL

	1992-93 Outturn £'000	1993-94 Total provision £'000	1994-95 Provision £'000
House of Commons: Administration Parliament and Privy Council			
A1 Office of the Speaker	**604**	**701**	**657**
A2 Department of the Clerk of the House Including the Vote Office and the Parliamentary Office of Science and Technology (net)	**21,430**	**25,406**	**25,230**
(1) Staff costs and other expenses of the Department of the Clerk including Select Committees and Delegations to International Parliamentary Assemblies.			10,697
(2) Staff costs and other expenses of the Vote Office.			14,982
(3) Staff costs and other expenses of the Parliamentary Office of Science and Technology.	—	—	156

SUBHEAD DETAIL

	1992–93 Outturn £'000	1993–94 Total provision £'000	1994–95 Provision £'000
Less:			
(4) Fees on Private and Provisional Bills, Taxation of costs, etc.			50
(5) Receipts from sales of publications.			551
(6) Receipts from the House of Lords.			4
A3 Department of the Serjeant at Arms (net)	**18,496**	**18,385**	**22,041**
Staff costs and other expenses including the costs of security, postage, telecommunications, and other services.			22,051
Less:			
(1) Receipts from the House of Lords.			10
A4 Department of the Library (net)	**7,022**	**9,288**	**7,795**
(1) Staff costs and other expenses including the cost of purchase, binding and repair of books and other Library services.			7,850
Less:			
(1) Receipts from the House of Lords.			55
A5 Department of Finance and Administration (net)	**5,913**	**6,208**	**6,883**
(1) Staff costs and other expenses.		3,823	4,460
(2) Cost of superannuation allowances paid to retired staff of the House.		2,898	3,002
Less:			
(3) Contributions from the Parliamentary Contributory pension Fund towards staff costs, and contributions in respect of widows' etc, pensions.	510	513	579

SUBHEAD DETAIL

	1992–93 Outturn £'000	1993–94 Total provision £'000	1994–95 Provision £'000
A6 Department of the Official Report	3,393	3,468	3,754
A7 Refreshment Department			4,470
Staff costs and other expenses.	4,291	5,176	5,153
Less:			
(1) Recoveries in respect of banqueting etc from the Refreshment Department Trading Fund.	350	350	683
A8 Broadcasting Services	407	702	801
Cost of televising the Chamber, Select, and Standing Committees.			866
Less:			
(1) Receipts from the House of Lords.			65
Gross total	61,556	69,334	71,631
Less:			
AZ Appropriations in Aid Recovery of input VAT.	—	—	2,590
Net total	61,556	69,334	69,041

The main group of estimates are usually presented to the Commons in March. They cover several volumes and in 1994–95 ran to over 1000 pages and cost almost £225. However, estimates of expenditure on supply services change as the financial year progresses. Consequently supplementary estimates need to be presented – usually in batches in June, November and February. Supplementary estimates can themselves be large volumes covering enormous sums of money – for example the February 1993 supplementary estimates ran to almost 300 pages and asked Parliament for just short of an extra £2.6 billion.

In 1993 the government acknowledged that the estimates were not very satisfactory documents: in their view, they were too long and complex and contained too much of the wrong information and too little of what MPs really wanted to know. Radical changes were proposed: from 1995, main estimates would be reduced in size to two volumes; estimates and spending plans in departmental reports would be fully aligned, and information would be presented in a standardised form across votes. Although there would be less detail in the estimates, what was there would be of greater clarity and higher quality. In a 1994 Report the Treasury and Civil Service Select Committee endorsed many of the government's objectives, but expressed some reservations about the detail of the proposal. It is not likely that any change will be introduced before 1996.

The change to a unified budget presented in November would have led to an imbalance in the timetable for presenting financial information. This has been remedied by the presentation in June of a *Summer Economic Forecast*. The first of these was presented in 1994, and the contents of the document are still evolving.

Other information with financial implications is given to Parliament in a whole range of ways, including statements in the House, memoranda submitted to select committees and the financial memoranda attached to bills. Important information on how public money is spent is, of course, received by the Committee of Public Accounts from the National Audit Office.

What does Parliament do with the information?

With the possible exception of a few confidential memoranda given to select committees, none of the financial information which is given to Parliament is given exclusively to MPs and peers. Formally, out of courtesy, the departmental reports, the budget statement and the estimates are all presented to the Commons first, but they are immediately put on sale to the public and subjected to intense analysis by the financial press and all the others who have an interest in the way government money is raised and spent.

Other than ease of access to these documents, MPs have no special privileges in terms of information.

However, at a series of different levels, Parliament is able to hold the government to account in its raising and spending of money. Formal control rests with the House of Commons alone, and a self-denying ordinance based on historical tradition means that the House of Lords does not involve itself with the various pieces of financial legislation. However, the Lords do become involved in the sense that they might debate matters of general policy with expenditure implications – inner-city problems, for example – and say 'Money has to be spent to alleviate this problem'.

We will begin by looking at the formal supply procedure in the Commons.

Supply procedure

At its most basic level, supply procedure consists of four stages:

1   the government presents supply estimates which request money and explain how it will be spent – this, broadly, is the information stage which has been described earlier;
2   the House of Commons votes on the estimates;
3   Parliament passes an Act which authorises the Bank of England to make the cash available;
4   after the money is spent, there is an audit.

The procedure is very complex and understanding it is not helped by the fact that the calendar year begins in January, the financial year in April, and the parliamentary year – usually – in November. Estimates cover one financial year, but they are not voted at the beginning of the year. For this reason, 'votes on account' are presented in the preceding November. When these have been authorised, they will allow about 45 per cent of the amounts authorised in the previous financial year to tide the government over in the new year. Sometimes estimates voted in a year do not cover all supply expenditure. When this happens, 'excess votes' are presented about eleven months after the end of the financial year to which they relate. In this way, actual authorisation of supply expenditure for one financial year lasts over a two and a half year period.

During the course of a session, main estimates, at least three sets of supplementary estimates, votes on account and excess votes will all come before the House of Commons. They will relate between them to three different financial years. In a normal session, there are usually three occasions when these estimates are formally voted upon – (a) not later than 6 February (and normally before Christmas), votes on account for the coming financial year and supplementary estimates for the current year; (b) not later than

18 March, supplementary estimates for the current year and excess votes for the previous year; and (c) not later than 5 August, the total of outstanding estimates. These occasions will be followed swiftly by the introduction of confirming bills which are the culmination of the supply process. These bills (known as 'Consolidated Fund Bills') are not debated in the Commons (though a vote could be held on their second and third readings – there is no committee stage) and they are invariably passed without debate or vote by the Lords. All stages are usually taken on the same day, and proceedings are formal.

The consolidated fund is the government's general 'bank account' at the Bank of England. The Bank can only issue money out of the fund if it has statutory authority to do so. There are some payments which it has standing statutory authority to make (for example, payments to the EU), but the majority of payments are subject to the authorisation of the annual Consolidated Fund Acts. The most important of the Consolidated Fund Bills is the one which will eventually become the Appropriation Act. As well as authorising the issue from the consolidated fund of the amounts sought in the main estimates and the summer supplementaries, the Appropriation Act 'appropriates' to individual purposes these amounts and the ones authorised by the two Consolidated Fund Acts which precede it. This 'appropriation to individual purposes' means that a maximum sum is allocated to each of the 160 or so votes which the supply estimates contained, and money which is provided to government for one purpose cannot be spent on another. The total sum contained in Part I of each estimate (see page 159) is reproduced in the Appropriation Act. However, the details contained in subsequent parts of the estimate are not part of the Appropriation Act, and, with the agreement of the Treasury, the global sum of money allocated can be redistributed. For example, Class IV, Vote 9 in the 1994–95 estimates was in respect of the Office of Fair Trading. Once this estimate had been given statutory authority by the Appropriation Act, the £19.6 million which it allowed could only be used for the maintenance of the Office of Fair Trading. However, the total could be redistributed inside the office (e.g. more spent on consumer affairs and less on competition policy). What the government cannot do is to decide to spend £1 million which was allocated to the Office of Fair Trading on, say, the Office of Gas Supply instead.

The timetable for the voting of supply and the passing of the Consolidated Fund Acts can be disturbed by general elections or extra sets of supplementary estimates. But in its most classic form, the timetable for 1984–85 shows the year's routine. It is set out on page 166.

In the autumn, appropriation accounts for the previous financial year are presented showing how the money voted has been spent.

The voting of 1984–85 supply

	Presented	Voted	Authorised
Vote on account	November 1983	December 1983	Consolidated Fund (No.2) Act 1983[1]
Main estimates	March 1984	July 1984 }	Appropriation Act 1984
Summer supplementary estimates	July 1984	July 1984	
Winter supplementary estimates	November 1984	December 1984	Consolidated Fund (No.2) Act 1984[2]
Spring supplementary estimates	February 1985	March 1985	Consolidated Fund Act 1985[3]
Excess votes	February 1986	March 1986	Consolidated Fund Act 1986[4]

Notes:

[1] This Act also authorised the sums contained in the winter supplementary estimates of 1983–84.

[2] This Act also authorised the vote on account for 1985–86. The sums covered by the winter supplementary estimate which it authorised were appropriated by the Appropriation Act 1985.

[3] This Act also authorised the excess votes for 1983–84. The sums covered by the spring supplementary estimate which it authorised were appropriated by the Appropriation Act 1985.

[4] This Act also authorised the spring supplementary estimates for 1985–86.

These are certified by the Comptroller and Auditor General. Money not spent in one financial year cannot normally be carried over, but must be surrendered to the consolidated fund.

If emergencies arise, there is also a contingencies fund. This is limited by law to 2 per cent of the previous year's total authorised supply expenditure. Any money drawn out of the fund must be repaid.

This system is clearly very complex, but how does Parliament really exercise its control over the sums set out in the estimates? After all, the system was originally designed to ensure control by the Commons of the government's spending, and if the House of Commons has power over the purse strings it might be thought to exercise them here in the control of supply expenditure. The House of Commons does, of course, have the ultimate deterrent: it can reject the government's estimates as a whole or defeat the second or third reading of a Consolidated Fund Bill. If it did so, the government would receive no money and a general election would take place. No government in recent history has been refused supply in this way, though the Labour government of Gough Whitlam in Australia in 1975 was threatened with the refusal of supply under a similar system and he was ultimately dismissed by the Governor General.

Rejection of the estimates in total would only occur when there was a crisis of confidence in the government. On a day-to-day basis, a more realistic form of control would be one where the House of Commons was able to assess each estimate and increase or decrease the sums it contained as it thought appropriate.

Increasing estimates is, however, not permitted. One of the fundamental rules of Commons' procedure is that money is only voted on the initiative of the government – that is, the monarch had to ask for supply, the Commons would not volunteer money. There is no reason in principle why this should be so, and the practice of permitting increases is allowed in Germany. In the USA, Congress has much greater freedom, though some argue that this is a cause of US budgeting problems. In France individual estimates may be varied up or down so long as the total remains the same. Suggestions that the Commons' practice should be altered have been resisted by the government, and a special committee which looked at supply procedure in the 1980–81 session pointed out that, if increases in estimates were to be permitted, this would have consequences for taxation and other matters. As some members of the committee recognised, the present system 'derives more from tradition than logic', but it seems likely that no change can be expected.

The Commons can in theory reduce estimates. On any of the days when estimates are considered, any backbencher can table an amendment to reduce any estimate by any sum of money.

However, few amendments are tabled, and here, as in other areas, the Speaker has the power to select which will be put to the vote. In recent years, only a very occasional amendment moved by a backbencher has been discussed. However, new procedures were introduced in 1982, and under these there have been several occasions when a proposal to reduce an estimate has been before the Commons.

The new procedures partly resulted from the 1981 Procedure Committee report. The committee talked of the 'myth of effective control', and proposed a system whereby the departmentally related select committees (which will be described in the next chapter) scrutinised each department's estimates. Eight 'estimates days' on the floor of the House were to be set aside for considering and voting on the estimates. The discussion would be based on the information the select committees had gleaned, and the House might well vote to reduce estimates to which committees had taken exception. In fact, when compromise reforms which met government objections were introduced, only three estimates days were allowed. Nevertheless, the particular estimates which are debated on these days *are* effectively chosen by a committee consisting of select committee chairmen (the Liaison Committee), who assess competing claims for debates from their committees.

But committees have not been keen to look at the details of the estimates and they have found it difficult to base their enquiries into economy and efficiency in government on the bare and unilluminating figures presented in the estimates. Instead, what they have chosen to do is to link with estimates topics which they believe should be debated. The estimates day can then be used for what amounts to a general policy debate rather than a discussion of whether the particular estimate is too large, too small or should be altered in some way. A typical example of this was the debate initiated by the Trade and Industry Committee in 1985 which was strictly on an estimate but which was used to discuss more general questions about trade with China, a subject comprehensively investigated by the committee. On the occasions when reductions have been proposed, this has often just provided a handle for debate: for example, when the Education Committee proposed a reduction in the Home Office vote in respect of prison education in 1984, the committee's spokesman made clear that they did not actually wish the government to forfeit money, but simply for the adequacy of its work in the field to be discussed. What are called estimates days are to all intents and purposes simply days when the select committees decide the agenda.

Procedural reformers have often called for proper scrutiny of the estimates by the Commons, and the introduction of estimates days in 1982 was intended as a step in that direction. The system of departmentally related select committees has resulted in more questions being asked of civil servants and ministers about the details of departmental spending, and most committees do now devote several sessions a year to their department's spending plans as set out in the departmental report. But select committees are not equipped to delve into detail across the board or rework estimates for particular government services. They do not have the capacity, time or – in most cases – the inclination to do so. That said, the system does allow a vigilant select committee to home in on an aspect of spending which it finds disturbing for some reason, take oral and written evidence about it from ministers, civil servants and others, persuade the Liaison Committee that the subject should be discussed, and table an amendment reducing the relevant estimate on one of the estimates days. That is a powerful potential weapon in parliamentary scrutiny of government policy, but it does not amount to a proper system of thorough scrutiny of each year's estimates by the House of Commons.

Budget and Finance Bill procedures

Formally, the House of Commons also exercises control over a large part of the government's money raising. This role is confined to taxation, though not all the money government spends is raised in this way – government borrowing is another means of raising funds, though, as we will see later, this escapes parliamentary scrutiny altogether.

The opening event in the session is the budget. The Chancellor of the Exchequer is photographed outside his official residence at 11 Downing Street with his battered Victorian despatch box, arrives at the House of Commons and immediately after question time, usually on a Tuesday and since 1993 in November rather than in March or April as previously, opens the budget. Budget plans are drawn up in some secrecy, and there is a great deal of expectation about the occasion. In his speech, which lasts upwards of an hour, he (as *Erskine May* puts it) 'develops his views of the resources of the country, communicates his calculations of probable income and expenditure, and declares whether the burdens upon the people are to be increased or diminished'. Less elaborately, he makes a speech about Britain's economic situation and lets everyone know whether taxes are going up or down. It is a great media occasion broadcast live and commentated upon by each television and radio station. Since the advent of the unified budget in 1993, the Chancellor has announced government spending plans in his budget as well as taxation proposals, but media interest – at least in the initial stages – still concentrates on the taxation side. Historically, the budget was a much grander event – Gladstone and Lloyd George were noted performers who delivered speeches lasting several hours. Even in the last twenty years, it used to be usual for MPs to mark the occasion by dressing up a little.

After the Chancellor's speech, the leader of the opposition begins a debate which lasts over four or five days. (An extra day was added in 1993 to compensate for the absence of an Autumn Statement debate). At the end of that debate, the House of Commons is asked to vote on a number of 'Ways and Means' resolutions (over 50 of them in most years) which will form the basis of the taxation elements in the Finance Bill. Some of these Ways and Means resolutions are complex, some almost curt (for example, Resolution 27 in 1993 just read 'that corporation tax shall be charged for the financial year 1994 at the rate of 33%'). Once they have all been agreed, the Finance Bill, which incorporates the budget proposals, is presented to the House. This is generally debated for one day at second reading. Thereafter it proceeds as a normal public bill, except that part of its committee stage is taken on the floor of the House (two days in most years) while the less controversial parts are dealt with in standing committee (sittings of the standing committee take at least ten days, with many of the sittings lasting well into the evening). Two days are spent on the report and third reading stages of the Finance Bill and these days' sittings can be long. Finally the bill is passed to the Lords. There consideration is a debate on second reading which amounts to a general economic debate. It receives Royal Assent sometime in the late spring.

It is the Finance Act which gives final authority to the taxation proposals in the budget, but many of these will have entered into effect within hours of the Chancellor's budget statement. For example, in 1993 taxes on petrol increased at 6 p.m. on budget day – just over an hour after the Chancellor sat down. This is permissible because of the provisions of the Provisional Collection of Taxes Act 1968. As soon as the Chancellor sits down, a motion is moved in the Commons which, if approved, allows specified alterations to come into effect straight away. This must be confirmed by the House agreeing within ten days to the Ways and Means resolutions which apply to these taxes and by the passage of the Finance Bill into law by 5 May (or within four months in the case of budgets not introduced in November or December).

A word needs to be said about Ways and Means resolutions. The name is a vestige of the old Committee of Ways and Means which was important in the Commons' history. Nowadays proposals to increase tax rates or to impose new taxes are the main types of business which must be preceded by Ways and Means resolutions. There are a sprinkling of Ways and Means resolutions throughout the parliamentary year, but the bulk of them come after the budget. They appear to offer nothing more than an opportunity to vote against a taxation proposal before the bill is introduced which will give effect to the resolution. However, only ministers are allowed to move Ways and Means resolutions, and any bill founded on these resolutions cannot be amended in such a way as to put the bill outside their scope without a new Ways and Means Resolution being moved. For example, we quoted a Ways and Means Resolution of 1993 which set the rate of corporation tax at 33%. No amendment to increase the rate to 40% would be allowed during the committee stage of the Finance Bill, though amendments to *reduce* the rate would be in order. Generally speaking, MPs may table only amendments to the Finance Bill which alter the taxation levels downwards and even here they are usually prohibited from discussing amendments to exempt or zero-rate any item as far as VAT is concerned.

Even taking into account these restrictions on the amendments which may be discussed, it is sometimes said that MPs have a particularly important role to play in amending the Finance Bill. Because of budget secrecy, affected groups only hear details of the budget when the Chancellor delivers his speech. They can brief MPs who are members of the Finance Bill Committee and try to convince them of their case. The MPs can then advance that case by amendments to the bill. However, the government is even less willing to accept substantial amendments to the Finance Bill than it is in the case of other legislation, although disquiet among government backbenchers can cause changes, whether following defeat on a vote, as in the case of the scrapping of the second tranche of VAT on domestic fuel in December 1994, or by the government altering its proposals in advance of possible defeat, as in the halving of the increase in petrol duty which was proposed in the 1981 budget. Less dramatic changes also regularly occur as a result of debate on the Finance Bill in standing committee.

The government is dependent at each stage of the Finance Bill procedure on maintaining a majority in support of its proposals. An individual proposal comes before the House on as many as three occasions when it can be put to the vote. Of course, government party MPs who are unhappy about elements of the budget package will think carefully before attempting seriously to defeat these proposals because they understand that the budget *is* a package and voting to decrease revenue in one area necessarily implies voting to increase revenue elsewhere – or to reduce public expenditure. In the same way as MPs do not have the resources to take on the Treasury over the details of public spending in their consideration of the estimates, so the House of Commons does not have the ability to draft an alternative budget. This does not prevent occasional – and sometimes effective – rebellion by government backbenchers.

Scrutiny of public money in general

We have described the separate – and elaborate – procedures which the House of Commons uses to deal with the estimates and with the Budget and Finance Bill. In both of these areas control theoretically rests with the Commons, though effectively the initiative for and details of budget and expenditure are set by the government. There are other fundamental reasons why it cannot be said that the House of Commons exercises full financial supervision.

As we saw on page 158 supply expenditure only makes up around 70 per cent of public expenditure in total. The other areas are subject to much less parliamentary control, if any. For example, local authorities' expenditure is only partially controlled by annual debates on reports, not subject to amendment, which set the level of the extra finance government provides the local authorities. Furthermore, long-term expenditure is not easily controlled by Parliament, even if it comes within supply procedures based on annual figures, nor are the estimates suitable tools for judging efficiency and effectiveness in public spending.

On the income side, the 1981 Procedure Committee commented:

A substantial part of the cash disbursements of the government is met from loans raised by the government, and not from taxation authorised by the House. A variable but sometimes substantial part of the government expenditure is met by creating new money through the mechanism of short term government indebtedness to the banks. These means of financing government expenditure do not come before the House at all, still less does the House exercise any control over them.

The Conservative government has also raised money through asset sales – privatisation of British Telecom, for example. Although Parliament must approve the legislation authorising privatisation, it has no control over the price at which the asset is sold and therefore of the income it generates. Despite the unified budget, Britain is also unusual in having no formal connection in its parliamentary processes between control of expenditure and control of the way in which the government obtains its income.

It would always be possible to devise new procedures which could re-assert the House of Commons' 'power of the purse'. However, these procedures would take up a great deal of time in the House and in committee, and MPs would need the back-up of better resources if they were to be responsible for alternative estimates and alternative budgets. The budget and expenditure would need to be better integrated, and the variety of ways in which different elements of public expenditure and of income-raising are within – or outside – parliamentary control would need to be regularised. There is little evidence of major pressure for far-reaching reforms of this nature. Parliament is not really equipped to do the work of the Treasury.

What recent years have seen is not so much control but the use of the House and its committees to inform public debate about financial matters. The Committee of Public Accounts' traditional work of monitoring value for money has been supplemented by the departmental select committees' examination of the spending of the departments under their supervision. Although this work has increased across all committees, who seem to have found the departmental reports reasonably user-friendly, the Treasury and Civil Service Committee has a special responsibility. It has evolved the practice of holding macro-economic enquiries each year in which evidence is taken from Treasury officials and ministers. Although the Treasury and Civil Service Committee has been reluctant to make recommendations in the areas which are within the responsibilities of other committees, these annual enquiries have been of great importance in the public scrutiny of the way the government conducts its financial affairs. Nevertheless, the committee is holding the Treasury's work up to examination, it is not pretending to devise an alternative detailed macroeconomic policy.

The Treasury Committee's reports have also been important for the general debates which the Commons have on the government's financial policies – whether in specific debates on the budget or the summer economic forecast or in more general debates on the Queen's Speech or on appropriate bills and government and opposition motions. There is also the monthly Treasury question time and the twice-weekly Prime Minister's question time where matters relating to the economy are frequently raised.

The formal backbone of the financial procedure – approving the estimates and the Consolidated Fund Acts and Appropriation Act – gives Parliament, and in particular the Commons, its ultimate authority over the government, and is the basis for the theory of ministerial accountability. The House of Commons *can* throw out the budget; it *can* refuse ministers supply. But these are long-stop powers which are the ultimate guarantee that government must respect the will of the democratically elected Parliament.

Of course, the battle is not normally constitutional, fought between government and Parliament, but political, where the combatants are the political parties. Whether more should be spent on defence and less on social security is a question which divides parties, not Parliament from government. On a day-to-day basis, the House of Commons may cause alterations in small parts of the budget package and may even one day vote against an individual estimate, but its main role is to act, through its committees and in its Chamber, as a sounding-board for the nation in its general scrutiny of government finance and economic policy.

CHAPTER 8

The inquisitorial function: parliamentary questions, MPs' letters and petitions

What are questions?

Erskine May tells us that 'the purpose of a question is to obtain information or to press for action'. As has already been made clear, the people who have the information – and the ability to act on it – are government ministers, and it is they who have to answer questions. Some parliamentary questions are asked (or – in parliamentary language – 'tabled' – or 'put down') which are answered by MPs who are not ministers but who speak on behalf of bodies like the House of Commons Commission or the Church Commissioners, but the vast majority of questions are tabled by backbenchers to ministers and answered by them. Many government supporters might like to ask questions of the leaders of opposition parties, but they cannot do so by means of the parliamentary question system. Questions, then, are part of the process by which the government is held to account. They are one of the best known, but misunderstood, features of the House of Commons, and it is on the procedures in that House that we will concentrate. Questions are also asked in the House of Lords, but their numbers are small compared with the Commons. Lords do not, however, labour under all the rules about questioning which restrict MPs, and which we will now describe.

Rules about questions

MPs are not free to table anything they wish. Questions must cover only areas for which ministers are directly responsible. This is not always clear-cut. There is no doubt that the Ministry of Defence, for example, is responsible for the Trident nuclear submarine. But a Conservative MP wanting to deride Labour Party policy on Trident would not be allowed by the rules to ask 'whether the government will assess the threat to Britain's security which is posed by the Labour Party's Trident policy', even though the minister would be happy to answer. Ministers are responsible to Parliament only for justifying their own policy, not for attacking the policy of the opposition. For that, so the theory goes, they are responsible to their party. But if the questioner asks 'whether the government will assess the benefits to Britain of the government's Trident programme', then the question *does* ask the minister about a matter for which he or she is responsible and the minister's reply may well take a side-swipe at the policy of the Labour Party. There are whole areas of public life where ministers are not responsible to Parliament – for example, the decisions of the courts, the day-to-day operations of the police, and the activities of local authorities. All these bodies do things which cause public concern, but the MP will not be able to table questions in Parliament to try to deal with that concern.

As well as this fundamental rule about ministerial responsibility, there are many other restrictions on questioning. No questions may be asked about matters which are subject to action in the courts (the *sub judice* rule). This rule helps to guarantee a fair trial, not one prejudiced by earlier statements in Parliament. There are also subjects about which ministers decide themselves not to answer questions, either because they think it would divulge commercially confidential information or because it would be too expensive or 'not in the public interest' to do so. In 1994, ministers could decide that providing an answer would be disproportionately expensive if doing so would cost over £450. The first ruling made by a Speaker about questions, more than 200 years ago, was that ministers did not *need* to reply to questions, and subsequent Speakers have always refused to comment on the way in which ministers answer – or avoid answering. Despite this, many backbenchers feel that it is unfair that ministers can decide without any independent check to refuse to answer particular questions which everyone accepts come within their responsibilities. Obvious examples of areas where probing may be undesirable are defence secrets or the detailed work of the security services, but there are many less obvious areas where ministers have consistently refused to answer questions. Examples include the tax affairs of individual companies, the identities of licensed vivisection establishments, the quantities of particular drugs prescribed in the National Health Service, the destination of armaments sold to overseas countries, the reasons why particular individuals were or were not appointed as magistrates, or the predicted level of unemployment.

In the case of questions they *do* answer, ministers can give whatever reply they think appropriate. For example, in one exchange (*Hansard*, 28 February 1984) a Labour back-bencher asked the Chancellor of the Exchequer 'if he will publish in the Official Report, or place in the library, the letter he has sent recently to the banks proposing the imposition of the composite rate of interest for interest-bearing personal accounts'. The minister's reply was 'In the course of his duties as Chancellor, my Right Hon. Friend has confidential exchanges with many bodies and it is not his practice to make them public'. The MP had heard a rumour about a change in policy which was indeed later announced in the budget. He was concerned and asked a question. The question was answered, but the answer avoided the specific point raised altogether. It can hardly be described as revealing!

There have regularly been concerns about evasive answers to parliamentary questions, but governments have always maintained that they are scrupulous in their replies. In 1994 the Prime Minister was asked (in a parliamentary question) what his policy was on 'providing in full the information sought by honourable Members in parliamentary questions'. His reply was as follows

Except for matters which are confidential or on which successive Governments have refused to answer questions upon grounds of public policy, or when a reply is not given on grounds of disproportionate cost, answers should give the information sought and should be accurate and truthful and not misleading.

Accurate, truthful and non-misleading answers may not, of course, reveal the whole story.

If an MP does ask about a matter for which a minister is responsible and which the minister has not refused to answer, there are still more restrictions of a technical kind. A question cannot argue a case. A question must not criticise the royal family or judiciary. A question may not ask a minister to comment on a press report, or to interpret the law or comment on the legality of an action, even of one of the minister's civil servants. A question cannot be asked if it repeats a question already answered unless there are reasonable grounds for supposing the answer may have changed.

Oral questions

Questions are not all answered orally in the House at question time. The great majority are only replied to in writing. In the 1992–93 Session, for example, no fewer than 63,684 questions were asked, of which just 7,134 were oral questions. And of the oral questions, only 3,141 received oral answers in the House. The rest received written replies.

Until the beginning of the twentieth century, written questions did not exist and there was no time restriction on oral answers. Even after time restrictions were introduced, almost all questions tabled for oral answer received oral replies. But after 1918 more and more oral questions were tabled, and the 'supplementary question' developed. Question time was not long enough to accommodate all questions and supplementaries and procedures were developed to share question time among ministers and among MPs with some degree of fairness.

These days, oral questions are answered from about 2.35 p.m. until 3.30 p.m. on each Monday, Tuesday, Wednesday and Thursday. The Order Paper sets out the questions tabled for the day in numerical order. The Speaker calls the first, the member rises and says 'Number 1, Madam Speaker' and the minister gives a reply drafted by the civil service. The Speaker then calls the member who tabled the question to ask a supplementary question. This is a question related to the original question and which might, typically, challenge the minister's answer, or congratulate him or her on it. It is through the supplementaries that question time comes alive, especially as other members are called from both sides of the House to ask further supplementary questions, before the Speaker decides to move on to the second question, when the procedure is repeated. An average of three or four minutes is spent on each question, so there is no opportunity for detailed and sustained interrogation. The minister is briefed by civil servants about the potential supplementaries but has to think quickly to respond to awkward points, and it is here that backbenchers hope to shine on the occasions when they catch a minister unawares or are able to expose an area of policy which is embarrassing to the government.

Part of the Order Paper for 1 November 1994, containing the questions set down for answer that day is reproduced below:

QUESTIONS FOR ORAL ANSWER

* 1 **Sir Thomas Arnold** (Hazel Grove):   To ask the Secretary of State for Education, if she will make a statement about nursery education.

* 2 **Mr Roger Knapman** (Stroud):   To ask the Secretary of State for Education, what has been the change in spending on books and equipment for schools since 1979.

* 3 **Mr Tony Banks** (Newham North West):   To ask the Secretary of State for Education, which countries of the European Union have a higher percentage of under-fives in nursery education than Britain.

* 4 **Mr Geoffrey Clifton-Brown** (Cirencester and Tewkesbury):   To ask the Secretary of State for Education, how many pupils are now being educated in self-governing grant maintained schools; and what was the same figure one year ago.

* 5 **Mr Peter Viggers** (Gosport):   To ask the Secretary of State for Education, what are the latest figures she has for the number of 16 year olds participating in part- or full-time education; and what were the comparable figures for five years ago.

* 6 **Mr Peter Kilfoyle** (Liverpool, Walton):   To ask the Secretary of State for Education, how many schools have opted for grant maintained status in the last year; and what was the figure in the previous year.

* 7 **Mrs Margaret Ewing** (Moray):   To ask the Secretary of State for Education, what steps she is taking to ensure equality of research funding throughout further and higher education establishments; and if she will make a statement.

* 8 **Mr Oliver Heald** (North Hertfordshire):   To ask the Secretary of State for Education, what are the key objectives being sought under the National Education and Training Targets Initiative.

* 9 **Mr Tim Rathbone** (Lewes):   To ask the Secretary of State for Education, what discussions she has had with private providers of nursery schooling in preparation for the introduction of the government scheme.

* 10 **Sir David Madel** (South West Bedfordshire):   To ask the Secretary of State for Education, what representations she has received from Bedfordshire County Council for increases in capital expenditure on maintained schools for the period after 1994–95; and if she will make a statement.

* 11 **Mr John Whittingdale** (South Colchester and Maldon):   To ask the Secretary of State for Education, what action she is taking to combat drug abuse in schools.

* 12 **Mr Stephen Byers** (Wallsend):   To ask the Secretary of State for Education, what percentage of primary school inspections planned by OFSTED for this term will not take place during this term.

* 13 **Mr David Evennett** (Erith and Crayford):   To ask the Secretary of State for Education, what steps she is taking to improve the levels of discipline in schools.

* 14 **Mr James Clappison** (Hertsmere):   To ask the Secretary of State for Education, what proportion of young people are now entering higher education; and what was the comparable figure 10 years ago.

* 15 **Mr Matthew Taylor** (Truro):   To ask the Secretary of State for Education, if she will make a statement on the level of capital expenditure approved for schools in Cornwall.

* 16 **Jane Kennedy** (Liverpool, Broadgreen): To ask the Secretary of State for Education, what assessment she has made of the effect of the reduction in the worth in real terms of student grant on the welfare of students.

* 17 **Mr Roy Hughes** (Newport East): To ask the Secretary of State for Education, what discussions she has had with teachers' unions concerning pay levels in the profession.

* 18 **Mr Tim Devlin** (Stockton South): To ask the Secretary of State for Education, what steps she is taking to recruit lay inspectors of schools.

* 19 **Jean Corston** (Bristol East): To ask the Secretary of State for Education, what measures she is taking to ensure proper accountability of the use of public money by higher education institutions.

* 20 **Mr Spencer Batiste** (Elmet): To ask the Secretary of State for Education, what steps she is taking to ensure uniformity in the standards of degrees between universities.

* 21 **Mr Richard Ottaway** (Croydon South): To ask the Secretary of State for Education, what support she proposes to give to those schools that wish to develop a specialism in music, art, languages or other areas of the curriculum.

* 22 **Mr Richard Burden** (Birmingham, Northfields): To ask the Secretary of State for Education, what plans she has to improve the funding available for nursery education.

* 23 **Mr Matthew Carrington** (Fulham): To ask the Secretary of State for Education, what is the latest estimate she has of the amount of money being tied up in maintaining surplus school places; and what steps she is taking to reduce the number of surplus places.

* 24 **Mr Andrew Miller** (Ellesmere Port and Neston): To ask the Secretary of State for Education, what representations she has received regarding the Student Loans Company.

* 25 **Sir Anthony Grant** (South West Cambridgeshire): To ask the Secretary of State for Education, what steps she intends to take to ensure that all children aged between five and 16 years play competitive sports in schools.

* 26 **Mr Simon Hughes** (Southwark and Bermondsey): To ask the Secretary of State for Education, what is the most accurate assessment she can make of (a) the number of parents who secure for their children their first choice of nursery, primary and secondary schools and (b) the satisfaction of parents about the current systems for choosing nursery, primary and secondary schools.

* 27 **Mr Nick Raynsford** (Greenwich):   To ask the Secretary of State for Education, what assessment she has made of the number of potential students in further or higher education who have been or are deterred from undertaking or completing a course for financial reasons.

* 28 **Mr William O'Brien** (Normanton):   To ask the Secretary of State for Education, if she will make a statement on the percentage of three and four year old children receiving full time nursery provision.

* 29 **Mr Archy Kirkwood** (Roxburgh and Berwickshire):   To ask the Secretary of State for Education, what representations she has received on the financial hardship experienced by students in receipt of student loans; and if she will make a statement.

* 30 **Mr Jerry Hayes** (Harlow):   To ask the Secretary of State for Education, if she will retain the assisted places scheme.

Questions to the Prime Minister will start at 3.15 p.m.

* Q1 **Mr George Stevenson** (Stoke on Trent South):   To ask the Prime Minister, if he will list his official engagements for Tuesday 1st November.

* Q2 **Mr Mike Hall** (Warrington South):   To ask the Prime Minister, if he will list his official engagements for Tuesday 1st November.

* Q3 **Mr Geoffrey Clifton-Brown** (Cirencester and Tewkesbury):   To ask the Prime Minister, if he will list his official engagements for Tuesday 1st November.

* Q4 **Sir Michael Neubert** (Romford):   To ask the Prime Minister, if he will list his official engagements for Tuesday 1st November.

* Q5 **Mr Geoffrey Hoon** (Ashfield):   To ask the Prime Minister, if he will list his official engagements for Tuesday 1st November.

* Q6 **Mr David Evans** (Welwyn Hatfield):   To ask the Prime Minister, if he will list his official engagements for Tuesday 1st November.

* Q7 **Mr Jim Cunningham** (Coventry South East): To ask the Prime Minister, if he will list his official engagements for Tuesday 1st November.

* Q8 **Mrs Angela Knight** (Erewash):   To ask the Prime Minister, if he will list his official engagements for Tuesday 1st November.

* Q9 **Mr Alan W. Williams** (Carmarthen): To ask the Prime Minister, if he will list his official engagements for Tuesday 1st November.

We also reproduce an extract from *Hansard* which deals with the last question to the Secretary of State for Education which was actually answered orally on 1 November, and the first question answered orally by the Prime Minister.

14. **Mr Clappison**: To ask the Secretary of State for Education what proportion of young people are now entering higher education; and what was the comparable figure 10 years ago.

Mr. Boswell: The Government's policies have led to record student numbers in higher education. More than 30 per cent. of young people entered higher education in 1993, compared with around one in eight 10 years ago.

Mr. Clappison: Will my hon. Friend join me in welcoming the fact that Britain how has a higher graduation rate than many of our European Union competitors and that 50 per cent. more students now gain a first degree than in 1979? Does my hon. Friend agree that instead of carping, Opposition Members and their Commission on Social Justice would have done better to study the successful Conservative policies which have enabled that to take place?

Mr. Boswell: My hon. Friend is entirely right in pointing to our achievements in that direction and, in particular, the fact that we now have the highest graduation rate in Europe. That does not entirely transmit itself into the Opposition Benches. Every time an Opposition Member comes up with a sensible proposition, someone tends to end up being sacked.

Mr. Bryan Davies: After that orgy of self-congratulation, and after Prime Minister's Question Time, will the Minister take his fellow ministerial team to No. 10 Downing Street to discuss a petition received by the Prime Minister this morning, presented by my hon. Friend the Member for Sheffield, Brightside (Mr. Blunkett) and myself, on behalf of the higher education sector—students, staff, administrators and vice-chancellors—protesting at the under-funding of higher education by the present Government?

Mr. Boswell: I congratulate the hon. Gentleman on the reten-tion of his somewhat dangerous portfolio. He has never told the House what proposals he would make for the resourcing of higher education. I can tell the House that, in the last public expenditure survey, we were able to produce a real terms increase, to a record level, in the proportion and amount of higher education funding in this country. We have nothing to be ashamed of. We have the highest student numbers and the best resourced higher education in our history.

Mr. Batiste: Are the Government committed to the principle of uniformity of standards across each class of degree across all universities in the country? If so, how does the Minister intend to ensure that the principle is observed in practice?

Mr. Boswell: We are absolutely committed to the maintenance of high standards. It is, of course, primarily for the academic community, through its higher education quality council, to ensure that degrees mean what they say and are uniform throughout the various institutions, and that is a matter to which it is giving the closest attention.

PRIME MINISTER

Engagements

Q1. **Mr. Stevenson**:   To ask the Prime Minister if he will list his official engagements for Tuesday 1 November.

The Prime Minister (Mr. John Major):   This morning I had meetings with ministerial colleagues and others. In addition to my duties in this House, I shall be having further meetings later today.

Mr. Stevenson: Will The Prime Minister confirm the complete absence of any mention of privatisation of the Post Office in the last Tory party manifesto? Is he aware of the complete absence of any public support for that latest piece of Government dogma? Will he now take this opportunity to do the country a service and rescue the President of the Board of Trade by withdrawing that absurd proposal?

The Prime Minister: As the whole House knows, we are considering the results of the consultation exercise that was launched in the summer. *[Interruption.]* I am surprised to hear Opposition Members scoffing. I thought that in the new politics the Labour party favoured consultation.

Mr. Brooke: If Mr. Al Fayed requires a forgery from *The Guardian* to resolve his conscience, what, in my right hon. Friend's mind, does that tell us about Mr. Al Fayed or *The Guardian*, or both?

The Prime Minister: I think that many conclusions may be drawn from that, some of which may well be drawn from the investigation that the Serjeant at Arms himself is carrying out into the affair. Certainly, whatever is uncovered I doubt whether it will be to the credit of the principal people concerned.

Mr. Blair: To return to the Prime Minister's response to my hon. Friend the Member for Stoke-on-Trent, South (Mr. Stevenson), on Post Office privatisation, there is more than a whiff of retreat in the air. If the Prime Minister does retreat—*[Interruption.]* Is he aware that if he does retreat on that he will be acting wisely, because if he is going to consult the British people, the vast majority of them—and, I believe, a majority in this House—want a modern Post Office with greater commercial freedom, delivering a cheap and reliable service, and that the best way of achieving that is to retain it in public ownership, run it as a public service and serve the public interest?

The Prime Minister: I can certainly share with the right. hon. Gentleman the wish to make the Post Office business strong, competitive and able to deliver the services that people need. Of course, a large number of improvements have been made over the past few years, most of them opposed at the time by Opposition Members. In 1981, we separated out Telecom and introduced the £1 monopoly limit, introducing competition and allowing a thriving courier industry to develop. In 1990, we sold Girobank. All those changes were opposed by the Opposition, who now take credit for the success of the Post Office as a result of our policies.

Sir Archibald Hamilton: Does my right hon. Friend share my concern about the actions of Mr. Preston of *The Guardian*? Not only has he been using House of Commons writing paper to forge letters; he has been forging other people's signatures—and this from a man who is on the Press Complaints Commission. Should he not resign from that body at once?

The Prime Minister: Over many years, *The Guardian* and its present editor have from time to time thundered against general standards in public life. It is, of course, the right of the press to do that; I simply invite its members to observe their own standards.

Mr. Ashdown: But is the Prime Minister satisfied with the promptness, accuracy and frankness with which his Chief Secretary to the Treasury has responded to questions over past weeks and months? Are those the standards by which he would wish his Government and their Ministers to be recognised?

The Prime Minister: The right hon. Gentleman, and some other hon. Members, may be wholly satisfied with their own blameless pasts in every respect. My right hon. Friend the Chief Secretary has made the position entirely clear, and I accept his word.

Sir Wyn Roberts: Does my right hon. Friend agree that so-called investigative journalism has sunk to a new all-time low? Does he also agree that, if a newspaper is found to have used the name of the House to give false authority to its activities, that newspaper deserves to lose the respect and confidence of the House?

The Prime Minister: I believe that a diverse and wholly independent press is a very important protector of our system of democracy. I hope that there is no dispute about that.

What is particularly sad is the casual abuse of what were once high and expected standards. If it is now commonly accepted in journalism that the end justifies any means, I believe that journalism will regret stooping to that standard. I hope that this is not the case; I believe the honest, factual journalism remains important to our democratic system. Systematic deception, fraud and collusion are certainly not what we expect from a free press.

Education questions and questions to the Prime Minister were answered on 1 November because it was a Tuesday. Each oral question day is allotted on a rota to one major department of State. On Mondays, the Welsh Office and the Departments of Transport, Social Security and National Heritage answer questions; on Tuesdays the Departments of Health, Education, Defence, and Employment answer; on Wednesdays it is the turn of the Scottish Office, Foreign and Commonwealth Office and the Departments of Trade and Industry and Environment, and on Thursday, of the Home Office, the Northern Ireland Office, the Treasury and the Ministry of Agriculture, Fisheries and Food. Each of these Departments thus answers questions once every four weeks. On Tuesdays and Thursdays the major department answering gives way at 3.15 p.m. to the Prime Minister, who is the only minister to answer questions more often than once every four weeks – he answers twice every week.

On each day MPs can only ask two oral questions each, and these must be addressed to two different departments. This limit goes only a small way to reduce to manageable proportions the number of oral questions tabled. To introduce a further element of rationing, MPs have to follow a procedure which only allows them to give notice of an oral question from 10 a.m. ten sitting days (normally a calendar fortnight) before it is due to be answered. So the questions for 1 November were tabled from 10 a.m. on the 18 October. And to have any chance of an oral reply, a question must be tabled before 5 p.m. on the first day tabling is allowed. This is because all questions received between 10 a.m. and 5 p.m. ten sitting days in advance are shuffled, no longer physically, but by computer, and appear on the Order Paper in the random order determined. The modern pressure on question numbers means that almost all questions which actually receive an oral answer are at least a fortnight old, and in some cases after a period when the House has had a holiday adjournment, rather older than that.

Fortnight-old oral questions cannot be burningly topical and are therefore usually relatively bland. If, for example, a dockers' strike is looming, the tabled question might be 'if the minister will make a statement on the dock industry'. The member hopes, when called, to be able to ask a topical supplementary, perhaps about an incident which happened that day. MPs started to table very uninformative questions asking ministers when they were next proposing to meet the Chairmen of nationalised industries, or EC Commissioners or others and nothing more, but the Speaker has ruled that these questions are too uninformative. Now oral questions must contain at least a small clue to the interests of the questioner, but it need not be more than 'if the minister will meet the Rail Regulator to discuss investment in the railways' – and the supplementary could be anything from the provision of buffet services, through the electrification of the line from Edinburgh to London to the Channel tunnel.

Some oral questions do still ask for information, but in the main they are pegs for mini-discussions, lasting just a couple of minutes, on issues which are part of the adversarial business of politics. Question time comes in the prime time of the parliamentary day, and is well attended by the press. It is not dominated by the frontbenchers, and any MP who attends has a fairly good chance of being called to put a supplementary. Putting down a question, or asking a supplementary, does not require as much work as writing a speech or preparing for a select committee, and each question time is devoted to a particular area of government policy in which particular MPs may specialise. It is understandably popular, but it is more to do with advancing the political argument than monitoring the work of government by careful questioning. A few minutes per question makes for adversarial argument rather than inquisitorial investigation.

Many MPs devise and table their own oral questions, but syndicates have also arisen in both major parties through which groups of MPs arrange to have questions drafted collectively – though they must still be physically tabled by individual MPs. The growth of syndicates has played a large part in the growth in the number of questions. Until very recently, all oral questions which were tabled were also printed, though many of those who had tabled an oral question, especially through the syndicates, were not so much interested in the answer as in taking part in the political argument that question time provides. On many days, over 200 questions were printed, though barely 20 would receive oral replies. In the case of questions to the Prime Minister, the numbers tabled for each Tuesday and Thursday rose from under 50 in 1978 to almost 200 in 1989. Nowadays only the first 30 questions tabled to the Departments answering first on Mondays, Tuesdays and Thursdays, the first 40 to the Departments answering first on Wednesdays, and the first ten to other ministers (including the Prime

Minister, but excluding the Chancellor of the Duchy of Lancaster, to whom the limit is 15) are treated as valid notices of questions. This has cut down enormously on the wasted time and effort taken in printing (and preparing answers to) questions which had no hope of an oral reply.

Since the beginning of Session 1994–95, occasional oral question times are held in the Scottish Grand Committee (see page 244).

Prime Minister's questions

It is not surprising that the fifteen minutes each Tuesday and Thursday when the Prime Minister answers is popular. It is the time when the adversarial nature of the parliamentary process is at its most obvious. The value of this half-hour is hotly debated. The House is noisy and rumbustious – when Prime Minister's question time was first broadcast many listeners wrote to the then Speaker to complain about the noise and barracking. Everyone is looking out for slip-ups or unguarded remarks, whether from the Prime Minister or opposition leader. Those who believe in confrontational politics tend to value Prime Minister's question time, and those who favour consensus look a little askance at what has been described as 'ritual confrontation'. What no one should expect is that the questions and answers in Prime Minister's question time should be simply a straightforward information-gathering exercise.

In the past, Prime Ministers tended to refuse to answer questions which dealt with matters under the control of a departmental minister. These were transferred to the responsible ministers, and answered by them and not by the Prime Minister. This led to the development of the transfer-proof questions, the most famous variants of which were questions which asked the Prime Minister what his official engagements were for the day, or if he would visit a particular town. These related so personally to the Prime Minister that he could not easily transfer them. The MP's supplementary question could then raise any issue under the sun – could the Prime Minister find time in his day to consider famine in Bangladesh or the British steel industry or could he visit the MP's constituency to see the effects of unemployment or the ravages of Dutch elm disease. (These questions would have been transferred to the Secretaries of State for Foreign Affairs, Trade and Industry, Employment and the Environment respectively if they had set out their real purpose in the tabled questions rather than in the supplementaries.) Mrs Thatcher announced that she would not normally transfer oral questions and John Major has followed her lead, but this has done little to suppress these questions about official engagements or visits. For example, in February 1994, of the 80 oral questions to the Prime Minister which were printed, all but three were in the form 'If he will list his official engagements for the day', and of these three, one was an 'official visit' question. MPs have seen the value of surprise and topicality which these 'shot in the dark' questions allow them. Effectively, the list of questions to the Prime Minister is little more than the announcement of who has won a ballot.

Some MPs have grumbled about this, and John Major made it plain in June 1994 that he would welcome a reform of Prime Minister's questions with questions of a substantive nature tabled by MPs, possibly the day before they were asked. What is certainly true is that MPs would not be happy to lose the chance open to every backbencher to engage the Prime Minister himself twice a week in matters of topical political concern. Although we no longer know the numbers who enter the ballot, there is a good deal of envy for those who achieve a place in the top ten, and great competition to emulate them.

Not that Prime Minister's question time serves the interests of backbenchers alone. The leader of the opposition almost invariably is called to ask two or three supplementaries, and leaders of the other parties have a good chance of being called. The person who frequently does best out of the twice weekly exchanges is the one who speaks the most – the Prime Minister. Prime Ministers in the past have spoken about their anxiety in facing question time, but a politician who is skilful enough to become Prime Minister is able to exploit question time to his or her advantage, by stating and re-stating their own policy and by attacking their opponents' views and so getting through to the electorate. What is seen is a kind of political gladiators' match, with the Prime Minister equipped with the heavy weapon of power and the shield of civil servants' briefing (and often helped by sympathetic questioning from MPs on his or her side of the House), while the leader of the opposition has to manoeuvre more nimbly.

Private notice questions

Often events occur at short notice which MPs think are so important that they should be considered immediately in the House. The government itself will sometimes initiate statements which are followed by supplementary questions, and MPs also apply for emergency adjournment debates. These procedures are described elsewhere. Another opportunity to raise important topical issues is by means of private notice questions (known as PNQs). These are questions which the Speaker considers so urgent that she allows them to be asked without written notice at 3.30 p.m.

Applications are made before noon, and the Speaker decides soon afterwards. Very little warning is given to the department, whose minister must attend the House a few hours later and make a public statement on matters which can sometimes be very delicate. In many ways, PNQs can be seen as statements which are not initiated by the government.

The discretion of individual Speakers to allow or disallow proposed PNQs means that the number in each session varies considerably. Only seven were permitted in the 1982–83 session, for example, but a different Speaker allowed 48 in the (admittedly longer) 1983–84 session. In the two calendar years following the 1992 General Election, 31 PNQs were allowed. Some of these dealt with disasters such as the floods in Wales in December 1992 and in Scotland in January 1993, while a number arose from developments in the war in Bosnia or the aftermath of the Gulf War. But many were more political, especially those which concerned incidents which had arisen in the national health service. The majority of PNQs are asked by opposition frontbenchers – all but six of the 31 in the two years up to April 1994, for example. Of these six, just two were asked by government party MPs. A particular additional type of PNQ is the one to the Leader of the House allowed each Thursday, asking what the proposed business for the coming week will be. It is almost a more relaxed extension of the Prime Minister's question time, with topical matters raised by backbenchers with a senior minister by the device of asking whether the Commons' business can be altered to include discussion of the matter which concerns the MP asking the supplementary.

Written questions

We have already seen that most questions receive a written answer, some because they were not reached in oral question time, but the majority because they were intended for written answer. Of the 63,684 questions in the 1992–93 Session, 56,550 were for written answer – an average of 236 a day.

Written questions are divided into two types – ordinary written questions and questions tabled for answer on a named day. The latter type were known until 1993 as 'priority written' questions. However, there was no objective standard by which priority could be judged, and in 1992–93, no fewer than 42 per cent of the written questions tabled were priority written questions, a figure paralleled in previous sessions. This high level of use of the priority system led to concern that MPs were indiscriminately marking their questions as priorities when they did not really warrant urgent replies. Consequently, the priority label was removed. In reality, priority questions had become little more than what they are now called –

questions for answer on a particular day. This was because priority questions tabled with a very short period of notice (48 hours was the minimum) often received 'holding replies' along the lines of 'I shall reply as soon as possible'. The substantive reply was then delayed for days or even weeks. The advantage of tabling questions for a named day is that MPs can be sure of an answer on a day they choose – perhaps because they have tabled a series of questions or because they have a meeting the following day. With ordinary written questions, they do not have this security. It remains possible to choose a named day for reply just 48 hours after tabling, so named day questions can still be used to elicit urgent answers.

Written answers serve a whole variety of purposes. If we take a random day, 3 May 1994, we find 294 questions due for answer. Many of these were intended purely to gain information, perhaps to help the MP pursue a political case (for example, the question from a Labour MP tabled to each government department on the costs of consultancy fees) or perhaps to help an MP in a case he or she is making on behalf of an interest group (for example, a question from a Conservative MP on the value of the music recording industry for the United Kingdom economy). Other questions may ask for information, but make a point in themselves: for example, a question asking for the level of pensions paid to war widows in a number of countries including Britain was partly intended to demonstrate that British war widows were unfavourably treated. On 3 May, a number of questions dealt with constituency issues, or issues which arose from constituency concerns, ranging from planning permission for telecommunications masts and support for the Taunton apple industry to council house sales in Nottinghamshire, defective building in Flint and European funding for East Anglia. Some questions raised minor, but important, matters which the MP would be unlikely to raise on the floor of the House – diseases of pigs, for example. Others followed up earlier answers to questions (an MP wanted to know what precisely a Foreign Office Minister had meant when he had replied to an earlier question that he wanted the European Community to be more accountable) while others raised issues (the suspension of two civil servants in Plymouth, for example) for which the minister was responsible but about which he or she might have known nothing. Finally, there are always the purely political questions: when an MP asks the Prime Minister if he will dismiss a particular minister, the questioner would be as surprised as anyone if the answer were 'yes'.

One particular advantage of written questions over oral questions is that they can be pursued much more relentlessly. A series of written questions can follow up in detail, almost as a lawyer would in a trial, the precise conduct of government policy in a particular area. One of the best exponents of this technique has been the Labour MP Tam Dalyell, who has asked hundreds of questions about the Falklands and Gulf Wars and their aftermaths, as well as on many other topics.

Written questions are often tabled (perhaps two or three times each day, and many more times before holiday adjournments) by arrangement with ministers to allow a written statement to be printed in *Hansard* in reply. This statement will usually be on an issue which is thought not to merit an oral statement. These questions are sometimes called 'planted questions'.

The value of questions

'Obtaining information' and 'pressing for action' were the basic objectives of questions according to *Erskine May*. We have seen another purpose – of advancing the political argument. Generally this is the purpose of oral questions, while the traditional purposes are still the principal objectives of written questions. We have seen that 'obtaining information' is not always effective. Governments give half-answers or refuse to answer particular questions at all. 'Pressing for action' is also not always effective: an MP may find writing to a minister or lobbying in some other, more private, way has better results.

Despite their disadvantages, MPs still ask questions though different MPs put different values on them. In recent years, about one in five MPs has asked fewer than 10 questions, while a small minority of MPs have asked over 400. In the year to 28 February 1994, one MP asked 983 questions and one no fewer than 1323. Broadly speaking new MPs ask more questions than senior backbenchers, and opposition MPs more than government supporters, but there are some new opposition MPs who ask very few questions, and some senior government supporters who ask a good many.

Questions are a useful weapon in the backbenchers' armoury. In oral question time, the frontbenchers do play a much larger role than they did twenty or thirty years ago, but Speakers have ensured that they do not dominate, even if some backbench contributions are made in co-ordination with the front benches, especially at Prime Minister's question time. Written questions are almost entirely in backbenchers' hands. MPs can ask questions without their party's approval, about matters which interest them individually. If they have the inclination, they can try to ask an oral question four days a week, enter the ballot for Prime Minister's questions every time and table half a dozen written questions every single day. Alternatively they may ask only a couple of questions a year and still do their job effectively by other means. It is up to each individual.

Questions achieve publicity, most obviously at oral question time, but also through the publication of written answers in *Hansard*: ministers' answers are on the public record. Perhaps most valuable of all, questions are (with one important exception, which we will return to later) answered by ministers. This is not just a statement of the obvious. Inside a government department, each parliamentary question is put into its own file with its draft answer and background briefing material. This file goes upwards through the civil service hierarchy, and eventually will be seen by the minister who will approve the draft answer, or perhaps ask for changes or further information. Run-of-the-mill 'political' questions are not going to cause the minister much thought, but questions which deal with small, constituency matters or which expose anomalies in government policy or unnecessary government expenditure may make the minister ensure that policy is changed to meet the MP's grievance. Ministers are held publicly to account for their answers, and are not going to endorse blindly their department's policy if they can see merits in an MP's case. The minister, not just officials, will consider the need for better geriatric services in a particular city, or a pedestrian crossing at an accident blackspot, or better consular provision in a popular Spanish resort, or more aid to goose farmers, or whatever the concern of the MP tabling the question is.

The important exception to the rule that questions are answered by ministers comes in the case of written questions which deal with matters within the responsibility of executive agencies. Although these agencies remain staffed by civil servants and are ultimately answerable to ministers, their day-to-day workings have been placed at arm's length from ministerial involvement. To emphasise this, the Conservative government decided that ministers would reply to written questions which raised issues for which agencies were responsible by saying simply that the minister would ask the chief executive of the agency concerned to write a letter to the MP. This would constitute the substantive reply to the question. Initially, the texts of these letters were not published in *Hansard*, but following mounting pressure from those concerned at the apparent dilution in ministerial responsibility to Parliament, it was decided in autumn 1992 to include the text of chief executives' letters in *Hansard*. It has been noticeable that chief executives' replies are often fuller than ministerial replies, and for this reason the change may have improved the quality of information MPs receive. However, there remain those who are concerned that an area has grown up for which ministers are responsible, but for which they do not always account directly to the House of Commons by replying to parliamentary questions themselves.

The process of questioning costs money. In early 1994, the government's estimate of the average cost of answering a written question was £97. This suggests that questions answered in the 1992–93 session cost over £6 million. In some ways this figure is misleading: civil service costs would not disappear if no questions were asked. But expressed as an average cost per MP per sitting day, the cost of parliamentary questions in 1992–93 is the much more modest £40. This is hardly an expensive way of enabling Parliament to fulfil the scrutiny task the electorate gives it.

The great constitutional theorist Ivor Jennings described parliamentary questions as 'of the utmost constitutional importance'. Others have described them as a farce and just a game. As usual, the truth is somewhere in between. They are important, but they should not be overrated. The fact that backbenchers asked in each of the last ten years almost 100 questions a year each shows that they are regarded as useful tools.

Questions in the House of Lords

The House of Lords also has a variety of ways of scrutinising the action of, and eliciting information from, the executive by means of questions. These questions are always addressed to Her Majesty's Government. (Questions on domestic House of Lords matters are usually addressed to the Leader of the House or Chairman of Committees.) Fewer questions are tabled in the Lords than in the Commons and the rules governing their content are less strict. It is ultimately for the House itself to determine what is in order and what is not. But there are some conventions nevertheless. Questions casting reflections on the royal family or relating to the Church of England, or to matters which are *sub judice* are inadmissible, as are questions phrased offensively. And it is considered undesirable to table questions on nationalised industries except for those asking for statistical information or on matters of urgent public importance. It is also undesirable to incorporate statements of fact or opinion in the text of a question.

Questions for oral answer (starred questions)

Every day at the beginning of a sitting up to four questions may be put to the government. They are marked on the Order Paper with a '*' and may be tabled up to one month in advance. As in the Commons, questions in the Lords were losing their currency from being tabled too far in advance and some members were, it was felt, hogging the Order Paper by tabling too many, too far ahead. In recent years the Procedure Committee have recommended that no member should have more than two on the Order Paper at any one time; that no Lord may have more than one question on any one day; and, as an experiment, that the fourth question each Thursday should be a Topical Question, drawn by lot by the Clerk Assistant on the preceding Tuesday. No starred question may be tabled less than twenty-four hours before it is to be asked. Unlike the Commons, questions are not limited to any particular government department on any particular day and there is, of course, no equivalent to Prime Minister's questions. Every member asking a question is allowed one supplementary before other members' supplementaries are put. Supplementary questions must be in terms confined to the subject of the original question but frequently go wider. They must not give rise to debate. 531 starred questions were asked in the 1990–91 session. There is no time limit to the question period but it is deemed 'undesirable' for it to last longer than half an hour.

Questions for oral answer after debate (unstarred questions)

A question which may give rise to debate may be put down for any sitting day and is taken at the end of business. It is not marked by a '*' on the Order Paper. Any Lord may make a speech upon the question but after the minister has replied on behalf of the government there is no right of reply. Unstarred questions are normally taken when business appears to be relatively light and, though less frequent, they are in many ways akin to Commons adjournment debates (see Chapter 9). In 1990–91, 42 unstarred questions were answered in debates. Since March 1993, it is now possible to table unstarred questions for debate in a dinner break. An hour's time limit is imposed so that the resumption of legislative business is not delayed.

Questions for written answer

Members of the House may also obtain written answers by tabling questions on the Order Paper under the heading 'Questions for written answer'. The minister concerned will then write to the Lord and the answer will also be published in *Hansard*. There is no limit to the number of questions a Lord may ask in this way, though members are discouraged from tabling large numbers of questions or multiple requests for information masquerading as a single question. Questions for written answer are answered within a fortnight. The government itself often uses the medium of a written answer to a question to make an announcement or publish information. 1304 written questions were answered in the 1990–91 session. Written answers on matters delegated to executive agencies are filtered through an appropriate member of the government and printed in the Official Report in letter form. The answer is not, however, protected by parliamentary privilege.

Private notice questions

A Lord may ask a question on a matter of urgency on any day, just like an MP. But it is the Leader of the House who, in the first instance, decides whether the question is of sufficient urgency to justify an immediate reply. Notice of such a question must be given by noon on the day it is proposed to ask it. Private notice questions are rare and there are seldom more than one or two a session. But answers to many Commons' private notice questions are repeated as statements in the House of Lords if the opposition requests it.

MPs' letters

MPs' letters to ministers can be seen as a part of the questioning process, though they are not strictly 'proceedings in Parliament'. The level of correspondence between MPs and Ministers is enormous, as the table below shows.

Department	Number of letters from MPs in 1992
Agriculture	11001
Customs and Excise	682
Defence	5189
Education	15192
Employment	3797
Environment	18103
Foreign and Commonwealth Office	7921
Health	16353
Home Office	21939 (1991 figure)
Inland Revenue	2859 (1991 figure)
National Heritage	2007
Northern Ireland	6255
Overseas Development Administration	5500
Social Security/Benefits Agency	35044
Scottish Office	3393
Trade and Industry	28129
Transport	16987
Treasury	1241
Welsh Office	3022

Note: The figures for Education, Northern Ireland Office and Trade and Industry include all ministerial correspondence, not just letters to MPs.

In an average month, then, at least one letter is written to a Minister by each MP each working day – and the number of letters greatly exceeds the number of questions. Although some of these letters deal with broader policy issues, many of them arise from MPs' case work. It is not therefore surprising that the most popular destination for letters is the Department of Social Security, or that other departments with responsibilities which concern the ordinary lives of constituents – health, law and order, education, transport – receive a correspondingly high post-bag. On the other hand, the Ministry of Defence, despite its vast budget, receives comparatively little correspondence.

Typically, an MP receives a complaint from a constituent, say that the constituent was discharged from hospital too soon, or has a fiancée who is not being allowed to immigrate from Pakistan or has a son who is being kept in atrocious cell conditions in a remand prison. The MP cannot investigate these complaints personally. He or she could ask parliamentary questions, or could apply for an adjournment debate. But the MP may start by forwarding the constituent's letter to the minister responsible and asking for comments. The constituent could have written directly to the department, but the intervention of the MP on his or her behalf should ensure that the issue is dealt with at a more senior level. Until quite recently, virtually all letters from MPs received replies from ministers personally. Although the reply had been drafted by civil servants, it could be assumed that the minister would have given at least some attention to the case before signing. In some departments (the Department of Social Security, for example) MPs are now encouraged to take up cases with the officials with hands-on responsibilities (the manager of the local benefits office, for example), while the growth of executive agencies has meant that (as happens with parliamentary questions) letters dealing with agency responsibilities receive replies from agency chief executives.

MPs are divided on what some see as the watering down of ministerial responsibility to Parliament implicit in this new way of dealing with correspondence. Others regard it as a welcome recognition of reality. It does seem to have led to somewhat more rapid replies. In the past there were many complaints from MPs about inordinate delays in replying to their letters. When the whole issue was reviewed in 1990 by the government's Efficiency Unit, they found that the cost of replying to letters was £17 million, and they pointed to the tension between the expectation by MPs that they should receive full and speedy replies, and the ability of departments, with their finite resources, to cope. Devolving, where appropriate, the responsibility for replying was one of the solutions they proposed. They also suggested that each department should publish targets for the time taken to respond to MPs' letters, and should regularly reveal performance against targets. Statistics are now published annually. In 1992, for example, major departments had target reply times ranging between 10 days (for example, Foreign and Commonwealth Office; Department of Trade and Industry) and 20 days (for example, Health, Education and Social Services). Percentages of replies within target ranged from 96 per cent (Employment) to 22 per cent (Home Office). Delay does remain one of the greatest disadvantages of letters in comparison with questions.

But letters have several advantages. First of all, they can be sent at any time. Questions can be answered only while the House is sitting, which means that ministers have a long summer holiday away from questions, while they continue to answer MPs' letters. Unlike questions, there are no restrictive rules about what an MP can say in a letter, but, of course, a minister is not obliged to give any more forthcoming an answer to a letter than to a question. The contents of these letters are private unless one of the parties releases them. The minister by convention does not do this unless the MP does, but ministers are aware that MPs may always 'go public'. Nevertheless, confidential matters can be raised in letters. There are no such things as confidential questions. MPs frequently 'go public' when they are not satisfied with the answer they receive to letters. The classic procedure is to raise an issue with a minister by letter, to put down parliamentary questions if the reply to the letter is inadequate, and finally to try to obtain an adjournment debate if the reply to the question is not satisfactory. Letters, then, are often the springboard for proceedings in Parliament.

In this section, the reader will notice that we have written about MPs' letters rather than backbenchers' letters. This is because all MPs, including government ministers and the Speaker (who are, of course, not able to table questions or raise matters in adjournment debates), use letters as part of their work on behalf of their constituents.

Letters from peers to ministers are treated in the same way inside government ministries as letters from MPs. There are no figures about their numbers, but they are likely to be many fewer. Peers, after all, have no constituency casework.

Petitions

One of Parliament's oldest functions was to redress the grievances made known to it by the petition of the subject. If letters to MPs are one way the constituent can bend the ear of government, this ancient way – the public petition – also remains open. The historical origin of petitions has meant that many of the rules surrounding them are ancient and still appear obscure despite some modernisation of them in 1993 (for example, a petition must be handwritten).

The use of petitions dropped off dramatically in the twentieth century: there were about 34,000 petitions in 1893, but only one in 1939–40. More recently there has been something of a revival. Individuals or small groups have petitioned in respect of their needs – a prisoner who wants parole or a village needing a by-pass. Pressure groups have also organised country-wide petitions which they then ask each MP to present on behalf of the constituency. The number of petitions in five recent sessions is set out in the table below.

Session	Number of petitions
1988–89	227
1989–90	960
1990–91	183
1991–92	452
1992–93	2651*

*Figure artificially inflated by presentation of 1500 identical petitions.

An MP can present a petition to the Commons simply by putting it in a large bag kept for the purpose behind the Speaker's Chair. If the MP wants to present it in the Chamber, he or she is restricted to a very short speech. All petitions are printed. Government departments may (but are not obliged to) make observations on them, and these observations are also printed. No committee considers petitions, and they are not a prelude to an investigation of the complaint by an outside body such as the ombudsman. In many ways, therefore, petitioning is not a fruitful exercise. But petitions do achieve publicity, and well-organised petitions, whether they express individual, local or national grievances, ensure that the constituency MP and government departments know that views are strongly held and have to be taken into account in decision-making. Petitions may also be very therapeutic in allowing the petitioners to get their grievances off their chests!

Petitions may also be addressed to the House of Lords, but in that House they are largely defunct.

CHAPTER 9

Debates

The dictionary definition of debate is 'the formal discussion, argumentation and resolution of a motion before a legislative assembly according to the rules of parliamentary procedure'. The proper title of *Hansard*, the daily record of the Chamber, is *Parliamentary Debates – Official Report*, and one could describe most of what happens while the House is meeting as 'debate' as the dictionary defines it. However, in this section we are going to use a more narrow definition, excluding debate in the broad sense of political argument and the legislative process. In our definition, debates take place when the House is considering a motion which is not connected with legislation. This motion can either be a substantive motion or a motion 'that this House do now adjourn' – an adjournment motion. We will describe each of these in turn, and then ask more general questions about the purposes and value of debate.

Almost all debates take place on the floor of the House, although it is possible for debates relating exclusively to Scotland or Wales or England or Northern Ireland to take place in specially constituted standing committees where all the MPs from those countries are entitled to sit. The most common standing committee debates take place in the Scottish Grand Committee, the Welsh Grand Committee or the Northern Ireland Grand Committee. These met to debate topics on six, three and one occasions respectively in the 1992–93 session, and general topics were discussed ranging from crime in Scotland to unemployment in Wales. The decision whether these committees should meet rests entirely with the government, and it is not possible to take any binding decisions in them. New procedures adopted in the case of the Scottish Grand Committee (see page 243) should mean more debates on Scottish business from session 1994–95 onwards.

Substantive motions

A substantive motion is one which expresses an opinion about something. This can range from 'This House has no confidence in Her Majesty's Government' through fairly colourless motions like 'This House takes note of the Report of the Royal Commission on

Criminal Procedure' to the full-blooded 'This House is appalled at recent press reports that the government made a deal with Chile'.

As the word suggests, a motion is 'moved', or proposed by the MP who sponsors it. This is done in a speech outlining the MP's view of why the House should adopt the motion or proposition. A debate then takes place, in which the Speaker calls MPs to speak, usually alternating between those in favour and those against the motion. The Speaker may also select an amendment to the motion, which one of the supporters of the amendment will move. When the time for the debate runs out, the Speaker asks the House to decide, by votes if necessary, whether any amendment should be made to the motion, and then whether the motion, as amended if it has been, should be adopted (or 'agreed to') or not adopted. If the motion is agreed to, it becomes a Resolution or an Order of the House.

This sounds complicated, but a practical example will make it easier. On 23 July 1993, following a government defeat the previous day, the House of Commons debated a motion in the following terms:

That this House has confidence in the policy of Her Majesty's Government on the adoption of the protocol on social policy.

The Prime Minister spoke first and moved this motion. The next speaker was the leader of the opposition. He was called to move an amendment to the motion, to leave out all the words after 'That' and to add instead these words:

in the opinion of this House, Her Majesty's Government should not deposit the Articles of Ratification of the Treaty of European Union with the Government of the Italian Republic until such time as it has given notification to the European Community that it intends to adopt the Agreement attached to the Protocol on Social Policy.

Mr. Major and Mr. Smith each spoke for half an hour, and they were followed by 21 other speakers (10 Conservatives, nine Labour MPs, one Liberal Democrat and one Scottish National Party MP) before the debate was wound up by the Shadow European Affairs spokesman and the Foreign Secretary. Two votes were taken, one to reject the opposition amendment and the second to agree the government's motion. The whole debate took some seven hours.

Although that debate was a more exciting occasion than many, with several heavy-weight speakers, including former Prime Minister Sir Edward Heath, being called to speak, the way in which it progressed was typical.

Substantive motions are normally tabled for discussion on the 20 days each session which are given to the two main opposition parties (17 to the largest opposition party). The issues which these debates deal with are wide-ranging, and reflect the opposition leadership's view of the issues which are important at the time, and which the government may find embarrassing. The government itself also initiates a number of debates on substantive motions each session. In addition to purely procedural matters or matters like MPs' pay and conditions, in the 1992–93 session there were twelve whole day debates on substantive motions which were initiated by the government. These dealt with matters like public expenditure, the coal industry, defence and the European Community.

In the 1992–93 session, about 6 per cent of the time on the floor of the House was taken up with opposition-initiated debates on substantive motions, and about 5 per cent with similar government-initiated debates.

Two special annual debates on substantive motions must be mentioned. These are the four or five-day debate on the budget proposals, and the six-day debate on the Queen's Speech with which each session begins. In a sense, these are both pre-legislative general debates – the first on the proposals which will be included in the Finance Bill, the second on the whole of the government's legislative proposals for the session.

Most debates on substantive motions are initiated by the government or the opposition. However, the Standing Orders provide for four half-days and ten Fridays to be given over to private members' (or backbenchers') motions (the number of days given over each session to private members' motions is normally reduced each session, and the number of days for private members' bills correspondingly increased). MPs are chosen by ballot to introduce substantive motions on each of these days. The MPs who win the ballot must give at least nine days notice of as broad, or as narrow, a subject for debate as they choose. Normally the subject chosen is fairly narrow, and reflects the interests of the MP who has won the ballot. In 1992–93 subjects as disparate as the Arab world, the civil rights of the disabled, sport and toxic waste disposal in Wales were raised. Backbenchers can push their motions to the vote, though this is rarely done. Backbenchers have in the past valued the opportunity of these debates to force the House to consider issues which may be less 'political' than the subjects chosen by the government and the opposition. However, backbenchers can – and from time to time do – table highly contentious motions for debate.

Private members' motions take up less than 4 per cent of the time of the House, and the debates on them are poorly attended as they occur during the first part of a Monday afternoon and during Friday, when many MPs are in their constituencies.

As part of the package of the 1995 experimental reforms following the Jopling report, days set aside for debating private members' substantive motions will cease to exist. They will be replaced by extra opportunities for backbencher-initiated adjournment debates on Wednesday mornings.

Early day motions

Just because there are few opportunities for backbench MPs to debate their motions does not mean that they have nothing to say. In recent sessions every sitting day has seen an average of over 10 motions tabled 'for an early day'. These are known as 'early day motions' or EDMs. Most are tabled by backbenchers who have no expectation that they will be debated (though, very occasionally, as in the case of an 1989 EDM on war crimes, important EDMs are given debating time). The purpose of EDMs is to put debating points across in a written form, and then to see what support the views expressed get. Other backbenchers who agree with them can sign the EDM, and each day in the first ten days after an EDM is tabled, whenever a new signature is added, the EDM is reprinted in the day's parliamentary papers with the running total of signatures added. Thereafter added names are only printed on Thursdays.

EDMs can be a useful source of intelligence for the whips. For example, in the 1985–86 session a large number of Conservative MPs signed an EDM critical of the bill to de-restrict Sunday trading – the Shops Bill. This was one of several indications which government business managers received that the bill would have a rough ride. EDMs can also be used by MPs to defuse pressure from constituents and others to be seen to be doing something about some issue, or to put material on the parliamentary record under the protection of parliamentary privilege.

The growth in the number of EDMs, the apparently trivial subjects with which some of them deal and the cost of publishing them have led some to question the value of what have been described as 'parliamentary graffiti'.

Adjournment motions

Over one-fifth of the time of the House of Commons is taken up with debating the question 'That this House do now adjourn'. This may appear rather odd, not to say indecisive. In fact it has very little to do with whether the House will adjourn – the times of the day and the times of the year when the House sits are effectively determined, as we saw, by the government.

Adjournment motions had a glorious history in the nineteenth and eighteenth centuries. Nowadays, in practical terms, moving the adjournment is no longer an option for the ordinary backbencher wishing to frustrate government business or to have a debate on a topic of his or her choice. Much of adjournment debate time is, however, regarded as backbenchers' time. There are different types of backbenchers' adjournment motions, and rather more than a tenth of the sitting hours of the Commons is taken up with them.

Backbench adjournment debates

The first type occurs daily (see Chapter 5) at the end of business, and normally lasts for half an hour. The adjournment motion is moved formally by a government whip, and then a backbencher speaks for fifteen minutes or so on a topic which he or she has previously notified. A minister then replies for fifteen minutes, no vote is taken and the House adjourns. The backbencher initiating the debate is chosen by ballot, except on Thursdays when the choice is made personally by the Speaker. The MP may raise any topic which is the responsibility of the government. The main restriction is that the MP's main request must not be for legislation. Topics raised in a randomly chosen week (7–11 March 1994) were: public awareness of faulty gas supplies; long service awards for ambulance personnel; psychiatric killings in Doncaster; an individual's *ex gratia* claim against the Lord Chancellor's Department, and the M11 link road.

Under the experimental arrangements for sittings which will take place in 1995, the new Wednesday mornings will be devoted to a series of backbench-proposed subjects debated on the adjournment – normally two subjects for one and a half hours each, and three subjects for half an hour. The subjects will be chosen by Speaker's ballot, and the motion for the adjournment will lapse at 2.30 pm. These Wednesday morning adjournment debates will replace private members' motions and three other traditional types of debate. One of these is the three hour debate held a week or so before each holiday adjournment (that is, four times a year). At this debate the House agrees the date of the holiday but, before doing so, backbenchers have the chance to raise a variety of topics. The other types of debate which are to be discontinued are adjournment motions moved on the last day before a holiday, when the day has traditionally been given up to a series of half-hour backbencher debates similar to the daily adjournment debate, and the adjournment debates held after the three main annual Consolidated Fund Bills. The ending of this type of debate will remove three all-night sittings since the Consolidated Fund adjournment motion is debated from the early evening until 9 a.m. the following day (8 a.m. if the following day is a Friday).

Government adjournment debates

Important and sensitive issues can sometimes be raised during backbench adjournment debates, but they are usually concerned more with an individual MP's particular concerns, and poorly attended – the last half-hour of the day frequently sees only the Deputy Speaker, the minister, a whip and the backbencher initiating the debate, in the Chamber. By contrast, very major debates often taken place when the government initiates an adjournment debate. The most famous of these took place in 1940 and led to Churchill replacing Chamberlain as Prime Minister. The advantage, from the government's point of view, in debating a major topic 'on the adjournment' is that the House cannot reach any decision except whether or not to adjourn. This is because no amendment can be tabled to the motion 'That this House do now adjourn'. The opposition cannot offer an alternative proposition to the House which may encourage dissident government back-benchers to vote with them. Frequently no vote even takes place, but when it does and the House votes to adjourn, no one can really say what this implies. For example, when the government policy for airports to serve London was debated 'on the adjournment' in February 1985, although the government was criticised by many of its own supporters who joined with opposition members to carry the motion 'That this House do now adjourn', no one could claim that the House of Commons had expressed a particular definite opinion about airport policy. On other occasions, government adjournment motions are tabled so that the House can have a wide-ranging debate about general areas of policy. A list of the topics debated on government adjournment motions in the first six months of 1993 gives an idea of the sort of topics where these adjournment motions are moved: the three armed services; Welsh affairs; international peacekeeping; Bosnia; and government support to exporters.

Emergency adjournment debates

A final type of adjournment motion is one of exceptional political sensitivity. This is the emergency debate – Standing Order No. 20 adjournment motions. In the description of the Commons' day, we have mentioned how MPs make applications for Standing Order No. 20 debates. Very few of these are successful – in recent times, fewer than one a year. They are allowed at the discretion of the Speaker, sometimes in response to backbenchers' requests, more usually to opposition frontbenchers'. The subject of the debate must be 'a specific and important matter that should have urgent consideration', and the topics allowed in the 1988–89 to 1992–93 sessions were an industrial dispute in the ambulance service and the refit of the Trident nuclear submarine. The atmosphere is always highly charged, and a vote almost invariably takes place. Standing Order No. 20 debates are unexpected – normally only 24 hours' notice is given, though in cases of exceptional urgency, the debate can take place at 7 p.m. on the day the application is made – and they are normally unwelcome for the government.

Occasionally the government will rearrange its business to allow an emergency adjournment debate in government time. This happened in April 1986 when the US bombing raids in Libya were debated on the adjournment a couple of days after they happened. Government announcement of this debate preempted any need to apply for a Standing Order No. 20 debate. During the Gulf War in 1990, the House was recalled during the summer adjournment to discuss the crisis on a motion for the adjournment.

Debates in the House of Lords

About a quarter of the House of Lords' time is taken up with debates. Some, as we have seen already, arise on 'unstarred questions' and take the form of short debates at the end of the day's business, rather like adjournment debates in the Commons. There are opportunities from time to time to debate reports of select committees or important government documents. But most debates take place on Wednesdays when, as we saw in Chapter 5, motions have precedence over bills and other business. Most of these Wednesdays are given over to the political parties to initiate debates, usually on a neutral 'motion for papers' (a procedural device to raise a subject with a right of reply to the mover of the motion; the motion is invariably withdrawn), or a 'take note' motion.

Occasionally motions are tabled – motions for resolution – which if passed constitute a formal resolution of the House on the matter. These are rare but can be effective. One such motion adopted by the House on 9 February 1983, and moved by Lord Shackleton, influenced the government's decision to delay setting up a trading fund for the Ordnance Survey.

Days for these Wednesday debates are allocated to the various parties by agreement between party whips. They are not time limited. However, where the mover of the motion considers it expedient he can ask the Leader of the House to move a Business of the House motion limiting the time. This is often done by the political parties so as to create the opportunity for two debates to be held. The limit on a single debate is usually five hours: the limits where two debates are held can vary but must not exceed a total of six hours. In the earlier part of the session, up until the spring recess, one Wednesday a month is set aside for two short debates limited to two and a half hours each which have been initiated by backbenchers or crossbenchers. The subjects are chosen by a ballot conducted some weeks beforehand by the Clerk of the Parliaments in the presence of chief whips and the Convenor of the Cross Benches. The order of speaking in debates is drawn up by the government whips' office, following consultation with the opposition and the Liberal Democrats. If a debate is time limited or a balloted short debate, the list of speakers carries a reminder of the time available for speakers. Extra time is made available for the mover of the motion, closing opposition speakers and the minister in reply.

There is greater opportunity for the backbench peer to raise subjects of personal or specialised interest than is available in the House of Commons – as peers who have formerly been MPs often appreciate. Many peers feel that they can use debates to discuss dispassionately the great issues of the day, and the sessions are often well attended and benefit from important contributions from Lords who are able to draw on their considerable experience and knowledge. For example, in January 1985, the House of Lords discussed the government's social and economic policies in a memorable debate lasting about ten hours. The 43 peers who spoke included two Cabinet Ministers, eight former Cabinet Ministers (including one former Prime Minister), three bishops, industrialists, trade union leaders, academics and a general medical practitioner who is a hereditary peer. The debate was the first to be televised, and attracted considerable publicity. Other Wednesday debates are on more specialised subjects, but the membership of the House of Lords is wide enough to cover most topics. For example, a three-hour debate on the work of the Research Councils in November 1984 heard contributions from the former Chairman of the United Kingdom Atomic Energy Authority, two former Cabinet Ministers, two former University Vice-Chancellors, the Chairman of the Agricultural Research Council, two former Masters of Cambridge Colleges, and a hereditary earl who is a Fellow of the Royal Society, as well as other peers. It would be difficult to assemble such expertise elsewhere, and it is common to contrast the high quality of debate in the Upper House with the less successful debates sometimes held at the other end of the Palace of Westminster.

Purpose and value of debate

In the Commons, the Speaker frequently begins a debate by appealing for short speeches. Too many MPs have told her that they wish to speak for her to fit them all in. Why are debates so popular? In a school debating society, good speeches may change the opinions of the listener. Relatively few parliamentary speeches do this. MPs do not speak in the hope that their political opponents will be convinced by them and change their policies as a result. But MPs and peers do in general speak in order to influence opinions, both of ministers and civil servants and of interest-groups and the public outside government. Parliamentarians can use the springboard of parliamentary debates to give publicity to a point of view or a proposal. Through the reporting of their ideas in the local and national press, they can satisfy constituency and interest-group pressures on them to support a particular cause. For example, if the government decided on a debate on policy towards wildlife and the countryside, a Conservative MP from a rural constituency might make a speech explaining why farmers need to keep down the number of foxes while an inner-city Labour MP might call for more access to the countryside for town-dwellers. Both MPs are favourably reported in their local press, and, of course, have expressed views generally held by their constituents. By speaking in debate they are helping themselves by helping their constituents. Through them, conflicting views get publicity, and the two sides – inside and outside Parliament – are each aware of the other's position. The decision-takers in government may not be affected by individual MPs' speeches in debate, but debate in the House is one of the important ways in which they can gauge the strength of the arguments and the support for them. Eventually some government may ban fox-hunting, or some other government may stop ramblers from entering farm land. The debates in Parliament will not have caused the action, but will have helped to influence it.

Rarely, debate can result in decisions. This happens at two levels. The individual case raised on the adjournment by a backbencher – say a failure to pay an allowance to a particular constituent – will only be known to the minister personally because of the debate. He or she may decide that their officials have acted too harshly or unfairly and reverse or alter their decision. In this way the half-hour adjournment debates are like MPs' letters to ministers or parliamentary questions, though more searching than these because the minister has to speak publicly for fifteen minutes or so to defend the departmental line. The minister will think carefully about the policy he or she is about to defend before doing that. At the other extreme, the vote at the end of a debate can result in major political change. Mr Callaghan's government was forced to call a general election in 1979 after all the opposition parties had agreed to support a motion of 'No Confidence' in the government. One of the conventions of the British constitution is that a government defeated on a question of confidence must resign. A motion expressing no confidence in the government is the most obvious example of a question of confidence, but the government may also declare any other matter to be one of confidence. This was done in November 1994 when the Prime Minister announced that any amendment of substance to the European Communities (Finance) Bill would be so treated. In cases such as that of 1979, it is not, of course, the debate itself which matters, but the vote at the end – and the vote only mattered in 1979 because the Labour Party did not have an overall majority in the House. This is unusual: since 1955, only the Labour governments of 1964–66, February to October 1974 and 1974–79 and the Conservative Government elected in 1992 have had majorities of fewer than 30. Major debates in situations of large majorities do not usually result in unpredictable decisions, but a debate where strong feelings are expressed, especially across party lines, can close options for the government – for example, the strength of feeling about airport development and the cross-party vote at the end of the debate on the subject, although it was an adjournment motion, in February 1985, meant that the government needed to take parliamentary opinion very seriously before it announced its decision, and concessions were made to meet the views expressed.

Debates are, of course, an important opposition weapon. The legislative programme of a session is largely controlled by the government, who also control the timing of policy announcements. This means that the government are normally able to choose the territory on which to fight. When opposition parties initiate debate, they for once are in the stronger position – and they can and do challenge the government to debate the areas of their policy and administration which the opposition think are embarrassing and on which the government might prefer to remain silent.

So, is debate part of the inquisitorial function? Debates are blunderbusses. Normally neither House debates a small and specific question in a substantive motion. A debate on the floor of the House cannot be a detailed enquiry. But debate does force the government (and to a lesser extent, the alternative governments represented by the opposition parties) to give an account of themselves and to defend their policies in a public forum, where what is said is reported in the media and will influence the electorate in the view it holds of its political leaders.

CHAPTER 10

Select committees

The House of Commons has a confusing system of committees. We have already dealt with Committees of the whole House and standing committees. Very different from these are the select committees whose name simply means that their members are *selected* from among the membership of the House. There have been select committees for hundreds of years, but their functions and responsibilities evolved as time went on and Parliament's needs altered. All committees, inside and outside Parliament, are responsible to a superior body which defines their tasks. Indeed, the very name 'committee' indicates that a task or function has been 'committed' or given to that body. Nowadays the House of Commons asks its select committees to perform an important and increasing part of its inquisitorial function. This is mainly through the departmental select committees, and most of this chapter will deal with them. But first there are other select committees which have to be described.

Select committees other than the departmental committees

The first group of these committees are what have been described as 'narrow gauge' committees concentrating on particular narrow areas of government action and producing concise, regular reports. They are monitoring actions of government on behalf of the House, some almost in a judicial capacity. Briefly, these committees are:

Committee of Public Accounts

This committee ('PAC') has existed since 1861 when it was established by Gladstone. Except for the Committee of Privileges, it is the oldest of the present committees. According to standing orders, its function is the 'examination of the accounts showing the appropriation of the sums granted by Parliament to meet the public expenditure, and of such other accounts laid before Parliament as the committee may think fit'. In fact, its principal work in recent years has been in the area of value for money audit – looking at the economy, efficiency and effectiveness with which government departments use their resources and the controls they exercise on spending. The PAC publishes a wide range of reports each session. In 1992–93 there were no fewer than 63 of these, on subjects ranging from cervical and breast screening to the BBC world service, countering VAT avoidance and the administration of student loans. The 15 members of the committee (customarily chaired by a senior opposition backbencher: Harold Wilson was chairman from 1959 to 1963) are not experts in all the subjects which come before them. But they are able to rely on the well-researched preliminary reports of the National Audit Office (NAO) (a department of about 1000 officials, many of whom are accountants, and headed by the C&AG, whose special relationship with the Commons we described earlier). The PAC usually follows up NAO reports in what can be hard-hitting evidence sessions with the most senior civil servants – the permanent secretaries and agency chief executives – in the government departments concerned. There is often great media interest in NAO reports and subsequent PAC evidence sessions and reports. There is more information on the work of the C&AG on pages 32 and 34.

Committee on the Parliamentary Commissioner for Administration

The Parliamentary Commissioner for Administration (PCA) is the ombudsman. His work has been described on page 34. The small committee on the PCA considers the reports he and the Health Service commissioners make to the House. From time to time they report on topics which have been highlighted by the PCA – as they did in 1993, for example, on the vexed subject of compensation to farmers for slaughtered poultry.

Select Committee on Statutory Instruments

The importance and growth of delegated legislation has been described in Chapter 6. The Select Committee on Statutory Instruments usually meets jointly with its Lords counterpart and looks at all delegated legislation except Northern Ireland and local instruments – not to decide whether the policy behind the instrument is acceptable or not, but whether the procedures involved in making laws by means of statutory instruments have been correctly followed. The Commons committee meets alone if the instrument concerned has been laid before the Commons only.

Deregulation Committee

The Deregulation Committee will consist of 16 MPs who will have responsibility for reporting to the House on draft instruments laid before the House under Chapter 1 of the Deregulation and Contracting Out Act 1994. The Committee will be set up for the first time in the 1994–95 session. As explained on page 150, its work is an extension of that of the Joint and Select Committees on Statutory Instruments, and it may provide an interesting precedent for future development, though until it has been operational for some time, it will be too early to judge.

European Legislation Committee

More and more legislation originates in the European Community. The purpose of this committee is to sift this legislation, decide which proposals are important, politically or legally, and to recommend which should be considered further before being agreed to by British ministers in Brussels. The committee's work is described in more detail in Chapter 11.

Others

Some of the committees of the House have a less public role. A number of these are described earlier (see pages 31, 74 and 96). In brief, the Finance and Services Committee is responsible for the money which the House spends on its own administration and services and has the job of monitoring the financial performance of the House's departments. It also reports to the House of Commons Commission or the Speaker on the financial implication of recommendations made by the Committee on Broadcasting (with its variety of executive functions concerned with the broadcasting of the House and its Committees) and by the four domestic committees which have delegated executive functions in the specific areas of accommodation and works, administration, catering and information (including library services and information technology). There is also a committee on the financial interests of MPs and other people connected with the House (MPs, their staff and parliamentary journalists are obliged to register their financial interests). This is known as the Members' Interests Committee. The Committee of Selection, with its responsibility of nominating members of Standing Committees, private bill committees and departmental select committees is itself a select committee. Finally, the Committee of Privileges has been appointed regularly since the seventeenth century to consider complaints about breach of privilege. The committee does not hold regular meetings, but considers individual questions referred to it by the House from time to time. Its seventeen members are among the most distinguished in the House.

Other committees may be established to meet particular needs. The House of Commons is always dissatisfied with its procedures, and a select committee to examine ways of changing procedures has been set up in most sessions over the last few years. This is called simply the Procedure Committee. Other 'domestic' issues like MPs' pay (1980–81 and 1981–82), the televising of the House (1988–90), sittings of the House (1991–92) (the 'Jopling Committee') and the conduct of members (1975–76) (arising out of allegations of corrupt conduct by particular MPs after the jailing of John Poulson) are set up as the need arises. Since the departmental select committees have become part of the scene, it is less likely that *ad hoc* select committees would be set up to deal with particular wider public issues, but the facility to do so is always there, and could be used again. For example, around 100 MPs in 1984–85 signed an early day motion calling for a select committee to consider human embryo research and human genetic engineering. Issues which *ad hoc* select committees have considered in the past include obscene publications (1957), the royal family's pay and expenses (1971–72), a possible 'wealth tax' (1974–75), abortion (1974–75), and violence in the family (1975–76).

Departmental select committees

A system of powerful permanent select committees covering each aspect of government policy has been an aim of parliamentary reformers for some time. Select committees evolved during the 1960s and 1970s but did not provide both comprehensive cover of government departments *and* specialisation. Some experiments did not work. An Agriculture Committee was proposed in December 1966 but ceased to exist in February 1969, having been opposed bitterly by government departments. The recommendation of permanent, comprehensive cover was finally made by a Procedure Committee in 1978: there should be twelve departmental select committees; eight days a year should be devoted in the Chamber to debating their reports; and the MPs who chaired the committees should be paid a small additional salary. The Leader of the House at the time was Michael Foot, 'not an enthusiast for' select committees as he has described himself, and the proposal seemed doomed to failure. However, an election took place in May 1979 which the Conservatives won, with a manifesto commitment to parliamentary reform. The new Leader of the House, Norman St John-Stevas, was in favour of select committees and, despite opposition from some of his Cabinet colleagues, he allowed the House to debate a slightly watered-down version of the 1978 recommendations. The proposed committee structure was approved by 248 votes to 12, and the committees began their work in 1980.

There have been a number of refinements of the system since

1979, with the departments which originally had for varying reasons been treated differently (principally the Lord Chancellor's Department, which no committee covered, and the Northern Ireland Office, responsibility for which was shared across departmental committees) being brought within the system. Changes in the structure of government – for example, the demise of the Department of Energy and the creation of the Department of National Heritage and an Office of Science and Technology after the 1992 election have also been reflected in the Committee structure.

On 1 November 1994, seventeen departmental Committees were operating. Their composition is set out in the following table. The total number of MPs from each party who serve on a Select Committee reflect the party composition of the House as a whole.

| Name of committee | Chairmanship | Number of members | | | Total |
		Conservative	Labour	Other parties	
Agriculture	C	6	4	1	11
Defence	C	6	4	1	11
Education	C	6	5	0	11
Employment	L	6	5	0	11
Environment	C	6	5	0	11
Foreign Affairs*	C	6	5	0	11
Health	C	6	4	1	11
Home Affairs*	C	6	5	0	11
National Heritage	L	6	5	0	11
Northern Ireland Affairs	UPU	6	2	5	13
Science and Technology	C	6	5	0	11
Scottish Affairs	L	6	3	2	11
Social Security	L	6	4	1	11
Trade and Industry	L	6	4	1	11
Transport	C	6	5	0	11
Treasury and Civil Service*	C	6	4	1	11
Welsh Affairs	L	6	3	2	11

*These Committees have power to set up one sub-committee.

One area of government activity is not covered by the departmental committees. This is the work of the intelligence services. A number of MPs would like to see this secret area of government work opened up to normal select committee scrutiny, but this has been resisted by government. However, the Intelligence Services Act 1994 did provide for a statutory committee made up of nine non-ministerial members of both Houses. This Committee was appointed in late 1994 by the Prime Minister in consultation with the Leader of the Opposition and will report to him.

How they work

The Standing Orders of the House set out each committee's responsibilities and powers. They are to 'examine the expenditure, administration and policy' of the relevant government department and of 'associated public bodies'. They have powers to 'send for persons, papers and records . . . to adjourn from place to place' (that is, to travel away from Westminster) and 'to report from time to time'. They can appoint specialist advisers. These are very extensive powers. Theoretically, a committee can pick any topic it likes within its broad frame of reference, appoint a batch of specialist advisers to assist it, and spend its whole time travelling round the country demanding not just evidence from anyone it likes but the disclosure of any private documents it happens to fancy seeing. Of course, it doesn't work like that in practice.

First of all committees have to be very selective about the topics they choose to investigate. The MPs on the committee have other calls on their time besides the committee. On average, they can probably devote five or six hours a week to the select committee – although a busy committee may demand more time. Most committees therefore meet once a week, perhaps three times a fortnight and very seldom more than twice a week. There are very few meetings during parliamentary recesses. Furthermore, committees' theoretical area of responsibility is mind-bogglingly large. For example, the Defence Ministry has around 120,000 civilian and 250,000 forces employees. The Defence Committee – eleven MPs backed by a permanent staff of five – cannot hope to investigate anything more than a tiny proportion of the ministry's work. Once the topic is chosen, the committee has to set itself some timescale in which to reach decisions – it may, of course, run a number of inquiries simultaneously. Normally most committees want to conclude each inquiry within a matter of months, and in some cases much more quickly, especially if they are investigating a topic in the news. Within that timetable, the committee has to receive evidence, in writing or orally, obtain detailed memoranda from the appropriate government department, pay any visits which it thinks are essential and discuss and agree a report which will be published.

The first job is to decide who should be asked to give evidence. Anyone is free to offer advice (formally called 'evidence') to the committee and many people who have an interest will write in without an invitation. These may not be the people whom the committee thinks could help it most, so it will decide what viewpoints it wants to hear, and invite particular representatives of these viewpoints to submit evidence – typically, representative pressure groups from different sides will be asked. For example, the Home Affairs Committee agreed a report in 1993 on juvenile offenders. As well as taking evidence from civil servants and ministers, the committee held oral sessions with the Association of Chief Police Officers, the Police Superintendents' Association, the Police Federation, the Council of Circuit Judges, the Magistrates' Association, the Association of Chief Officers of Probation, the National Association of Probation Officers, the Association of Directors of Social Services, the British Association of Social Workers, the Howard League for Penal Reform, the National Association for the Care and Resettlement of Offenders, the Prison Governors' Association, the Prison Officers Association, the National Intermediate Treatment Federation, the Standing Committee for Youth Justice and the National Children's Home. Not surprisingly, sessions lasted from February to May! In addition, a whole range of other organisations submitted written evidence.

Normally witnesses invited to give evidence are willing to do so. If they are not, the committee can invoke its formal power to call for persons, papers and records. In 1982, for example, the Energy Committee (which monitored the work of the then Department of Energy) ordered Arthur Scargill to give evidence to it the following day after it appeared that he would not do so voluntarily. In recent years, not many formal orders have been made, and none has been ignored, but if a witness disobeyed an order of a committee, or refused to answer questions, the House would be asked to uphold the order. In 1992, the Social Security Committee ordered the two sons of Robert Maxwell, Ian and Kevin Maxwell, to attend a hearing in its inquiry into pension funds. The two brothers did attend, but refused on legal advice to answer questions. The Committee reported their conduct to the House, but the 1992 General Election prevented any further action taking place. If the witness disobeyed an order of the House, the House has the power to imprison him or her. As well as ordering individuals to give evidence, the power to send for persons, papers and records allows committees to insist on being shown copies of documents which are relevant to their enquiries – the Trade and Industry Committee used this power in 1984 and 1993 forcing first a reluctant British Shipbuilders and then an equally reluctant British Coal to show the committee their corporate plans.

These formidable powers are restricted in one important area. Committees cannot demand the attendance of other MPs or of Lords. Mrs Edwina Currie only agreed to give evidence before the Agriculture Committee in its inquiry into the salmonella in eggs affair in 1988 following considerable pressure and after the committee had indicated that it would report the matter to the House if she did not do so. Another MP, Sir Hal Miller, declined to appear before the Trade and Industry Committee in its inquiry into the Iraqi supergun affair in 1991. Both Mrs Currie and Sir Hal were backbench MPs at the time, but the rule that committees cannot compel members of either House to give evidence is potentially at its most problematic so far as ministers are concerned. Since all government ministers are members of one House or the other, this means that committees cannot insist that a particular minister should give evidence to them. Normally, the government will send *a* minister when requested, but it is ultimately the Prime Minister who decides which minister should attend, not the committee. A second restriction in dealing with government is that committees' powers to send for papers and records do not extend to papers and records held by government departments. However, although committees' powers do not stretch in theory to government, two important undertakings have been made by the Leader of the House. These were (in 1979) that every minister would do all in his or her power to co-operate with the departmental select committees, and (in 1981) that a debate would be provided in government time on the floor of the House 'when there is evidence of widespread general concern in the House regarding an alleged refusal to disclose information to a select committee'.

Select committees, of course, will always try to apply pressure gradually in any disagreement with the government. In its investigation in early 1986 of the Westland affair (a major political crisis which resulted in the resignation of two Cabinet Ministers), the Defence Committee originally intended to hear evidence from certain named senior civil servants. They did not appear, but the committee did secure the attendance of the most senior civil servant of all, the Secretary to the Cabinet, Sir Robert Armstrong. Again, although it had no formal power to do so, the committee eventually forced the government to hand over two crucial internal government documents. Disputes between the committee and government were resolved without a debate on the floor of the House – though the critical report which the committee eventually produced did not mince words, and the government's response to the report hinted at proposals, later modified, to restrict committees' examination of civil servants in the future.

If there is time, witnesses are frequently asked to submit a written memorandum before they give their oral evidence. On the basis of this, as well as other information they have, the committee's staff will prepare a brief for MPs on the committee which suggests what the oral evidence session should be used for. This oral session may then last two hours or so with the witnesses asked to express their opinions and then tested on them. It can be a harrowing experience – the witness is interrogated by eleven politicians under the gaze of the press, television and public, and cannot refuse to answer or just get up and leave. Of course, witnesses are often politicians, senior civil servants or experienced business people or senior professionals. They can normally hold their own and can sometimes get away with saying very little or with escaping really probing questioning on the views they are putting across. Every committee has suspicions from time to time that witnesses are being – at the very least – economical with the truth.

Some people believe that the formal evidence sessions are not necessarily productive, especially where the committee is looking at a sensitive issue. When confidential or security matters are involved, evidence can be taken in private, which allows the witness to relax a little. But it is also possible for committees to meet informally with people who have something to say about the topic of the inquiry and to discuss the issue off the record. Another way in which committees can learn about the topic they are investigating is by travel away from the familiar atmosphere of the committee rooms at Westminster. There is always press criticism of committee visits to far-off or exotic countries, but each visit abroad is vetted by a committee consisting of all committee chairmen which must be convinced that travel will add to the value of the inquiry. Committees are able to travel more freely inside the United Kingdom. For example, in 1993 the Agriculture Committee visited Lowestoft, Brixham, Plymouth and Aberdeen as part of its inquiry into the effects of conservation measures on the British sea fishing industry, while the Environment Committee went to Newcastle, Glasgow and Northern Ireland as part of its inquiry into energy efficiency in buildings. Such domestic visits provide opportunities to meet people with first-hand experience of the problems the committees are tackling and useful insights are almost always gained.

After the evidence has been taken, the visits made and a study made of papers submitted, the committee meets in private to discuss the areas it wants to cover in its report. Usually the staff of the committee provides a skeleton outline of a report as a basis of discussion. When agreement is reached on the opinions to be expressed, the staff are normally asked by the Chairman to produce a draft report reflecting the committee's thinking. The clerk of the committee does this with the assistance of the specialist advisers, and the length of what is produced can vary greatly, reflecting (usually) the amount of time which the inquiry has previously taken up. The Chairman of the committee will study this draft report and alter it if he or she thinks necessary, so that it accurately reflects their opinion and that of the committee as they see it, and it will then be submitted to a private meeting of the committee. It is discussed paragraph by paragraph, and any members of the committee can suggest amendments to the Chairman's proposals, if necessary pressing their suggestions to a vote, where a simple majority is enough to make a change. (A Chairman of a Commons committee does not vote unless there is a tie.) When the report has been gone through in this way, there is an opportunity for a final vote before the report is formally made to the House. Officially there is no such thing as a minority report, but any member can propose a draft report to the committee as an alternative to the Chairman's. This is voted upon and incorporated in the minutes of proceedings. The committee are not restricted to discussing the Chairman's draft. When the report has been agreed, arrangements are made for it to be printed and published. It is put on sale, and is freely available to MPs, and is usually launched into the public domain at a press conference held by the Chairman. In due course – a couple of months or so – the government is expected to respond, normally by means of a Command Paper or a detailed memorandum, to the points made in the committee's report.

What purpose do they serve?

Having explained how they go about their work, we ought to ask a more fundamental question: what is the purpose of this work? Some cynics say that MPs have to do *something*. There are 651 of them, and not all of them can be ministers or shadow ministers, so select committees have a therapeutic value in keeping MPs out of trouble. The evidence of the first 15 years of their existence is, however, that the committees have not generally opted for the quiet, uncontroversial backwaters of public life. If anything, their work has created trouble for government rather than simply occupying the time of potential trouble-makers. On the other hand, the committees have not fulfilled the dream of some of their most passionate advocates by clawing back power to Parliament from the executive.

With their limited resources, committees cannot really expect to exercise any comprehensive scrutiny of government, although a hard-working committee can do a thorough job on particular subjects. Committees can point up issues by tackling subjects which the government would prefer them to leave alone and interrogate ministers and senior civil servants in a way which is not possible through the use of parliamentary questions. Certainly the departmental committee system has resulted in a more thorough exposure of civil servants and officials of public bodies to examination in public than the country has ever seen in the past. For this reason, supporters of more open government tend to support the committees' work.

This scrutiny does not necessarily lead to direct changes in policy by government. One criterion by which committees are sometimes judged is the number of their recommendations which are accepted by government or which result in such changes. This is a potentially flawed measure. First of all, many recommendations may be so widely acceptable that no government would have any difficulty in agreeing with them. Secondly, recommendations vary greatly in their importance: a simple statement that a report contains, say, 40 recommendations means little – it may be much less wide-ranging than a report which contains four. Thirdly, committees may excite media interest most when they oppose government policy, but that does not mean that recommendations which they make in opposition to government are particularly meritorious. But if governments do not always change their policies directly as a result of departmental select committees' reports, a well-argued report may push ministers one further step along in the direction of change – and at least ministers always make their policy decisions in the knowledge that they may be cross-examined about them by the select committees. Ultimately, too, they may be forced to change their policies by a vote in the Chamber: as we saw in Chapter 7, select committees since 1982 have had three days a year at their disposal on the floor of the House which they can allocate to discussion about, and a vote upon, departmental estimates. We have discussed elsewhere the way in which the government controls the business of the House. When the whips are on, the government does not normally fear defeat. But although the government has not been challenged yet, days controlled by select committees are potentially worrying for them: if a select committee, with a majority of members from the government party, wants to vote against the government, they may persuade other select committees to join them, especially if their dispute with the government is about a 'select committee issue', for example, the lack of seriousness with which the government has treated a committee recommendation. There is no evidence, however, that this 'select committee consciousness' has grown up yet.

Perhaps the most important work departmental select committees do is in advancing political discussion. Informing the House of current issues and contributing to the debate on current issues are viewed by the MPs who have served on committees as their most important functions. Government, politicians, pressure groups and the public speak to the committees, and the committees' recommendations are addressed back to these groups. Issues are aired, opposing points of view are tested against one another in a public forum, and at the end of the day the committee's conclusions may not be as important as the simple fact that they conducted an inquiry. Public and political opinion is usually better informed at the end of an inquiry – and, incidentally, the MPs on the committee usually understand the issues better themselves.

In this context it is worth noting the importance of the relationship between the media and the select committees. Journalists have become aware that select committees are an alternative focus for news about political issues, and can expose matters which otherwise might escape scrutiny. Committees, on the other hand, realise that media support and interest in their inquiries makes it more difficult for their evidence sessions and reports to be ignored. Membership of a select committee can thus enhance an MP's media profile: committee members, and especially chairmen, are increasingly asked to speak on radio and television on topical issues within their committee's terms of reference, whether or not a formal inquiry is being undertaken.

This relationship with the media is one of the factors which attracts MPs to see committee membership as an important part of their work. As committees' expertise develops, the quality of their work will improve, and the committees will become more respected and so more influential. This said, much depends on the quality of the committee's membership and the efforts individual MPs put in. MPs are appointed to select committees by the House on the recommendation of a committee of senior MPs known as the Committee of Selection. They nominate committees which will reflect the party strengths in the Chamber, but, other than that, the reasons for their choice of particular MPs to serve on particular committees are not made public. Sometimes MPs who want to serve on particular select committees are not given the opportunity, while 'difficult' MPs – including at least one former chairman – have been removed from committees. There is also sometimes a large turnover in membership – for example, there was no less than a 54 per cent turnover in the membership of the Agriculture Committee in the 1985–86 session and a 45 per cent turnover in the Transport Committee in 1992–93. Attendance by the MPs nominated is also variable: in the 1992–93 session, most committees had attendance records in the 80–85 per cent range, but one was 89 per cent, while another committee went as low as 68 per cent. Another important limitation on the departmental select committees is in their staffing provision – on average just under 4 staff per committee or sub-committee, including secretaries and clerical staff. Despite the power to appoint additional specialist advisers, this power is used sparingly, with an average cost in the financial year 1992–93 for pay and expenses of specialist advisers and for work commissioned from them of only £7400 for each of the committees. There is an interesting contrast here with the regulatory organisation Oftel, which regulates the telecommunications industry. In 1995, Oftel had a staff of over 170. Another comparison is with the US Congress of 1992–94: the House Committee on Energy and Commerce there, for example, had a staff of around 130, though the work of congressional committees is much more extensive than their Westminster equivalents, involving legislative and budgetary work.

With these limitations on back-up and the 101 things besides select committee business which MPs have to do, it is surprising how much committees achieve. In the 1992–93 session, over 2100 witnesses were examined by departmental select committees, with over 4700 memoranda received by them (a large proportion being from the government and associated public bodies). The committees themselves issued 74 reports. (They issued 317 during the course of the 1987–92 Parliament, and the workload has increased session by session). Their choice of subjects was, of course, influenced by what was practical and politically rewarding, but committees of politicians cannot be expected to behave otherwise. Certainly they needed to be choosy, but without a quite different structure they cannot be more ambitious. The table below lists the subjects of the reports of the 1992–93 session and demonstrates the breadth of the subject matter covered.

Committee	Subjects of reports
Agriculture	1 & 2 Banana imports 3 Hill livestock 4 Beer 5 MAFF annual report 6 Fishing conservation
Defence	1 & 9 Defence estimates 2 & 5 Army commitments and resources 3 SA80 rifle and light support weapon 4 Peacekeeping and intervention forces 6 Trident missile 7 Royal dockyards 8 Navy commitments and resources 10 Reductions in forces numbers
Education	1 & 4 Departmental spending plans 2 Schools funding 3 Special needs
Employment	1 Employment in horseracing 2 Employment in coal industry 3 Maritime skills and employment
Environment	1 Forestry and the environment 2 Housing Corporation 3 Departmental spending and annual report 4 Energy efficiency in buildings
Foreign Affairs	1 & 2 Europe after Maastricht 3 The UN 4 Departmental spending plans 5 UNESCO
Health	1 NHS Trusts 2 Tobacco advertising 3 & 6 Community care 4 Dental services 5 Community supervision orders

Committee	Subjects of reports
Home Affairs	1 Security Service 2 Immigration delays 3 Domestic violence 4 Immigration advice 5 Legal aid 6 Juvenile offenders
National Heritage	1 & 2 Export of works of art 3 National lottery 4 Privacy 5 CD prices 6 News at Ten
Science & Technology	1 Office of Science and Technology
Scottish Affairs	1 Scotland-Europe transport links
Social Security	1, 4 & 5 Pension funds 2 Low income statistics 3 Disability benefits
Trade and Industry	1 Coal industry 2 Trade with Europe 3 Aerospace industry
Transport	1 & 2 Railways 3 Public transport in London 4 London bus deregulation 5 Departmental spending plans
Treasury and Civil Service	1 1992 Autumn Statement 2 Banking supervision 3 Monetary union 4 1993 Budget 5 Budgetary reform proposals 6 Role of civil service
Welsh Affairs	1 Work of Welsh Office 2 Ancient monuments 3 Rural housing

Some observers believe that select committees, whether or not they do the job well, detract from the essential purpose of the House of Commons – the political battle on the floor of the House between conflicting ideologies. They do this first of all by taking MPs away from the Chamber, it is claimed, and into committee rooms. Attendance in the Chamber has certainly fallen in the last 50 years, but academic researchers have produced evidence that there is no correlation between this and the growth in select committee work.

Some select committees have indeed tried to direct their work back at the events of the Chamber. Recently the Trade and Industry Committee's inquiry into the coal industry was debated particularly extensively on the floor of the House. This followed British Coal's highly controversial decision in 1992 to close 31 pits. An opposition motion calling for the closures to be stopped until the committee had reported was defeated on the floor, but the government amendment to the motion which was carried itself referred directly to the committee's inquiry. In the event, some members of the committee felt that insufficient regard was paid to the conclusions of their report, published in January 1993, when the government produced its White Paper in March that year. This was reflected in the debate on the White Paper that month. But the coal review was a particularly intensely fought-over issue of high political moment. More usually, select committees' relationship to the work of the Chamber is more low-key. The Treasury and Civil Service Committee makes regular reports on the government's financial proposals, and the Defence Committee reports on the government's Defence Estimates every year for the defence debates.

Many committees have tackled matters relevant to legislation passing through the House, occasionally going so far as to propose amendments to bills, as the Energy Committee did during the progress of the bill to privatise the gas industry or as the Home Affairs Committee did in 1994 during the passage of the Criminal Justice and Public Order Bill. The latter committee had an earlier success when the Football Offences Bill was enacted in 1991 – the Act was introduced as a private member's bill by the members of the committee following an inquiry into football hooliganism. Most committees find that at least one of their reports is each year 'tagged' on the Order Paper as relevant to the House's business that day. Generally, committees would welcome the opportunity to have their reports discussed more often on the floor of the House, but the decision on the numbers of such debates is outside their control.

More importantly, critics of select committees point out that they are much less managed by the whips than standing committees are, and tend to develop consensus views. Labour and Conservative members of the committee who need to work harmoniously together frequently agree on a common approach to the issue under discussion, and committees can often as a result produce controversial reports which are agreed unanimously without any votes having taken place inside the committee. Both sides may have had to compromise their party-political views to achieve this and many believe that the committees function best when they do not operate in a party-political manner.

Readers must make their own judgement: is co-operation with an opposing political philosophy desirable or should we always fight against a philosophy which we oppose? Certainly if we decide that politics is about confrontation, then select committees are not the best way of putting that into effect. In the inquisitorial process, the best results are achieved if the committee agrees among itself. Its confrontation will, on behalf of the House, then be directed against the powerful government departments and public bodies which the committee is supposed to monitor.

House of Lords select committees

Like the Commons, the Lords also have the more domestic, narrow-focus committees (for example, Privileges or Broadcasting or the Offices Committee, with its sub-committees). But the House of Lords has also made effective use of select committees on general subjects in the last 20 years, though it has no departmental select committee system. The nearest approximation to this is in the various sub-committees of its European Communities Committee, which are described in the next chapter. A Science and Technology Committee, with sub-committees, is active and has a membership which includes many distinguished scientists. Both committees continue from session to session. In addition, the House from time to time sets up *ad hoc* committees, either to consider the merits of bills (for example, the two charities bills in 1983 or the Infant Life Preservation Bill in 1987–88) or to consider *ad hoc* matters. In 1985 a committee considered overseas trade, specifically the trade deficit in manufactured goods, and in 1993–94 another considered medical ethics, specifically euthanasia. Such committees are not normally expected to continue in existence for longer than one session and usually try to fulfil their orders of reference in that time.

Select committees in the Lords operate in a way which is almost identical to Commons committees and they encounter many of the same logistical difficulties. They have an inherent power to send for witnesses; documents are produced voluntarily. An Order of the House would be required to compel witnesses to attend or produce papers and none has in recent times been necessary. They have power to meet concurrently with Commons Committees. After considering evidence a Lords committee reports to the House.

There are no minority reports in the Lords. Dissent – were there to be any – would have to be recorded by moving amendments and having these amendments printed in the minutes of proceedings. Lords committees usually succeed in achieving unanimity as members know that unless their conclusions can be supported by all they are unlikely to achieve the greatest impact. The Chairman in the Lords has no casting vote.

The House invariably finds time to debate the reports of its committees and through these debates the committee seeks to elicit a response from the government. In 1993–94 about 3 per cent of the House's sitting time was spent debating select committee reports. A written response is also provided – within two months for reports of the European Communities Committee and six months for all others. It is, of course, difficult to say how far government policy adapts to the findings of Lords select committees but where those committees produce reports which accord with government thinking, rather than being deeply critical, they seem to have effect. There are several examples of this happening in the case of the Science and Technology Committee, for example, in areas as diverse as hazardous waste disposal, the establishment of a national computer network for distributing data about remote sensing and regulation of biotechnology. The Science and Technology Committee was the first select committee of either House to propose, through one of its members, an amendment to a public bill – the Forestry Bill, in 1981. Also, in 1985 government support (but no government time) facilitated the passage through Parliament (under private members' procedure) of the Charities Bill which had been drafted by the Select Committee on Charities in 1984.

Whatever the response of the government may be to committee activity, the reports of Lords committees also reach a wider audience. Those of the European Communities Committee are frequently used by Members of the European Parliament – of all member states, and all parties. The report of the Select Committee on Overseas Trade – though its findings were on the whole rejected by the government: indeed the committee had the rare accolade of being referred to (unfavourably) in the Chancellor of the Exchequer's 1986 budget speech – received wide media attention after publication in October 1985 and ran through five editions. More recently, the report of the Select Committee on Medical Ethics also received wide media coverage because it proposed no change to the law governing euthanasia. Such reports did much to stimulate political debate.

There can be no doubt that committee work has featured conspicuously in the renaissance of the House of Lords in recent times. It suits the non-partisan temper and character of the House, and there has been demand from backbench and opposition front-bench members of the various parties for its extension. Against this background, the House appointed a committee on the Committee Work of the House. The committee reported in February 1992 having taken evidence from a wide variety of sources – Members of the House, the government, former specialist advisers, the EC Commission and leading public bodies. The picture that emerged was a flattering one in terms of the quality of reports and their utility. So far as select committees on general subjects were concerned, the principal recommendations of the committee were to confirm the complementary role that Lords committees should play in relation to Commons committees; and to establish a Liaison Committee under the chairmanship of the Leader of the House to monitor the select committee work of the House and to allocate resources between select committees. The Liaison Committee, in an attempt to diversify the House's committee work, has since reduced the number of sub-committees of the European Communities Committee from six to five and recommended the appointment of *ad hoc* select committees on a sessional basis.

CHAPTER 11

Parliament and the European Union

The relationship between the United Kingdom and its Parliament and the European Community (now European Union) has been an important theme of British politics since 1973 when this country joined what was then the European Economic Community, or Common Market.

The 1957 Treaty of Rome, which established the Community, and to which Britain subscribed when Parliament passed the European Communities Act 1972, had set the objective of an ever-closer union of the peoples of Europe, but its effects in the early years were principally seen in commercial and economic areas such as agriculture, competition policy and coal and steel reorganisation. Two important – and controversial – moves since 1973 have brought a deeper union closer. The first of these was the Single European Act of 1985 with its added restrictions on individual member states' rights and greater impetus for a single market within the Community. The second was the Treaty on European Union, otherwise known as the Maastricht Treaty, of 1992. The Maastricht Treaty introduced the concept of a European Union, founded on three pillars – the old European Community, and new provisions for co-operation in foreign affairs and security and in home affairs and justice. The Treaty also included a timetable for monetary union and other measures to deepen the union. Both the Single European Act and the Treaty of Maastricht were given the force of law in the United Kingdom by Act of Parliament: the European Communities (Amendment) Acts 1986 and 1993.

The cumulative effect of these measures has been to make an increasing number of aspects of life in the United Kingdom subject to European Community or European Union decision – or, at least, discussion. As a consequence, British public opinion, politicians of all parties and Parliament itself have had to undergo a sometimes painful and acrimonious readjustment to the inevitable sacrifice of sovereignty which has resulted. And if Britain as a nation has had to sacrifice its sovereignty, that means that the British Parliament has also had to adjust and forego some of its primacy in legislative matters.

There is no formal role for national parliaments in the European decision-making process. Four principal bodies are instead involved. First of all, the European Commission can be seen as the Community's full-time bureaucrats. They have a number of responsibilities, including supervising member states' compliance with the treaties and negotiating on behalf of the Community. But they also have the job of proposing the initiatives which may ultimately become community law. Where the Commission cannot legislate directly, they must submit their proposals to the Council of Ministers (a council made up of the appropriate ministers from each member state, depending on the subject matter being discussed), and to the European Parliament (a directly elected body with numbers of members from each Community state roughly in proportion to population). The power which each of these bodies has depends on the subject matter of the proposal. Under the Treaty of Rome, all important European proposals needed only to secure the approval of the Council of Ministers. The effects of the Single European Act and the Maastricht Treaty have been to enhance the powers of the European Parliament, though the Council remains the institution primarily responsible for the adoption of community legislation. As well as its legislative role, the European Parliament has considerable control over the Community's budget, and can in the last resort sack the commissioners who head the Commission. The fourth European body is the Court of Justice which is the final arbiter of all legal questions falling within the scope of the Community Treaties (and, in certain cases, the Union Treaty). Some of its rulings have in effect amounted to decisions to overturn the domestic legislation of member states, as, for example, its decisions in 1990 on British fisheries legislation and in 1994 on British employment law. The court thus has powers in respect of primary legislation passed by the British Parliament which British domestic courts do not possess, at least so far as legislation other than directly applicable community law is concerned.

A hypothetical example will illustrate how law affecting United Kingdom interests can now be passed without the formal involvement of the British Parliament.

Let us imagine that the civil servants in the EC Commission decide that the growing industry of deer farming in Europe needs to be regulated. They discuss this internally, and consult with a wide range of interested parties – farmers' organisations, conservationists, independent experts etc. Different EC countries have different problems – and different views. The Commission drafts proposed regulations; these are presented to the European Parliament which discusses them in its Agriculture Committee. Amendments are suggested, and the Commission makes modifications. The modified proposals are then put to the Council of Agriculture Ministers. The Greek minister takes a different line from the French minister, but after some bargaining, agreement is reached. The regulation is made, and immediately has the direct force of law in each member state. A deer farmer in Scotland ignores the new regulations, which are bitterly opposed by people in the Highlands. The authorities in Scotland do nothing, but what is happening is reported in the German deer farmers' magazine. German deer farmers, who are obeying the legislation, are very angry. They put pressure on the German government, which brings the dispute to the European Court. The court orders the British government to enforce the regulation in Scotland.

Although this example is imaginary, similar real events have led to a gradual realisation inside Parliament that more should be done to enhance the contact between domestic legislators and the actors on the European stage. To help this process, since 1991 MPs have been given funding for one two-day visit per year to a Community institution in Brussels, Luxembourg or Strasbourg.

The least fruitful area for developing these contacts has probably been the Commission. At the top of the pyramid, at least one of the two British commissioners has always been a former MP, and, in the past, one of the commissioners has been a Lord (though, for procedural reasons and to comply with Community rules on the appointment of commissioners, he had leave of absence from the House of Lords). But at a more junior level, Commission staff have sometimes proved unwilling to discuss legislative proposals with national legislators rather than with members of the European Parliament, while neither British MPs and peers individually, nor their committees, nor either House, have any special standing if they comment on any consultative documents which the Commission may publish. A declaration attached to the Maastricht Treaty does, however, commit member states to ensure that national parliaments receive Commission proposals for legislation 'in good time for information or possible examination'.

The most obvious point of contact between Westminster and Europe might seem to be the European Parliament. Up until 1979 all Members of the European Parliament (MEPs) were also members of their national parliaments. When MEPs became directly elected, the interchange between the two parliaments lessened. Nevertheless, a number of peers have been directly elected as MEPs since 1979 (four were members before the 1994 European Parliament election, though only one was re-elected), and there have been a few MPs who have also been MEPs (two after the 1994 elections) – though there have generally been fewer of these 'dual mandate' MPs in the United Kingdom than in some other Community countries. Other personal contacts have arisen in a number of ways: quite a number of MEPs have served as MPs (six of those elected in 1994 had done so), while others are spouses or other relations of MPs (three spouses of MPs were elected as MEPs in 1994). And, of course, all MEPs have contact through their party organisations with domestic MPs. Moreover, since 1991 there have been limited rights of access to Commons facilities for MEPs. A number of MEPs and pro-European MPs have suggested that further steps need to be taken. Some elaborate proposals – such as to make MEPs temporary members of the House of Lords or to set up a Grand Joint Committee of MEPs, MPs and peers (similar to the Advisory Committee on European Questions in the Belgian House of Representatives) – have not been acted upon, nor have MEPs been provided with offices at Westminster as their German colleagues have in the Bundestag. And there is no consistent evidence of MPs and MEPs co-operating at the constituency level, especially across party. The future may see greater co-operation. Two declarations attached to the Maastricht Treaty referred to parliamentary contacts. One called for exchange of information and contacts between national and European Parliaments to be stepped up 'in particular through the granting of appropriate reciprocal facilities and regular meetings between Members of Parliament interested in the same issues'. This declaration has already resulted in a number of joint meetings of national parliaments and the European Parliament to discuss areas of policy – for example, scrutiny of criminal justice matters. The second declaration called for the periodic meetings of a conference of national and European parliaments, to be known as Assises. The conference would have the rather vague role of being 'consulted on the main features of the European Union.' A preliminary Assises took place in Rome in 1990. One other interesting example of co-operation across member states and with the European Parliament is the six-monthly Conference of European Affairs Committees at which the relevant national and European parliamentary committees discuss the techniques of scrutiny as well as wider policy matters.

The most important area of input into European Community decision-making as far as MPs and peers are concerned has been through influence upon the British ministers who will represent the United Kingdom in the Council of Ministers. Here some important adjustments have been made, principally in committee work, to accommodate the European dimension.

The House of Lords established its Select Committee on the European Communities in 1974. Its main remit is to scrutinise draft European Instruments, i.e. Commission proposals, and to draw the attention of the House to those which raise issues of policy or principle with a recommendation as to whether or not a debate is desirable. The Committee is empowered to consider the merits of proposals for EC legislation and it frequently takes advantage of the opportunity provided by the publication by the Commission of a consultative document or 'action programme' to undertake wide-ranging investigations of EC policy in a particular area and to make recommendations. Indeed, the Committee's wide terms of reference even permit it to undertake free-standing enquiries into EC issues in the absence of specific proposals.

The Committee has 20 members and an elaborate structure of five sub-committees roughly covering the principal areas of competence of the European Community. There is a total working membership (including co-opted members) of about 65 Lords and they normally consider whatever proposals are regarded as important by the Chairman of the Committee. These sub-committees take evidence and make reports which are often of a very high quality, reflecting the distinguished membership of the committees: for example, in 1994 the Finance, Trade and External Relations sub-committee had 13 members, including a former Secretary to the Cabinet, a former Permanent Secretary and Chairman of a merchant bank, two former EC Commissioners, two heads of Oxbridge colleges, a former General Secretary of the TUC, two former Leaders of the House, an ex-Chairman of a major clearing bank, and the Chairman of a major engineering company.

The reports are intrinsically useful as a source both of information and informed opinion. Although their target is, theoretically, the House and, through the House, the government minister and government policies, the Lords' reports also have a wider market in the EC institutions, including the European Parliament itself.

In 1993 (calendar year), 12 reports were debated, taking up just over two per cent of total sitting time. Whether a report is debated or not, it will be replied to in writing by the government within two months of publication. In 1993, 16 reports were made to the House; and a total of 178 documents referred for scrutiny by sub-committees out of a total of 759 instruments deposited and considered by the Chairman.

Since ratification of the Maastricht Treaty, the European Communities Committee has recommended that its scrutiny activity should be extended to any significant inter-governmental proposal under the two new 'pillars' of the Treaty – home affairs and justice, and the common foreign and security policy (CFSP). The Committee will pay particular attention to those proposals in these areas which would eventually require UK legislation, or impose legal commitments on the UK. Detailed arrangements for this parliamentary scrutiny of the pillars have yet to be agreed. The government have, however, indicated that many draft texts relating to home affairs and justice will be deposited in Parliament for scrutiny before they have been finalised at international level; they do not, however, envisage that it will be possible to deposit many similar documents under the CFSP pillar.

The Commons have gone down a somewhat different avenue from the Lords, and use a dual system of select and standing committees to scrutinise Community legislation. The key body in this is the 16-member Select Committee on European Legislation.

This Committee fulfils a sifting and highlighting role. It considers all Community documents, the most important category of which is made up of legislative proposals of the Commission to the Council of Ministers. The number of documents considered in the average year is about 900 to 1,000. The Committee's staff of ten prepares briefs on each of these, helped by the explanatory memorandum which the relevant government department is obliged to produce. The Committee then meets weekly to decide on the basis of these briefs what further scrutiny, if any, each document needs. In the case of most documents, the Committee reports, in effect, that their legal and/or political importance is not sufficiently great for them to need further consideration by the Commons. This marks the end of the scrutiny process for these documents. But in the case of about 50 documents a month, the Select Committee decides that their legal and/or political importance is great enough to warrant another stage of scrutiny. The Committee reports to this effect, and the relevant document automatically stands referred either to European Standing Committee A (which deals with documents relating to agriculture, fisheries, food, transport, forestry or the environment) or European Standing Committee B (other matters). These Standing Committees were first set up in 1990 and have, unlike other Standing Committees, a permanent membership of 13. Other MPs are permitted to attend and speak, but not to vote. On average, between two and six do so. In considering a document (several may be considered together), the Standing Committees normally begin with a question and answer session lasting up to an hour during which the appropriate minister is examined on the proposal. This question session can be very testing: the minister is questioned on one proposal for an hour, and (unlike Select Committees) civil servants are not permitted to help the minister out in his or her replies. Questions are followed by a debate, in which a resolution is moved by the minister and to which amendments may be proposed. A vote can be taken at the end of the sitting (which may not last more than two and a half hours in total), and the resolution adopted is reported to the House. A motion is then put to the House without debate and the scrutiny process is complete. Documents which the Select Committee believes should be debated on the floor of the House are automatically referred to one of the Standing Committees, but if the government agrees with the Select Committee's view on the need for a debate on the floor, the document can be 'dereferred' and so considered by the whole House. During the 1992–93 session, Committee A met on 24 occasions and considered 31 documents, while Committee B met 30 times and dealt with 51 documents. Subject matter of documents ranged from sheep and goat farming and timeshare to relations with Libya and company taxation. During the same session 17 documents were considered on the floor of the House in five debates.

Before the creation of the European Standing Committees, debates on European documents took place either on the floor of the House or in Standing Committees set up *ad hoc* as they are for statutory instruments. The European Standing Committees have proved a more successful means for scrutiny of the merits of documents, and their combination of a mini question time with traditional debating methods may encourage similar developments in other areas.

The scrutiny process is intended to influence the minister in the position he or she takes in the Council of Ministers. A resolution of the Commons passed in 1990 (replacing a similar 1980 resolution) makes it clear that in normal circumstances the British representative in the Council of Ministers should not signify British approval for a legislative proposal before the Commons scrutiny process is complete. If he or she does so, reasons must be given to the Select Committee if the proposal is awaiting the Committee's clearance, or to the House if the proposal is awaiting debate. A similar convention is observed by the government in the case of the House of Lords. It is not always possible to fulfil this commitment, and ministers frequently have to write to the occupant of the Chair of the Select Committees of the two Houses explaining, retrospectively, why some measure or other had to be agreed before debate could take place at Westminster. The British Committees cannot therefore put up an irremovable obstacle to ministerial action as, for example, the equivalent committee in Denmark can. Nevertheless, it is generally acknowledged that the British system of scrutiny is better developed than that in most other member states, and it is agreed across parties at Westminster that it is important for Community legislation to receive proper attention in both Houses.

The Select Committee in the Commons has power to establish sub-committees, and can report on issues which arise from its scrutiny role. It has from time to time recommended improved scrutiny procedures, and can be expected in particular to come forward with proposals for scrutiny of the pillars of the European Union which deal with justice and home affairs and foreign and security policy. At present, there is no systematic scrutiny in these areas.

There are other ways in which ministers can be held to account on EC matters, unassociated with the specialist select committee structure and the debates on their reports. An MP or peer who is interested in a Community proposal being considered by the Council of Ministers can use the normal inquisitorial methods of questions and (if he or she is a member of one) the Commons departmental select committees to hold to account the British minister involved. Questions, as we said earlier, can be useful, but not too much should be claimed for their effectiveness. There used to be a special question time set aside in the Commons for EC matters, but this was dispensed with in April 1985 because of its unpopularity. MPs clearly did not think that parliamentary questions were an adequate way of holding ministers to account. The use of departmental select committees is limited because the committees usually have a lot else to occupy them as well as Community policy in their field. Some other useful conventions have been developed. In the Commons the forthcoming business in the Council of Ministers is always announced in advance, normally by a written statement printed in *Hansard*. After the less important Council meetings, a written statement about the outcome is similarly made, but where the Council has been important – major discussions on the Common Agricultural Policy, or meetings of Foreign Ministers or of the Heads of Government, for example – the statement is made orally in the House. If desired, these statements are also repeated in the Lords and in each House they can be followed by something between half an hour and an hour of questions to the minister by backbenchers. In the Commons, it is also usual to have whole-day debates on European Community affairs in general and perhaps on the annual agricultural price settlement and the Community's annual budget. The debates usually take place on substantive motions and the motions are subject to amendment and to a vote.

These procedures taken together certainly amount to a measure of formal scrutiny. MPs and peers may feel frustrated that they are not able to amend European legislation, but ministers can be under few illusions about the true views of Parliament – as expressed in both Houses – when they come to discuss draft legislation in the Council of Ministers.

However, the British minister is only one of fifteen in these gatherings. The minister has to make compromises and will often settle for second best when British interests conflict with those of other countries. So whatever the preferences of the British government – even when they accord with those expressed in Parliament – they may well have to be departed from in the course of negotiations leading to a final text agreeable to all member states. Parliament can – and frequently does – come second to European 'realpolitik'.

Moreover, as more power passes from the Council of Ministers to the European Parliament so, paradoxically, the power of domestic parliaments diminishes. This concern about the role of the individual nation state and its institutions inside a European Union was at the heart of the debates on the Maastricht Treaty in 1992–93, and is likely to remain at centre stage as the next moves in the 'ever closer union' come forward for negotiation in 1996. The role of national parliaments in the law making processes of the EU is one of the many matters which will be debated in these negotiations.

The British Parliament does retain ultimate sovereignty – it could pass an Act to repeal the European Communities Acts and so withdraw the United Kingdom from the EU. But short of this extreme step, it will need to adjust its procedures to deal with the growing amount of EU business passing through Parliament, but not passed by Parliament each year, and to a new type of ministerial responsibility where the British government may have to account to Parliament for EU policies which they opposed in the Council of Ministers but on which they were outvoted.

A Treasury minister summed up the situation succinctly in 1988 after the European Court had ruled that the United Kingdom should impose VAT on spectacles. He said: 'The British Parliament can overrule decisions of British courts. If we wished to change decisions of European courts made under European directives, we should have to obtain the consent of our partners.'

CHAPTER 12

Parliamentary reform

This book has so far been mainly descriptive. In this final chapter, an attempt will be made to stand back and ask what could be improved in the way the British Parliament operates. Our present parliamentary system does have admirers. The Indian, Canadian and Australian federal and state legislatures, among others, regularly send officials to London to learn how Westminster operates. The new democracies of eastern and central Europe have also shown considerable interest in Westminister as they develop their own parliamentary institutions.

But few would argue that Parliament is perfect. The increased scepticism about politics and politicians which has been evident in the 1990s in Europe and North America (a 1994 survey of British 18 to 34 year olds found profound distrust and cynicism about conventional party politics) has affected British popular views of Parliament – the institution with which politicians are most associated. For example, a Gallup opinion poll in 1993 found that only a quarter of those questioned had 'a great deal' or 'quite a lot' of confidence in Parliament. In response to this criticism, Parliament at the very least can be expected to continue to alter as society changes, just as it has over the centuries. More radically, there are those who advocate a series of reforms ranging from alterations in methods of work through reform of the House of Lords to wholesale constitutional change.

Before we analyse these proposed reforms, we have to ask a fundamental (perhaps *the* fundamental) question: What is the job of Parliament? So far many of its tasks have been described, but we need to think what their ultimate purpose is. Of course, no clear constitutional text exists to prescribe the functions of Parliament so we do not have the useful starting point available in most other countries. For example, the German Basic Law says: 'The deputies to the German Bundestag . . . shall be representatives of the whole people' and 'All state authority emanates from the people. It shall be exercised by the people by means of elections and voting and by specific legislative, executive and judicial organs'.

These German definitions give us a hint about the first purpose of the British Parliament, through its dominant part, the House of Commons: to indicate that the United Kingdom is a democracy. The House of Commons is the only national body which is elected by all adult citizens, and it is because of this that Britons could say that their country complied with Article 21 of the Universal Declaration of Human Rights: 'Everyone has the right to take part in the government of his country, directly or through freely chosen representatives'. Other states, of course, do things differently, and a traditional Marxist might argue that democracy was displayed better in ways other than election to a bourgeois House of Commons forming part of the apparatus of a capitalist state. However, most British people would probably accept that having a Parliament is essential to democracy.

Parliamentary democracy does not imply parliamentary control. We saw in Chapter 4 that parliamentary sovereignty did not mean that the House of Commons, let alone Parliament, governed the country. Instead, government is exercised *through* Parliament. The next question we need to ask, then, is what the relationship between Parliament and government should be. The first point to remember is that the leading figures in government, the ministers, are drawn from Parliament, and are generally supported in their actions by their fellow party members in Parliament. Because of this, it is simplistic to talk about 'Parliament' and 'government' as if we had a separation of powers between the executive and legislature as in the USA. Those Members of Parliament who are members of the government will have very different ideas about government/Parliament relations from Members of Parliament who are not members of the government.

The kaleidoscope of Parliament can be turned other ways to give further perspectives on the institution's role *vis à vis* government. The breakdown of Parliament into government ministers and the rest has to be seen alongside breakdowns into representative parliamentarians (members of the House of Commons) and non-representative parliamentarians (Lords); all backbenchers and opposition frontbenchers (the latter have the hope of becoming ministers and so are likely to hold different views about government's role); backbenchers who have no realistic hope (e.g. nationalist MPs) or desire to become ministers and those who want – or even expect – their time on the backbenches to be as short as possible; those who are orthodox members of political parties; and those who have maverick views or (almost exclusively in the Lords) are non-party. Each of these groups can reasonably be expected to have a different answer to the question 'what should be the relationship between Parliament and government?'

There are some areas on which all the differing interest groups inside Parliament would agree. First of all, there is little, if any, pressure for a separation of powers in the United Kingdom. It is broadly accepted that a principal task of Parliament is to provide the personnel for government, and, through the opposition parties, personnel for alternative governments. It is also accepted that all

members of the House of Commons have a representative function
to take up issues with government on behalf of their constituents.
As we saw in Chapter 8, ministers, just like any other MP, write
letters to other ministers about constituency cases.
However, views differ radically over the extent to which government should be constrained by Parliament. Should, at one
extreme, strict party discipline in the House of Commons ensure
that a government, with a Commons majority, is backed in every-
thing it does, any House of Lords attempt at veto being overridden
by the use of the Parliament Acts or even the abolition of the
Chamber altogether? At the other extreme, should a government
be expected to fight every inch of the way and to accept that its
proposals may well be mauled or even rejected by a Parliament
which comes up with alternative proposals of its own? The range of
possible relationships stretches from mere democratic legitimation
by Parliament of government actions at one end of the spectrum
to active control and power over those actions at the other.
　Some parliamentarians and outside observers advocate one or
other of these extremes or think that they can discern them in
the current situation. The suggestion that the truth lies somewhere
between should not come as a surprise. The daily shifting business
of parliamentary politics cannot be neatly analysed. In line with
the conventional British tradition of fair play, Parliament seems
to combine two apparently contradictory roles: it gives democratic
authority to the government's actions, but also requires the government to account for these actions with the sanction that they
may not be endorsed. The old word for this second function was
'inquest'. We would probably now call it 'scrutiny'.
　Those who are in favour of parliamentary reform have usually
tried to suggest ways in which the scrutiny function could be
improved and Parliament's influence increased. But before we
examine some of their suggestions, we need to look at some
alternative approaches.

Strengthening government's hand

It is possible to argue for reform which will diminish Parliament's
powers of scrutiny and influence. We could say that the people elect
their government at general elections when clear policy manifestos
are put before them. Once a government is elected, Parliament
has no business preventing it from acting as it thinks fit. The
government, with all the resources of the State behind it, is in a
better position to decide about public affairs than MPs or peers
who may make capricious decisions on the basis of short-term
factors. Few people would argue that decisions in the conduct

of a war, for example, could be left for a democratic assembly: ancient Athens is an example of how not to behave. The theoretical extreme of this view would see no role for an opposition at all. A more moderate version would give the opposition opportunities to make their voice heard, but by definition they could not expect to see the government prevented from doing what it thought right. While the House of Lords might need to be curbed or abolished, the House of Commons would not really need *reform* to fit in with this model: Chapter 4 explained how the government controls that House at present. But it was also explained that this control was subject to the consent of MPs. All that this model of Parliament requires is that, in the Commons, those selected as parliamentary candidates could be guaranteed to support their party line in Parliament if elected, especially when their party is in government, and not to subject their leaders to any form of scrutiny. In some Commonwealth countries with Westminster-style legislatures, the dominance of party through the caucus system – which sometimes even includes the prior consideration of government bills by the caucus of the governing party – provides a version of this model. If Parliament were to move to a mere rubber-stamp role, we might begin to question the need for the institution altogether.

Referendums

Some advocate more direct involvement of the people in political decision-making, by-passing both Parliament and government and using referendums instead. A referendum is an opportunity for all electors to vote on a specific proposition. It can either be mandatory (that is, have the same effect as a law) or be merely advisory. The 1970s saw the main use of the referendum in the United Kingdom – in March 1973 in Northern Ireland on the province's constitutional future, in March 1979 in Scotland and Wales on the proposals for forms of devolved government for the two countries, and in June 1975, throughout the whole United Kingdom, on the issue of continued membership of the EEC. It is in the context of Europe that arguments for and against referendums have most recently been aired – in the debates about whether moves towards greater European union ought to be given effect without the popular support which a referendum is said to show. In Europe, Switzerland is the only country making frequent use of referendums but most democracies use them occasionally. Supporters of the referendum see it as a valuable method of controlling government and ensuring that its decisions are endorsed by the people, and they dismiss the criticism that referendums results are usually conservative, especially on social and moral issues, by saying that the people should be allowed to be conservative if that is what they want. Parliament has no business flouting popular wishes.

However, the referendum could be seen as an abdication of responsibility for decision-making by government and Parliament, and there are problems about its use in the United Kingdom. First of all, the referendums of the 1970s have been advisory. Could future referendums mandate Parliament without breaking the doctrine that only Parliament can make the law? Some supporters of the referendum believe that results should be binding. Secondly people dispute the circumstances in which a referendum should be accepted as a valid indication of popular opinion: does a given percentage of the electorate have to vote, or is a majority decision on a low turn-out equally valid, if less persuasive? Thirdly, who should be responsible for deciding that a referendum is necessary? The United Kingdom, without a written constitution, has no clear guidance about the circumstances in which referendums should be used (if, for example, we say they should only be used on constitutional issues, who decides what a constitutional issue is?) or about how the problems they present should be resolved. Finally, who should be responsible for setting the question to the electorate? Its phrasing may, after all, govern the result. And however deftly the question may be phrased, what is to prevent the referendum becoming a vote of confidence in the administration of the day? It is, for example, highly significant that of the 42 referendums held by the Commonwealth Government in Australia between 1906 and 1994, only eight have been responded to positively.

Referendums would alter the relationship between government, Parliament and people, but would be unlikely to replace Parliament altogether: the cumbersome business of consulting the electorate could only possibly take place if it was limited to a few major issues – though modern interactive information systems may offer new possibilities. Nevertheless supporters of the referendum are basically expressing dissatisfaction with the way Parliament represents – or fails to represent – their views.

Is internal reform enough?

Most of the rest of the reforms which this chapter discusses can be classified as proposals to strengthen Parliament's hand. But first we have to ask whether this can be done in isolation. Parliament must, of course, be seen in the wider economic, political and cultural context of the country. Some commentators believe that, because of this, if there are deep-seated problems in Britain, efforts to strengthen Parliament internally will just be so much tinkering or, as David Judge put it in his book, *The Politics of Parliamentary Reform*, when describing reform movements of the 1960s:

whilst the Commons was experimenting with toy boats in its own bath water in the Chamber, the international economic sea upon which the British welfare state had been floated became ever more turbulent and hostile.

The late Stuart Walkland, a long-time and often despairing student of the parliamentary process, wrote bluntly 'parliamentary reform cannot be effective in a vacuum or within the present political structure of the House'.

It is well outside the scope of this book to analyse the constitutional packages which have been proposed as solutions to Britain's perceived ills. However, several would have implications for the way in which Parliament works, and we need to look briefly at these.

Proportional representation

The first proposal is for the introduction of proportional representation (PR) for parliamentary elections. In Chapter 4 figures were produced to show that representation of the political parties in the House of Commons is not in the same proportions as the total votes cast for those parties throughout the country. Proportional representation is an important part of the Liberal Democrats' policy. It is now part of Labour Party policy to introduce PR for elections to the European Parliament (and for elections to the House of Lords and Scottish Parliament if reforms in these areas are brought forward). Some Labour supporters, however, remain opposed to PR, and the party has not settled its policy on PR for elections to the Commons. The Conservative party supports the existing electoral system, though individuals in the party are in favour of PR.

There are several alternative electoral systems which would result in a more proportionate House of Commons. (Of course, no one knows how voters would behave if PR were in existence. Many people may at present vote tactically because they understand the present electoral system.) The first of these is the single transferable vote system (STV). Under STV, there would be larger constituencies, each returning perhaps between three and seven MPs. Electors would mark candidates in order of preference. To be elected, a candidate would need to achieve a quota of votes. Votes surplus to the quota would then be distributed to other candidates according to the second preference, and so on until the required number of candidates was returned. The votes for candidates unable to reach the quota would be redistributed. This system operates for local elections and elections to the European Parliament in Northern Ireland. Under STV constituents would no longer have one particular MP to whom they could turn, and the special relationship between a constituency and its MP, which exists perhaps especially in rural areas, would disappear. On the other hand, the rivalry between the different constituency MPs might actually produce better service for constituents, and it would be more likely that a constituent would be able to discuss problems with an MP who shared his or her political views. Voters would also be able to choose between different candidates of the same party.

The second suggested method of PR is the one used in Germany – the additional member system (AMS) or a variant of it. This could involve the number of British constituencies being halved. The larger new constituencies would each return one MP on the existing 'first past the post' system. But electors would also have a second vote which they would cast for a party, not a candidate. All the 'party' votes throughout the country would then be totalled, and a number of 'party' MPs, equal to the number of 'constituency' MPs, would be declared elected. The number of 'party' MPs from each party would be determined in such a way that the total of constituency and party MPs from each party would be in the same proportions as the total votes cast across the country for the parties. The added 'party' MPs would be drawn from party lists submitted before the election. The dangers with this system are that two different classes of MPs would be created – ones with constituencies and ones without – and that the constituency MPs could be overworked in comparison with the others. Furthermore, smaller parties would have a higher proportion of non-constituency MPs; in Germany, for example, the Free Democratic Party had, in 1994, 47 seats in the Bundestag, but none of their MPs represented a constituency.

Advocates of PR are not primarily concerned about its effect on the constituent/MP relationship. They claim that PR is fairer, and that it is likely to produce coalition governments. These would have broader popular support and be more successful in tackling Britain's problems. This is not the place to comment on these claims. As far as the Commons is concerned, its membership under a PR system might well be split in such a way that no party would have an overall majority. This could mean that the House's powers would be strengthened because the government would continuously need to secure support for its actions from more than one party.

MPs are certainly potentially stronger in a hung Parliament where there is no overall majority, but, if PR were introduced, solid coalitions might result which, though multi-party, behaved in exactly the same way as a single party. The House of Commons would not necessarily find its actual powers enhanced. It will be of particular interest to see the effect PR has in New Zealand, where it will be introduced for the elections due in 1996.

Bill of Rights

Another proposed constitutional reform with important parliamentary implications is the argument for a Bill of Rights or a written constitution. In a 1976 book, Lord Hailsham described the British system as allowing an 'elective dictatorship'. A government, even if elected by less than 40 per cent of the voters, is in such a powerful position in the House of Commons, and through the House of Commons in Parliament, that it can guarantee that its legislation, however sweeping its nature, will be passed without anybody being able to prevent it, whatever constitutional conventions may be trodden upon in the process. The protection against this would be a Bill of Rights which would introduce constitutional guarantees enforceable by the courts. Because the courts could override legislation, parliamentary sovereignty would no longer exist. However, it is argued, Parliament is in fact not succeeding in checking the executive, and parliamentary sovereignty means no more than government sovereignty under our present arrangements. The Labour and Liberal Democrat parties are both committed to the introduction of a Bill of Rights as part of a package of constitutional reforms.

One problem with a Bill of Rights is that it would itself need to be introduced as an ordinary piece of legislation, and there is no clear way in which legislation could be 'entrenched' or protected against repeal in the future. This would mean that there is no real chance of introducing a Bill of Rights unless there is agreement across the political parties to do so, and unless there is agreement about the rights to be incorporated. And it is precisely because different political parties have different views about 'rights' that the call for a Bill of Rights originated in the first place. Furthermore, some politicians would be unwilling to see essentially political questions decided by unelected judges. Of course, a Bill of Rights *could* strengthen Parliament's position: Article 9 of our existing Bill of Rights of 1689 (which is, in fact, no more than a particularly revered Act of Parliament, despite its title) lays down that 'freedom of speech and debate on proceedings in Parliament ought not to be impeached or questioned in any court or place outside Parliament', and a new Bill of Rights could, for example, regulate Commons' procedures so that an opportunity existed to discuss every piece of proposed legislation.

Devolution

A third constitutional reform is devolution of power from London to the separate countries of the United Kingdom and perhaps also to the English regions. Devolution forms part of the programme of Labour and Liberal Democrat parties – though Plaid Cymru and the Scottish National Party seek a much greater measure of self-rule for their respective countries. The Scotland and Wales Acts of 1978 provided for devolved assemblies with differing powers in Scotland and Wales, but these never came into being because of the voting in the March 1979 referendums. Northern Ireland had a form of devolution from 1972 to 1986, and a more extensive form from 1922 to 1972.

The pressure for devolution principally arises among people who live in the parts of the country which are remote from London and who believe that central institutions, including Parliament at Westminster, do not understand or care about their problems – though the Orkney and Shetland Islands, which are further from London than Prague is, voted overwhelmingly against devolution in 1979.

So far as Wales and Scotland are concerned, the House of Commons has developed structures to consider their affairs. The Welsh Grand and Scottish Grand Committees, on which all of the respective countries' MPs are entitled to sit, meet to discuss specific matters (the Scottish Grand Committees, uniquely for House of Commons standing committees, meet from time to time in Scotland or Wales); there are annual days of debate given over to Scottish or Welsh affairs: Scottish and Welsh question times form part of the normal cycle, and there are select committees on Scottish and Welsh affairs. Advocates of devolution believe that these structures do not go far enough, and that it is wrong that English MPs can be whipped to vote on Scottish or Welsh business in a way which suits the government but which might not represent majority opinion in Scotland or Wales. This view received additional momentum after the 1987 election when the Conservatives won only 24 per cent of the popular vote in Scotland and 29.5 per cent of the vote in Wales, and was compounded in 1992 when these percentages were 25.7 and 28.6 respectively.

As far as Scotland is concerned, the government published proposals in March 1993 for enhancing greatly the role of the Scottish Grand Committee. New standing orders based on these proposals were endorsed by the House just before the 1994 summer adjournment and came into operation in November 1994. The new system is likely to result in 12 meetings a year of the Scottish Grand Committee (a committee consisting of all MPs with Scottish constituencies), some being held in Scotland (not just Edinburgh) and some at Westminster. The Committee will have a number of legislative responsibilities, effectively replacing the Chamber for the second reading of some Scottish bills; it will consider some statutory instruments, and it will also debate general matters. Some of these debates will be government initiated, but four debates will be initiated by the Labour Party and one each by the Scottish National and Liberal Democratic parties.

There will be periodic question times and opportunities to hear statements from Scottish Office ministers (including those who are not MPs). Half-hour adjournment debates will be taken at the end of business, and there will be a novel procedure (along the lines of Lords unstarred questions) for short debates with short speeches on particular topics raised by Scottish MPs. The government has also suggested that some Scottish bills should be considered by special standing committees. At the time of going to press, the way these fairly substantial reforms will work out in practice was not clear. Thus it remains to be seen how Scottish politicians and public will react. It is conceivable that the Grand Committee could become the embryo of a Scottish Assembly, though the reforms fall far short of the devolution of power which some people seek.

Some English MPs support devolution for practical reasons: removal of large parts of Scottish, Welsh and Northern Irish business from Parliament would ease the timetable considerably and allow Parliament either to meet for shorter hours or to spend longer on other issues. Britain is, after all, a more centralised country than France, Germany, Italy, Canada or Australia, let alone the USA.

As in the case of a Bill of Rights, it is difficult to see how devolution could be entrenched – the introduction of direct rule in Northern Ireland in 1972 shows how a devolved government could be 'called back' by London. There would also be disagreements about the powers of the devolved assemblies and on the duties and powers in the Westminster Parliament which MPs from Scotland and Wales should continue to have. Clearly any system of devolution would have wide constitutional implications affecting the nature of the State, but there would be a whole range of narrower, parliamentary implications also.

There is considerable political opposition, especially in the Conservative Party, but also among some Labour supporters, to the proposals for proportional representation, devolution and a written constitution. The interested reader is advised to follow through the issues each proposal raises in the more detailed works referred to in the bibliography. But it is important to note that there are supporters of fundamental constitutional change in Britain, and that any such change would be bound to have wider implications for Parliament. We also need to remember that some people push the argument a stage further – that constitutional change is a necessary condition for parliamentary reform.

House of Lords reform

Those in favour of constitutional reform must despair when they consider past difficulties in obtaining approval for schemes to reform the House of Lords. This has been in the air since the middle of the last century and came near to fulfilment following the report of the Bryce Commission in 1918. The Commission unanimously agreed a definition of functions of a reformed House of Lords which essentially holds true of the House today. It also proposed an Upper House partly elected by MPs and partly chosen by a joint committee of both Houses, so as to ensure the survival of a hereditary element, though some members dissented on this. Government proposals based on Bryce were put forward for debate in 1922 and 1927 but not pursued. And it is interesting to remember that in the early 1920s impending radical reform of the House was used as an argument for excluding women hereditary peers from taking their seats! There have been several substantial modifications in the powers and composition of the Lords nevertheless: the Parliament Act of 1911 limited the Lords' powers to delay public bills to two years – a period reduced by the Parliament Act 1949 to one year; the Life Peerages Act 1958 allowed the creation of peerages to be conferred on men or women which would not be passed on to the holders' descendants, but expire on their deaths; and the Peerage Act 1963 allowed all hereditary peeresses and all Scottish peers to sit in the House, as well as allowing reluctant hereditary peers to disclaim their peerage for life.

However, over 60 per cent of the members of the House of Lords, as we saw in Chapter 2, have their seats in Parliament because of an accident of birth. A feeling that this is inappropriate in a modern democracy lies at the root of the calls for Lords reform; but, despite many different proposals, the hereditary element remains. The principle has its defenders: for example, the argument is used that the monarchy would also be under threat if the concept of hereditary peerage were under attack. Another argument in favour of the *status quo* is that, irrespective of its anomalies, the House of Lords performs a useful function at present. As the Americans say, 'if it ain't broke, don't mend it'. Possibly also some of the calls for a reformed House of Lords result from dissatisfaction with the present House of Commons, and exasperation with the poor prospects for the constitutional reforms we have just discussed.

The most important functions of the House of Lords are to be a place where informed and expert opinion can be brought to bear reasonably dispassionately on problems of the day through committees and debates, to revise legislation brought from the Commons, to give first consideration to some legislation (principally, but by no means entirely, non-controversial) and finally to act as a check on the abuse of power by the Commons (the Lords could reject any bill to postpone a general election since such bills are not subject to the Parliament Acts).

The most radical reformers say that these functions could either be discharged elsewhere or are unnecessary. They believe the House should be abolished, and that the British Parliament, like those in New Zealand, Sweden and Denmark, should have only one Chamber, so becoming what is called a 'unicameral legislature'. Abolition of the House was official Labour Party policy from 1977 to 1989. The principal arguments against abolition are that it would strengthen the 'elective dictatorship' of the government in the Commons, and that it would remove an effective layer of parliamentary scrutiny, especially of those parts of bills or those EU proposals or statutory instruments which pass through the Commons without discussion. Abolitionists counter these arguments by saying that the un-elected Lords have no moral basis for undoing the work of the elected Chamber, and that Commons procedures could be changed to ensure that MPs had a proper opportunity to discuss the business which passes through their House. The ultimate safeguard the Lords give electors – their power to stop the Commons from postponing a general election – could be provided instead by legislation requiring a referendum before any extension of the life of a Parliament is put into effect.

Of course, abolition of the Lords would have several knock-on effects, of which account would need to be taken. For example, it would not be so easy to bring outsiders into a Prime Minister's team of ministers. At present one or two can be made life peers. The average age of MPs would also be likely to rise: a number of long-serving MPs move on to the House of Lords rather than trying to retain their Commons seat. And the Commons itself would need to be radically adapted to enable it to function properly on a 'unicameral' basis. Close scrutiny would have to be given to the way in which the Commons considers legislation and to the intervals between stages of consideration of bills, for there would be no second chances of 'getting the bill right' in the Lords. And with no second chamber, governments would be more constrained in the number of bills they could introduce, unless more legislative time could be found in the Commons – possibly by rigorous timetabling of bills or changes in legislative procedure.

An alternative to abolition is to neuter the House of Lords. It would be difficult to justify the House's existence at all if it had *no* legislative role – indeed, it would be of little practical utility. Less radically, there is obviously scope for whittling down the Lords' present powers. For example, they could be restricted to delaying bills for six months, or to being able to ask the Commons to think again only on one occasion. Their consideration of Commons' bills could be subject to a time limit, or their present absolute power to reject secondary legislation could be removed. The so-called Salisbury convention (that the Lords should not reject at Second Reading any proposal contained in a party's election manifesto) could be enshrined as a formal rule or extended to all government bills whether in a manifesto or not, though such provisions might be difficult to draft. Readers can invent further permutations of their own.

Similarly, there is no shortage of theoretical possibilities for how a reformed House of Lords might be constituted and what its powers might be. One of these deserves special attention because it came nearest to being achieved: the scheme outlined in the Parliament (No. 2) Bill of 1968–69. Although this bill had a majority of 150 in the Commons on second reading (its principal recommendations had previously been endorsed by 251 votes to 56 in the House of Lords), it was opposed for different reasons both from the left and the right (Michael Foot and Enoch Powell were among its opponents), and it was dropped after a protracted committee stage, taken on the floor of the Commons as is conventional for constitutional bills. Basically, the Parliament (No. 2) Bill proposed a two-tier House of voting and non-voting peers. Among voting peers, the government of the day would have had a small, but not absolute, majority. Hereditary peerages would gradually be phased out as future successors would no longer have the right to sit in the Lords. Delay of primary legislation by the House would be limited to six months, and the power to reject secondary legislation outright would be removed.

The Parliament (No. 2) Bill envisaged the House of Lords eventually consisting only of appointees, like the Canadian Senate. If the power of appointment was vested solely in the Prime Minister, this would be a considerable extension of the power of prime ministerial patronage. An alternative means of appointment would be by function or interest, as in the case of a proportion of the members of the Irish Senate or the membership of the French Economic and Social Council or the EU's Economic and Social Committee. There are vestiges of this in the Lords at present: the law lords and bishops are members because of their office. Certain industrialists, university vice-chancellors, trade union leaders, council leaders and other group leaders could also become members of a House of Lords because of the office they hold. Alternatively, particular bodies (the CBI, the TUC, etc.) could each have the power to nominate a number of Lords. This would be a way in which Parliament could recognise the corporatism of the modern state – after all, captains of industry and trade union leaders are sometimes already referred to as 'barons'. However, it is unlikely that it would be easy to agree which organisations should be represented in which proportions in a function-related House of Lords and, as time passed, ideas might change about what functions should be included. A Chamber composed of representatives of the institutions of the 1960s would be wholly inappropriate for the 1990s.

The removal of hereditary peers from the House or, alternatively, of their right to vote is an interim measure of reform currently being proposed by the Labour Party. It would have the effect of establishing a Second Chamber of nominated life peers. As a 'quick fix' it may seem appealing but the mode of future appointments would need to be fully considered for the reasons already stated – even though such a nominated Chamber might only be a temporary expedient pending some more radical reform. And if hereditary peers were allowed to attend but not vote, their role in proceedings, level of remuneration, and other privileges might need to be re-defined.

An indirectly elected House, chosen from among existing elected office holders, has also been proposed. This could consist of representatives elected by each principal local authority in the United Kingdom, perhaps with a certain number of nominees of the European Parliament. The Netherlands, for example, has an upper house chosen by an electoral college representative of local councils.

Other reformers propose a directly elected House. However, they recognise that elections at the same time and on the same basis as the Commons would be unnecessary duplication. In Norway and Iceland the upper houses are composed of a proportion of the elected members, the remainder constituting the lower houses. The party strengths are thus the same in both houses and the potential for conflict avoided. But this is not a genuinely bi-cameral system and were it adopted the current constitutional safeguards which the Lords provide would be lost. A variety of alternative systems are canvassed, including proportional representation based on national or regional lists of candidates, or lengthier terms of office, or a system of retirement by rotation so that, for example, there would be elections every three years to the Lords, but with only one-third of the membership up for election. Current Labour Party policy in the long term is to replace the House of Lords as it is composed at present with an elected second chamber and the party acknowledge that there is a powerful case for a bicameral rather than a unicameral legislature. They proposed a 322-member chamber elected through a Regional List system on a 135,000 person quota. The powers of the chamber would remain unchanged.

The election of a reformed House of Lords or Second Chamber, especially if on a different electoral basis from the House of Commons, will bring its own problems, however. An elected House would have enhanced authority (if proportional representation were involved, some people would claim it had *more* authority than the Commons), and would be more likely to come into conflict with the Lower House. This is already true in Australia where different voting systems are used for elections to each House of the Federal Parliament. It is for this reason above all that the idea of an elected chamber is likely to meet resistance. For example, the convention that the Prime Minister is the person who leads the majority party in the Commons might no longer necessarily hold if the Lords were also directly elected – why should the Prime Minister not be the leader of the largest party in the Lords? And what would happen if the largest party in the Lords were different from the majority party in the Commons? To keep the Lords in second place to the Commons, various combinations of directly elected and appointed members have in the past been suggested (and are currently practised in countries such as Ireland, Spain and Italy), but again there is no general agreement on such compromises.

It is always possible to design blueprints for replacing the House of Lords, but it is very much more difficult to produce a scheme which wins all-party approval. Abolition or curtailment of powers are harder to justify in the absence of any serious prospect of major reform of the House of Commons, and improving their Lordships' respectability by election would create a rival to the Commons. These difficulties may explain why neither of the two major political parties has in recent years placed Lords reform high on its political agenda. The Conservative Party, in spite of a very brief flirtation with the idea in the early 1980s, has no present intention to reform the House. The Labour Party, while it has a policy of reform, did not accord it high priority in its manifesto for the 1992 General Election – Lords reform was relegated to the work of a second Parliament, that is to say after yet another General Election and at least five years further on! At the time of going to press, however, Lords reform seemed to have been accorded a new priority by the Labour Party. Their proposal to remove the hereditary element from the Lords – or alternatively to remove their right to vote – will, they maintain, be enacted some time in the first Parliament following a Labour victory at a general election.

In the last 30 years the House has evolved in ways which make it a very different animal from that, say, of the immediate post-war period – even though its powers have remained unchanged since 1949. The creation of Life Peers, following the Life Peerages Act, has wreaked a curious evolutionary effect on the membership of the House, As we saw on page 16, over half of the most active members are now appointed, rather than hereditary, members. Moreover, just as the House's legislative powers largely complement rather than compete with those of the House of Commons, the House has developed other new activities on the same complementary lines. Thus the consideration of legislation has been modified by the setting up of the Delegated Powers Scrutiny Committee; more frequent use of Public Bill Committees; the possible forthcoming use of Committees of the Whole House off the floor; and the decision to institute Special Public Bill Committees for Law Commission bills. And a proposal to establish an elaborate select committee structure on departmental lines has been rejected in favour of concentrating expertise in areas which, in the past, did not overlap with House of Commons activity – like the European Communities, Science and Technology and *ad hoc* committees on particular issues. In the absence of any political consensus on major reform and, until recently, of any political party to commit itself to it strongly, it could be said that the Lords have already reformed themselves in terms of what they actually do and the way they do it – almost by stealth. Many peers believe that the Lords does a good job, and that, compared with their colleagues down the corridor, peers have no reason to feel ashamed about the way in which their oddly constituted House has been able to operate in recent years. As Lord Carrington once told the House, 'After all, it is not your Lordships' fault that you are unreformed.'

House of Commons reform

We have seen that some commentators believe parliamentary reform cannot be achieved in a narrow, procedural context, but we have also seen that major constitutional changes are not imminent. For the remainder of this chapter, we will accept that Parliament's function of scrutiny of government must be conducted within the present framework, but we will ask how that framework might be improved in the House of Commons. Can the House of Commons do a better job in keeping the government on its toes? Must backbenchers always be confined – in the splendid phrase of Labour MP Austin Mitchell – to the role of 'heckling a steamroller'? Does the House of Commons deserve the description Dafydd Elis Thomas, then President of Plaid Cymru, gave it in 1991: 'the most disorganised, inefficient, unaccountable, ramshackle, theatrical so-called legislature in the western world'?

There is no doubt that the Commons have sufficient powers in relation to the government if they choose to exercise them. Bills could be defeated, the estimates reduced, and even the government thrown out of office if the House of Commons decided on a vote that it had no confidence in them. More realistically, minor changes to legislation can be made or the government forced to back away from proposals it is canvassing because of the threat of rebellion among its supporters inside Parliament. In recent years, the Lords have shown the way in defeating government proposals, but action – or the threat of it – by Commons backbenchers has also been a considerable problem for government ministers on a diverse range of issues over the years – and these problems have intensified in periods, such as those following the 1974 or 1992 General Elections when government majorities have been small. The basis of Parliament's power has always been the vote. But are there more methodical ways for the Commons to scrutinise government than to swat the occasional legislative fly in the division lobbies? A great deal of hope still rests on the select committees. When Norman St John Stevas proposed the new system to the House in 1979, he said that he did so with the aim of 'altering the whole balance of power between Westminster and Whitehall'. If this ambitious aim has not been met fully, it is certainly the case that the haphazard system which existed before 1979 has been replaced by a much more comprehensive mechanism by which Parliament can hold government to account. Moreover there is no doubt that senior civil servants and ministers are aware of the high profile committees have – and thus the potential problems they pose. Reformers are now asking how they could be improved further.

Different committees operate in different ways, and some observers see a confusion among MPs who are members of select committees about their role. Some central direction would, they believe, help. The Liaison Committee, made up of MPs who chair committees, has the responsibility under the Standing Orders of 'considering general matters relating to the work of select committees', but it seems to have given comparatively little guidance to committees about how they should go about their work. There is some evidence of committees acting in concert over their examination of the spending plans contained in departmental annual reports. There may be opportunities for more central direction to committees, though individual committees will rightly remain jealous of their autonomy.

Direction from a central body, is not, however, likely to resolve one of the fundamental confusions: are select committees expected to operate on a bipartisan basis or to preserve the clash of party ideologies in their work? And if they do behave in a bipartisan way, does that make them either politically neutered or (depending on one's viewpoint on co-operation between the parties) politically dangerous? This problem is heightened the closer the committees come to the day-to-day business of the Chamber as the Trade and Industry Committee's report on the coal industry, to which we referred on page 222, seemed to demonstrate. If all legislation were referred to departmental select Committees, as some reformers wish, including legislation which is contentious in party-political terms, bipartisanship in the committees would be strained. Nevertheless, the example of the Public Accounts Committee, whose reports are normally agreed across the parties, shows that there are many areas of government expenditure and administration, if fewer areas of policy, which the select committees could scrutinise without too much party-political wrangling. To begin with, a lot more work could be done in looking at the details of government departments' expenditure plans.

To attempt more comprehensive coverage, the committees might need better resources in terms of staff and research. This would cost money, and would need to be justified in terms of the return it would bring. However, no one would want to see select committees so under-resourced that they were simply incapable of dealing with the problems they try to tackle. Many MPs who serve on the committees would themselves also need to devote more attention to committee work. They would probably only be willing to do this if select committees were generally regarded by politicians as an acceptable alternative career to being a minister or, indeed, a positive achievement on the road to ministerial office. The relatively high visibility in the media of MPs who chair select committees and the subsequent ministerial careers of a number of prominent select committee members may be factors which will make committees more attractive, but the proposal that occupancy of a select committee Chair should be rewarded with a modest additional salary may also need to be reconsidered.

Select committees will also need to develop links with the Chamber if their influence is to grow. Formal opportunities for the committees to put their views to the House would enhance their powers. But the most important reform of all would be the growth of a select committee consciousness among all MPs so that committee members' views were taken seriously because they were the whole House's nominated delegates on particular areas of public affairs. Unfortunately there is an element of chicken and egg in this: the committees' stature will grow because the whole House is inclined to accept their advice, but the House will only be inclined to accept their advice when it believes that their stature is sufficiently high. An enhanced role for select committees as part of parliamentary reforms is therefore likely to emerge only after a period of gradual development. It should also be remembered that it is up to committees themselves with their present powers and resources to make progress in this direction.

The parliamentary parts of the legislative process come in for frequent criticism – there was a particularly trenchant discussion of the subject in the 1992 Report of the Hansard Society Commission on the Legislative Process, to which the interested reader should refer. Most people accept that Parliament is not suited to be the principal initiator of legislation: among Western parliamentary assemblies, it is perhaps only the US Congress that fulfils this role. However, many MPs and peers feel that the decks are unfairly stacked against private members' legislation. As we saw in Chapter 6, it is very easy to kill a private member's bill, even though it may be supported by a large proportion of the Commons. Lords' private members' bills are even more vulnerable. Relatively minor procedural reform (principally allowing more time for the report stage of private members' bills) would redress the balance a little.

Proposals are often made for reform of the various stages through which public bills pass in the Commons but there are no universally agreed remedies. There is considerable support for the routine timetabling of legislation, with over half the MPs who replied to a questionnaire sent out by the Jopling Committee in 1991 favouring its greater use. The Committee recommended timetabling after second reading for all government bills committed to standing committee. However, MPs believe that timetabling would give an extra weapon to the government's armoury, and when the issue was last put to a vote on the floor in 1986, it was rejected by 231 to 166, with the split in opinion unrelated to party allegiance. But timetabling does not necessarily lead to less time for the consideration of a Bill: it can simply mean better use of the time available – it is widely agreed that legislation is at present often dealt with in too great a hurry and with insufficiently thorough debate. There is some evidence of a growing willingness for bills to be considered under a voluntary timetable, and this was acknowledged by both front benches as the way forward for the future when the experimental reforms of sitting hours was put to the House in December 1994.

Some reformers question the need for the traditional stages of public bills, or propose that more work should be done away from the floor of the House in committee. Perhaps, for example, the report stage could be taken in a special committee where all MPs could attend, speak and move amendments but where only a specified number would be entitled to vote.

Standing committees are not popular, although MPs may tend to focus on their bad experiences in standing committees where contentious party-political legislation is being considered and where the opposition has an interest in spinning out proceedings to as great a length as possible. The ideal of a committee stage is that the details of a bill should be carefully considered and where necessary improved. Sometimes standing committees live up to this ideal – for example, the 1986 Standing Committee on the Financial Services Bill was regarded as a workmanlike attempt to improve the legislation. The old-fashioned filibuster is increasingly rare, though it is still uncommon to see governments willing to agree to amendments which they have not themselves proposed, preferring instead to use their majority to maintain the bill in the form it entered committee. Moreover, as the Hansard Society Commission pointed out, even the best standing committees pay too little regard to the practicality of the legislation before them.

There are several possible aids towards achieving the ideal committee stage more often. First of all, the MPs who make up the committee could be better informed, though often there is no absence of briefing material from pressure groups: the use of special standing committee procedure or something else akin to select committee methods of work may do something to improve this, as might better research facilities. Another suggested reform is that the committee stage should be subject to a pre-arranged timetable, and that there should be an opportunity for each clause of a bill to be discussed. A third aid to the standing committee procedure would be a greater willingness by governments to accept amendments to legislation. Committee members should be able to feel that, if they present a good enough case, they have a real chance of changing the government's mind.

One way that this might be achieved more painlessly is by allowing Parliament to consider proposed legislation at an earlier stage than is normal at present. In Chapter 6 we described the lengthy work inside government before a bill is published. As part of this, a Green Paper is sometimes issued for discussion: recent examples include the 1986 Green Papers on personal taxation or on the financing of local government. These Green Papers can be considered by departmental select committees or debated in the House. Though urgency would not allow this in all cases, it might help parliamentary scrutiny if Green Papers became the norm when new legislation was under consideration and if draft bills were published some time before the actual bill. Parliament could reapportion its time so that more was spent on the pre-legislative stages. There is an interesting precedent in the publication of draft clauses on complex tax matters which the Inland Revenue wishes discussed before they are incorporated in a Finance Bill. Another precedent comes in the case of Northern Ireland legislation. Most of this is made by statutory instrument, and many of these are published in advance in draft. While it was in being, the drafts were considered by the Northern Ireland Assembly, and also occasionally by the Northern Ireland Committee (a standing committee) in the House of Commons.

Northern Ireland statutory instruments are a special breed, but there is no reason to prevent much more secondary legislation applying in Great Britain similarly being published in draft for preliminary parliamentary discussion. This would be one way of meeting concerns about the proliferation and other defects of secondary legislation covering so many important areas of policy to which we referred in Chapter 6. Secondary legislation is a minority interest at Westminster, but some of those who do pay attention to it feel that Parliament should be able to amend it, and also that the Commons (or, at least, a Standing Committee) should be able, as of right, to debate any secondary legislation which causes controversy. For the future, MPs have an easy remedy against the extension of powers to make law by secondary legislation: they can oppose any enabling clauses in primary legislation put before them which appear too open-ended. Reformers also believe that Commons' procedures for dealing with European legislation ought to be strengthened. This might partly be achieved by altering the functions of the present Select Committee on European Legislation and its potential sub-committees, but the levels of awareness and interest among all MPs of the rather arcane legislative methods and output of the European Union would need to grow: the Hansard Society Commission roundly criticised the 'head in the sand' attitude of many MPs in this area.

The arguments for providing Parliament with earlier and better information about legislative proposals are also advanced in respect of government financial affairs. Many political commentators have described how the Chevaline defence project – which would have cost billions of pounds – proceeded in the 1970s without any acknowledgement in Parliament of its existence, let alone specific authorisation of the expenditure. Chapter 7 described the general patchiness of information given to Parliament about public expenditure and the difficulties which MPs had in conducting any sort of detailed enquiry before voting supply. The government has gone some way to improving the quality of the information which Parliament receives by the introduction of departmental reports. More improvements may flow from the revision of the form of the supply estimates. However, MPs would be helped in their consideration of public expenditure if they were given considerably more detail, especially on the assumptions which lie behind plans, so enabling them to make judgements on the past and likely future effectiveness of the spending concerned. This detail would also need to be available earlier in the public expenditure planning process. Most MPs would also welcome greater help in this. The work of the independent National Audit Office in assessing the past economy, efficiency and effectiveness of government departments is an indication of what could be done by a parallel body assisting the Commons or its committees to assess spending plans in advance.

This would be one of the many reform proposals which would involve more parliamentary staff. A number of MPs and outside observers doubt that better levels of parliamentary staffing would be particularly cost-effective for the taxpayer, but other MPs believe that under-resourcing and lack of facilities are their severest handicaps. MPs' accommodation has improved substantially over the last twenty years, though it still lags behind some other countries. MPs' research and secretarial facilities are also much better than they were, and any MP who wishes can now probably employ one good-quality researcher and a personal secretary. Some believe that better facilities in the constituencies are also needed for MPs to discharge their ombudsman role properly on behalf of constituents, and many MPs favour the provision of office facilities for each MP in his or her constituency. Expansion of the research division of the House of Commons library would be an alternative – or from many MPs' point of view an additional – way of increasing the resources at MPs' disposal, and the select committees could be more ambitious if backed by larger staffs. There is also room for supplementing these Commons resources by greater access for MPs and Commons staff to information technology or by developing further initiatives, such as the Parliamentary Office of Science and Technology. Despite the advances of recent years, there also remains an argument for a uniform House of Commons administrative service, managed on more 'MP-friendly' lines.

MPs' pay has been a controversial subject for many years. Although this controversy has died down since the 1983 decision that pay should be linked to civil service rates, there are still those who argue that some candidates of high quality are reluctant to stand for Parliament because of the low level of the pay. Another argument heard is that if MPs devoted themselves full-time to their parliamentary duties and were not able to hold outside jobs, the quality of Commons scrutiny and rectitude would improve.

If there are limited resources, some people believe that they would be more effectively used if distributed among a smaller group of people. The former Conservative minister, Lord Rawlinson of Ewell, has called for a House of Commons containing half the present number of MPs; the former Speaker, Viscount Tonypandy, has suggested 450, and Sir Robert Rhodes James, the then MP for Cambridge, presented a bill in 1986 to limit the Commons to 500 MPs. The Foreign Secretary, Douglas Hurd, also suggested in 1994 that the Commons may be too large. If the government side of the House were not to be dominated by the so-called 'payroll vote', a reduction in numbers of MPs would probably need to be matched by a reduction in the number of MPs who are ministers or at least in the numbers who are parliamentary private secretaries – the half-way stage between being a backbencher and being a minister. MPs would also have proportionately more constituency work to do. Perhaps the principal reason why a reduction is unlikely is that many of the MPs who voted for it would be voting themselves out of work. A similar suggested reform – also unlikely – is that there should be a compulsory retirement age for MPs.

As well as the timetabling of bills, many MPs are in favour of more general reform of the Commons timetable. Late night sittings are unpopular, as is the uncertainty of the parliamentary year. Reform of these would obviously be personally convenient for those who are detained at the House late into the night, or who are unable to plan their summer holidays. Many of the ideas were, as we have said, endorsed in 1992 by the Jopling Committee, and a number of them have been put into operation on an experimental basis in 1995. But controversy remains over these proposals: a reduction in the number of days or hours the House sits would mean that certain classes of business would need to be dropped from the Commons timetable or have discussion curtailed. This does not sit easily with other reform proposals that, for example, more time should be made available for debates initiated by backbenchers or for topical debates. The solution of regular morning sittings is opposed by a large number of MPs, though it may seem a rational solution to outsiders.

How long a whole parliament should last – in other words, whether the Prime Minister should retain the effective right to time general elections as she or he thinks best – is a more complex constitutional issue. Fixed-term Parliaments might make MPs more inclined to vote against the government since they could no longer be threatened that the consequence of doing so might be an unwelcome early election. But an administration which was forced to remain in office without a working majority simply because the fixed term had not expired might not serve the country's best interests. More mundanely, knowing exactly when an election would occur would remove one of the favourite sports of political commentators, and make life a little less worrying for MPs who have marginal seats.

The final proposed reform is a little more esoteric, but has relevance to many of those previously discussed. Some see scope for the House of Commons Commission to develop into a body which independently assesses the House's needs on behalf of all members – each major interest group in the House is already represented on it. The Commission might ultimately be able to give a lead on the direction which the House and its committees could take. The Commission could also come to act rather like the Bureau or Committee of Elders of a number of European parliaments in setting the House's agenda. Such functions for the Commission would be a long way from its present role, and could perhaps only be achieved if the corporate sense of House of Commons identity develops in a way which allows a government minister, an opposition frontbencher and three backbenchers from different parties, under the Chairmanship of the Speaker, to arrive at a shared sense of purpose about the House of Commons' job.

Dissatisfaction with current procedures is common among MPs. While disadvantages can be found in any specific proposals for reform, the pro-reform climate has grown over recent years. In June 1994, the Prime Minister spoke of his hope that

we can find ways of enabling the Commons to do its business in more sensible ways, in more sensible hours without either unacceptably reducing the government's capacity to carry its programme or reducing the opposition's flexibility in deploying and proving its case against government legislation.

He believed that

this effort has very strong support on both sides of the House and very strong support outside the House from millions of people who follow our proceedings.

Although his aim that the way forward should be mapped out before the 1994 summer recess was not achieved, a number of the proposals of the Jopling Committee were adopted experimentally in 1995. But the steps taken were modest, and experiments do not necessarily lead to permanent change, as a 1967 experiment with morning sittings demonstrated. Even if the 1995 changes are adopted permanently, it is likely that dissatisfaction with other aspects of the way in which the Commons operates will remain. Movement in one area inevitably creates pressure in others.

The central dilemma remains. The British Parliament is not the product of one conscious design. The way it operates can be quirky and odd and it covers many competing interests and aims.

This book has attempted to describe the mechanics of Parliament. Throughout we have also tried to emphasise the human element. Perhaps that needs even more emphasis. There is an emotional aspect to the place. Westminster is the scene of national dramas where an account has been given over the centuries for the conduct of wars, foreign relations and economic management. Members of Parliament are part of a developing historical institution. But it is an institution just like schools and hospitals: it has an inward-looking life of its own where friendships are formed across the political parties. Life is not all politics, as on the one hand, the deep sense of a grief felt across both Houses on the day that John Smith died, or, on the other, the 1986 charity regatta on the Thames, the annual tug of war, and numerous Lords v. Commons matches all go to show in their different ways. There is much more humour and humanity than might appear in a dry description of procedures. As Ken Livingstone said in his maiden speech in July 1987: 'I cannot recall anywhere that I have been where there is such a degree of helpfulness, general good humour and pleasantness.'

Parliament has its faults. Few people are totally satisfied with it, and reform will always be debated. Perhaps no democracy worth its name would find its Parliament above reproach. But the vigorous discussion of how the British Parliament could be improved is an indication that the institution is alive, kicking and working – if not always in a manner which is to everyone's liking.

BIBLIOGRAPHY

Adonis, A., *Parliament Today*, Second Edition, Manchester University Press, 1993.

Beloff, M. and Peele, G., *The Government of the UK*, Second Edition, Weidenfeld & Nicolson, 1985.

Biffen, J., *Inside the House of Commons*, Grafton, 1989.

Bogdanor, V., *Multi-Party Politics and the Constitution*, Cambridge University Press, 1983.

Bogdanor, V. (ed.), *Representatives of the People?*, Gower, 1985.

Bradshaw, K. A. and Pring, D. A. M., *Parliament and Congress*, Quartet, 1981.

Butler, D. and Kavanagh, D., *The British General Election of 1992*, St Martin's Press, 1992.

Carstairs, C. and Ware, R. (eds), *Parliament and International Relations*, Open University Press, 1991.

Cocks, Sir B., *Mid-Victorian Masterpiece*, Hutchinson, 1977.

Cook, Sir Robert, *The Palace of Westminster*, Macmillan, 1987.

Crewe, I. and Fox, A., *British Parliamentary Constituencies: A Statistical Compendium*, Faber, 1984.

Critchley, J., *Westminster Blues*, Second Edition, John Murray, 1989.

Davies, M., *Politics of Pressure*, BBC, 1985.

de Smith, S. and Brazier, R., *Constitutional and Administrative Law*, Seventh Edition, Penguin, 1994.

Dod's Parliamentary Companion, Dod's Parliamentary Companion Ltd, 1995.

Drewry, G. (ed.), *The New Select Committees*, Second Edition, Oxford, 1989.

Englefield, D., *Commons Select Committees: Catalysts for Progress?* Longman, 1984.

Englefield, D., *Whitehall and Westminster*, Longman, 1985.

Fell, Sir B. H., Mackenzie, K. R. and Natzler, D. L., *The Houses of Parliament*, HMSO, Fifteenth Edition, 1994.

Franklin, Mark and Norton, Philip (eds), *Parliamentary Questions*, Oxford, 1993.

Garrett, John, *Westminster – Does Parliament Work?*, Gollancz, 1992.

Griffith, J. A. G., *Parliamentary Scrutiny of Government- Bills*, George Allen & Unwin, 1974.

Griffith, J. A. G. & Ryle, M. T., *Parliament*, Sweet and Maxwell, 1989.

Hansard Society, *Making the Law: the Report of the Hansard Society Commission on the Legislative Process*, November 1992.

Hollingsworth, Mark, *MPs for hire*, Bloomsbury, 1991.

Jennings, Sir I., *Parliament*, Cambridge University Press, 1969.

Jones, C., *The Great Palace*, BBC, 1983.

Judge, D. (ed.), *The Politics of Parliamentary Reform*, Heinemann, 1983.

Liaison Committee, *The Select Committee System* (First Report from the Liaison Committee) (1982–83) (HC Paper 92), HMSO, 1983.

Laugharne, P., *Parliament and Specialist Advice*, Liverpool, 1994.

Likierman, Andrew, *Public Expenditure*, Penguin, 1988.

Likierman, A. and Creasey P., *Structure and Form of Government Expenditure Reports*, Certified Accountant Publications, 1984.

Likierman, A. and Creasey, P., *Public Expenditure Documents Presented to Parliament*, Certified Accountant Publications, 1985.

Marsh, D. and Read, M. *Private Members' Bills*, Cambridge University Press, 1988.

Marshall, E., *Parliament and the Public*, Macmillan, 1982.

May, T. Erskine (ed. Sir Clifford Boulton), *Parliamentary Practice*, 21st Edition, Butterworths, 1989 (referred to in text as Erskine May).

Miers, D. and Page A., *Legislation*, Second Edition, Sweet and Maxwell, 1990.

Mitchell, A., *Westminster Man*, Thames Methuen, 1982.

Mitchell, A., 'Consulting the Workers: MPs on their job', article in *The Parliamentarian*, January 1985 (referred to in text as the January 1985 Survey of MPs' attitudes).

Morgan, J. P., *The House of Lords and the Labour Government 1964–1970*, Oxford, 1975.

National Audit Office, *Report by the Comptroller and Auditor General: Financial Reporting to Parliament* (HC Paper 576), HMSO, 1986.

Norton, P., *The Commons in Perspective*, Martin Robertson, 1981.

Norton, P., *Legislatures*, Oxford, 1990.

Norton, P. (ed), *Parliament in the 1980s*, Basil Blackwell, 1985.

Radice, L., Vallance, E. and Willis, V., *Member of Parliament: The Job of a Backbencher*, Second Edition, Macmillan, 1990.

Richards, P. G., *The Backbenchers*, Faber, 1974.

Roth, Andrew, *MPs Chart*, Parliamentary Profiles Ltd, 1992.

Rush, M., *Parliamentary Government in Britain*, Pitman, 1981.

Rush, M. (ed.), *Parliament and Pressure Politics*, Oxford, 1990.

Ryle, M. and Richards, P., *The Commons under Scrutiny*, Routledge, 1988.

Shell, D., *The House of Lords*, Second Edition, Harvester Wheatsheaf, 1992.

Shell, D. and Beamish, D. (eds.), *The House of Lords at Work*, Oxford, 1993.

Taylor, E. S., *The House of Commons at Work*, Ninth edition, Macmillan, 1979.

Walkland, S. A. (ed.), *The House of Commons in the Twentieth Century*, Clarendon Press, 1979.

A variety of factsheets are also available from the House of Commons' Public Information Office and from the House of Lords' Information Office.

INDEX